Commentary on the Creed of Najm ad-Din al-Nasafi

Sa'ad Ad-Deen At-Taftazani

Translated with Introduction & Notes by
Earl Edgar Elder

Dar Ul Thaqafah

Dar ul Thaqafah
www.darulthaqafah.com
https://twitter.com/darulthaqafah
Email: darulthaqafah@gmail.com

Find our titles on your favorite online bookstore using the keyword 'Dar Ul Thaqafah'.

2023 CE – 1444 H

Translation of the Qur'ān

It should be perfectly clear that the Qur'ān is only authentic in its original language, Arabic. Since perfect translation of the Qur'ān is impossible, we have used the translation of the meaning of the Qur'ān throughout the book, as the result is only a crude meaning of the Arabic text.

Qur'ānic verses appear in speech marks proceeded by a reference to the Surah and verse number. Sayings (*Hadith*) of Prophet Muhammad (saw) appear in inverted commas along with reference to the Hadith Book and its Reporter.

Preface

During recent years there has been a revival of interest in things mediaeval. The Neo-Thomist school of philosophy is but one evidence of this. Different scholars have reminded us that the Middle Ages are not a backwater nor a bayou having little connection with the great stream of intellectual movements in our civilized world. Nor can one fully appreciate this period in the history of Europe and ignore the contributions of Islam and Judaism. The dependence of the theologians of the three faiths on the metaphysics of Aristotle for terminology and expression made for a mutual exchange of thought that refutes forever the idea that the religions which thrived in the Mediterranean world existed in isolated compartments or dealt with one another only through war and persecution.

Etienne Gilson in his *Unity of Philosophical Experience* records the similarities in principles and conclusions between al-Ash'arī and Descartes. Spinoza, the Jew of Amsterdam, was influenced by Maimonides, the Jew of Cairo, who although a real Aristotelian was greatly indebted to Ibn Sīnā and other Muslim writers. Miguel Asin in various volumes has shown the influence of Ibn Rushd on the theology of Thomas Aquinas, of Ibn 'Arabī on Raymond Lull, and of Muslim eschatology on Dante's *Divine Comedy*.

The three groups, the Christians, the Jews, and the Muslims, used similar arguments to prove the *creatio ex nihilo*. Yet in spite of much agreement in the scholastic method, doctrines peculiar to each naturally persisted. The orthodox theology of Islam developed a unique theory for explaining the active relationship of the Creator to His universe. This contribution to the catalogue of cosmologies is not so well known in the West. Maimonides, to whom we are indebted for the best systematic statement of this doctrine,[1] agreed with a number of Muslim thinkers in considering these explanations of world phenomena as fantastic and as contrary to the accepted principles of Aristotle.

But it is just because this theory of Continuous Re-Creation and Atomic Time lies behind the explanations given by al-Taftāzānī of the Creed of al-Nasafī that this exposition of a Muslim creed is of great interest. The

[1] *The Guide for the Perplexed*, tr. Friedländer, I, chap. 73.

PREFACE

book is also valuable as a comprehensive and authoritative statement of Islamic belief made at the time when it had become crystallized. While the Western world has reveled in a new birth of ideas which continued through the Renaissance, the Reformation, and the Enlightenment the world of Islam has largely held with a tenacious grasp to the doctrines set forth here. Until the present day it has remained an authoritative compendium of the arguments setting forth an explanation of the articles of Muslim faith. As a textbook of theology it has long held a leading place among the scholars attached to the great Muslim University of Al-Azhar in Cairo.

The translation was first made as a part of the requirements for the degree of Doctor of Philosophy at the Kennedy School of Missions of the Hartford Seminary Foundation. I am greatly indebted to the late Professor Duncan Black Macdonald for having been my guide to the way of understanding many of the intricate problems of Muslim theology. My sincere thanks are due to Professor Harry A. Wolfson of Harvard University for assistance in translating many difficult portions of scholastic reasoning. Among others who have helped in this task I gratefully mention the late Professor W. G. Shellabear and Professor E. E. Calverley of the Kennedy School of Missions of the Hartford Seminary Foundation. I wish to acknowledge the help and advice of Professor Austin P. Evans, general editor of the Records of Civilization. Professor Arthur Jeffery of Columbia University has given valuable assistance, especially in reading the proof.

E. E. ELDER

Evangelical Theological Seminary, Cairo

Introduction

Just over a millennium ago Abū 'l-Ḥasan al-Ashʿarī (d. A.D. 935) formulated the doctrinal position of orthodox Islam. He is credited with having saved the faith from corruption and having silenced the heretics. Three centuries separate his death from that of Muhammad. In time of appearance and importance he occupies in Islam a place comparable in the history of Christian doctrine to that of the Council of Nicaea. There is something representative in these two, al-Ashʿarī, the individual, and Nicaea, the church council. In Islam creeds and expositions of dogma are written by men who though they claim to give expression to that which is according to the Approved Way of the Prophet and the Agreement of the Muslim Community have no more ecclesiastical authority back of them than their own pens. In the evolution of doctrinal statements one never hears of "church" councils and their decisions but only of learned men and their convictions as to the essential truths of the Muslim's belief.

Muhammad himself, as reflected in the Qur'ān and Traditions, gave little attention to the systematic arrangement and logical presentation of the revelations to which he laid claim. His message was theocentric, but he was not a theologian. As long as he lived there was no necessity for a reasoned, methodical statement of Belief, just as there was no need for a political constitution or a code of laws. As the medium of instruction and guidance Muhammad met events as they came. If necessity demanded, verses were abrogated by new ones, or a more detailed explanation left no uncertainty as to Allah's purpose and desire.

When the Prophet died, loyalty led his followers to seek guidance from the verses of the Qur'ān which he had given them although they were not yet collected into one volume. One interpretation of such verses as "This is a detailed explanation of everything" (Qur'ān 12:111) and "We have neglected nothing in the Book" (Qur'ān 6:38) was that this revelation through Muhammad was sufficient in itself for all times and occasions. But experience taught the community of Islam that even a book purporting to come direct from the Almighty and All-Wise was not enough. Recourse was had to the practice and commands of the Prophet, then analogies were drawn, and if guidance was still lacking one looked for the Agreement of the Muslim Community.

Orthodox Islam is accustomed to consider the days of the Companions of the Prophet and their Successors as the golden age when the use of dialectics was unnecessary. Because of their fidelity to Muhammad and because throughout their lives they were in the shadow of the memory of his presence, these early Believers are pictured as relying absolutely on his authority.

The reason given then for much of the early theological controversy is that people lost their first love. Fidelity to the dead Muhammad waned before loyalty to a living leader. Zeal for the faith degenerated into jealousy and party strife.

In reviewing the evolution of doctrine one might easily fall into the error of attempting to separate what in the West is designated theological speculation as being in a different category from political theory. But in Islam oftentimes the early differences on religious matters had their origin in diverse political opinions.

The adherents of the family of 'Alī and Fāṭima claimed the Khalifate as the legitimate right of the Prophet's descendants. This narrow claim has been rejected by the great Sunnite majority of Islam, but the Shi'ite minority through frustration and persecution has developed a passion motive that has colored much of their thinking.

Less than three decades following the Prophet's death there arose the Kharijites, who held that the headship of the Muslim community belonged not to some branch of Muhammad's family, nor to a certain Arab tribe, but to the one best qualified for it. This political revolt against the ruling powers produced theological discussions over the distinction between Belief and Unbelief, the meaning of Islam, and what actions make man a great sinner.

To support the position that questioning about theological subjects was unnecessary there are traditions from Muhammad which discourage the discussion of dogma. Not only would he have no system of theology in his time, but for all time as well. Just as his utterances, as the instrument of revelation, settled metaphysical problems during his lifetime, so they were to go on settling them for the community of the faithful who accepted him as Prophet. The traditions regarding theological speculation which are said to have come from him not only teach the futility of divisions over matters of belief but also the inherent wickedness of schisms. One tradition has it that he said that the Magians were divided into seventy sects, the Jews into seventy-one, the Christians into seventy-two, and the Muslims into seventy-three, only one of which would escape the Fire. The Prophet, when asked which sect this was, replied, "It is that to which I, myself, and my Companions belong." [1]

This attitude of mind that deprecated discussion and schism was responsible in the end for the formation of a school of thought, the Murji'ite, which counseled delaying judgment as to the real faith of a professed Believer. Because his final destiny rested with Allah, an evil-doer who professed Islam was still to be reckoned as one of the people of the *qibla*, that is, those who in worshiping Allah faced towards Mecca. This position was a result of their attitude towards the Umayyad rulers, whom they obeyed even though most pious Muslims were skeptical as to the real faith of such impious potentates.

Another explanation given for the rise of theological disputation is that suggested by Ibn Khaldūn.[2] It was the result of attempts to decipher the obscure and ambiguous passages (*al-mutashābihāt*) in the Qur'ān. One explanation of certain verses produced a crude anthropomorphic conception of Allah; other ingenuous interpretations saw in the Qur'ān the embryo of a pantheistic faith.

A third reason for the development of Muslim dogmatics was the necessity for an apologetic. Through the rapid expansion of Islam into other lands beyond Arabia it came more and more into contact with Greek and Christian thought. Centuries before, Christian teachers had laid the foundation for the science of dogmatics by using such philosophical propositions as suited their purpose. Now when Muslim parties saw in the writings of non-Muslims arguments which would defend their position they were quick to use them. The close resemblance between material that appears in the writings of John of Damascus and the Murji'ite and Qadarite [3] doctrines is proof of this. The Kharijite doctrine that those who were guilty of great sins were no longer to be considered as true Believers is essentially that of Christians who classify sins as mortal and venial.

It was in refuting the positions of the Mu'tazilite party that orthodox Islam finally came into its own and arrived at a mature expression of its Belief. Al-

---

[1] See al-Shahrastānī, *al-Milal wa 'l-Niḥal*, p. 3. Cf. also similar traditions about the sects of the Muslim community, Wensinck, *A Handbook of Early Muhammadan Tradition*, p. 47.

[2] *Al-Muqaddima*, III, 44 f.

[3] The party which taught that the creature has power over his actions.

though when al-Taftāzānī wrote five hundred years had passed since the great Mu'tazilites had flourished and but little less than that since they had been eclipsed by al-Ash'arī, he often presents the orthodox position by first answering the Mu'tazilites.

In spite of the fact that al-Nasafī makes no mention of them in his Creed, al-Taftāzānī used this accepted method of commentators.

The origin of the dissent of this school of thought from the orthodox position is given by al-Taftāzānī.[4] The name given them by their opponents meant Withdrawers or Secessionists, but the Mu'tazilites called themselves the People of Unity and Justice. It is around these two points that one may focus the peculiarities of their reasoning.

In early Islam there developed a remarkable reverence for the Qur'ān, largely because of its own witness to itself. It is presented as the very speech of Allah to Muhammad. Its style is oracular. In all probability from contacts with Christianity and its doctrines of the Logos, the idea that the Qur'ān was uncreated and eternal was adopted by Muslims. The Mu'tazilites held that this undermined the unity of Allah by establishing something eternal alongside of Him. It really meant the ascribing of a Partner to Him and was therefore to them the worst kind of infidelity.

In addition to Speech Allah had other attributes such as Life, Power, Willing, Seeing, and Hearing. Over against the accepted opinion that these were also eternal many Mu'tazilites said they were the essence of Allah itself, that is, His essence is said to be knowing when connected with things known. He wills but does not have the attribute of Willing. He speaks with a speech but it subsists in something that is other than He. They were not alone in this. Al-Ash'arī says, "The Mu'tazilites, the Kharijites, many of the Murji'ites as well as many of the Zaydites say that Allah is rich, mighty, great, majestic, grand, master, overpowering, seeing, lord, possessor, constraining, high, but not on account of might, greatness, majesty, grandness, mastery, lordship and constraint."[5] The orthodox on the other hand said that all these characteristics were to be predicated of Allah and that He possessed eternal or essential attributes (*ṣifāt azalīya* or *dhātīya*).

The relation of unity and plurality in God had also been discussed by John of Damascus and others such as the Pseudo-Dionysius, the Neoplatonic mystic, and their arguments are echoed in the Mu'tazilite controversy. Faced with the task of defining the exact relationship between the essence of Allah and His attributes, the Muslim theologians took refuge in the use of negative

---

[4] See below, pp. 8 f.   [5] *Kitāb Maqālāt al-Islāmiyyin*, p. 177.

terms as had other theologians before them. Although the attributes were eternal they were careful not to establish a plurality of eternals. "The attributes are not His essence itself, nor are they anything extraneous to His essence."

From their position on the attributes the Mu'tazilites showed themselves anxious to avoid any literal interpretation of the passages using anthropomorphic terms of Allah. They were vigorous in their denial of the Beatific Vision. This may have been the starting point for working out their doctrine of Allah's absolute uniqueness. From reading the Qur'ān and Traditions orthodox Muslims came to believe that they would see Allah in the next world. Among the Jews and the Christians there was often fear or doubt about the thought of beholding God. However, the Christian emphasis on the resurrection as well as Hellenistic mysticism had turned men's attention to the other world. In discussing its realities the matter of the Beatific Vision became in the early Middle Ages one of importance. But in Islam to accept this as a reality meant, if literally interpreted, that Allah had a shape, a face, hands, arms, and feet. Many of the early Believers accepted the verses but refused to comment further on their meaning. Mālik b. Anas, in answer to the question about Allah's seating Himself on His throne, said, "How it is done is unknown, it must be believed, questions about it are an innovation." [6]

The question of the justice of Allah, which was also a rallying point for the Mu'tazilites, went back to very early debates about the punishment of sins and man's responsibility for his actions. Christian teaching regarding predestination influenced these controversies even though discussion was inevitable from what appeared in the Qur'ān and Traditions. Allah is described as having created the world and established His decrees in eternity. Some creatures are destined to do good, others to do evil; some are Believers, others are Unbelievers. Men are also urged to repent and turn to Allah. Had it been possible to identify absolutely the body of Believers with those who do good and obtain entrance into the Garden, and the Unbelievers with those who do evil and deserve the Fire, there would have been little place for dispute. The Qadarites, who appear to have been forerunners of the Mu'tazilites, said that man possessed free will to choose good deeds. The Kharijites taught that one who committed a great sin must be an Unbeliever; the orthodox Muslims, influenced by the Murji'ite teaching which delayed judgment on sinners, since it is Allah who passes judgment,

---

[6] Macdonald, *Development of Muslim Theology*, p. 186.

said that the professing Muslim who is an evil-doer should not be considered an Unbeliever. The Mu'tazilite position also hinted at delay or at least uncertainty by saying that the evil-doer is in a middle position and not to be identified with the Believers nor the Unbelievers. In general they held that his final destiny rests on his actions and on the absolute justice of Allah. Faith is not granted freely to some and withheld from others. Allah acts for the good and the guidance of man. If man accepts he enters the Garden; if he refuses he receives the punishment he deserves.

Undoubtedly in reaching their position the Mu'tazilites were greatly influenced by Christian thought and Greek philosophy. They avoided hypostatizing the attributes of Allah, especially that of Speech, into anything like the persons of the Trinity, and they affirmed His absolute unity. Again they had recourse to Greek dialectic to support their positions.

The dialectic used by the Mu'tazilites and others to rationalize their religious tenets was called *kalām* (speech). Al-Taftāzānī reviews the rise of this science in Islam. At first the term was used by pious Believers in contempt of those who relied on logic and philosophy to give a rational explanation of their faith. Eventually it came to mean scholastic theology. The term Mutakallim (or one who used *kalām*), instead of being applied to heretics, was used of the ultra-orthodox who taught such a barren intellectualism that al-Ghazzālī (d. 505 A.H.) when he appeared voiced a vigorous protest against them.

The close of the second century after the Hijra ushered in the rule of the 'Abbāsid Khalifas, Ma'mūn and Mu'taṣim, at Baghdād. They not only favored the heterodox teachings of the Mu'tazilites but by persecution tried to impose these views on their subjects. During the reign of the latter an abridged edition of the *Enneads* of Plotinus by Porphyry of Tyre was translated into Arabic by a Christian of Emessa in the Lebanon, under the title of "The Theology of Aristotle." Unfortunately those who sought to harmonize the doctrines of Islam with Greek philosophy considered this book a genuine exposition of Aristotle's teaching. For them it was just as authoritative as the Qur'ān. Al-Fārābī, writing after the time of al-Ash'arī, was a combination of the loyal Muslim and the Neoplatonist and still looked on this work as authentic as did also his disciple, Ibn Sīnā. But the great work of translating the texts of Greek philosophy came after the heyday of the Mu'tazilites. The influence of Greek thought on orthodox theology from the fourth to the sixth centuries of the Hijra had only an indirect effect, for the mold for Muslim dogmatics had already been formed. When more light is thrown on the early period we shall doubtless see as well that Indian and Oriental philosophies too have played a part in producing the dogmatics of Islam.

To return to the beginning of the third century of the Hijra, even though the heterodox thinkers turn to non-Muslim sources for the rational statement of their position, the general attitude of orthodoxy remained as before. The use of logic and philosophy was an abomination. Al-Shāfi'ī held that certain men should be trained for defending the faith, but that it would be a great calamity if their arguments were disseminated among the common people. It is reported that he said, "My judgment is that those who use *kalām* should be beaten with palm sticks and led about among the clans and tribes and it should be said, 'This is the reward of those who have forsaken the Book and the Approved Way and have taken up with *kalām.'*" Abū Yūsuf held that whoever sought knowledge through *kalām* had become a *zindīq* (a dualist or an atheist).[7]

Aḥmad b. Ḥanbal, who died in the middle of the third century, led a reactionary movement that insisted on a literal interpretation of the Qur'ān and abhorred rationalizing. With him dogma had for its real basis the Qur'ān and Traditions that went back to the first generation of Believers. His popularity with the people saved the cause of orthodoxy for a time but it remained for Abū 'l-Ḥasan al-Ash'arī who called himself a disciple of Ibn Ḥanbal to give the *coup de grâce* to the Mu'tazilites by turning their arguments against them. *Kalām* instead of being despised as an innovation now became the handmaid of revelation, just as in Latin Christendom under Albert the Great, Bonaventura, Thomas Aquinas, and others, scholastic theology used Aristotle and any available Greek philosophy that suited its purpose. Being a convert from the doctrines of the Mu'tazilites, al-Ash'arī was able to use effectively their dialectic in defending orthodoxy. The well-known story of his conversion to the Approved Way is told by al-Taftāzānī in the opening section of his commentary.[8]

But al-Ash'arī was not alone in making a statement of Islam's belief which was supported by the arguments of scholasticism. Contemporaneous with him in Egypt there was al-Ṭaḥāwī, and in Samarqand Abū Manṣūr al-Māturīdī became the founder of an orthodox *kalām*. Both followed the legal school of Abū Ḥanīfa, the great interpreter of jurisprudence (*fiqh*),

---

[7] Macdonald, *Development*, p. 187; 'Alī al-Qārī, *Commentary on al-Fiqh al-Akbar*, pp. 2 ff.; 'I.D., supercommentary of al-Isfarā'inī (Cairo text of A.H. 1335) on al-Taftāzānī, p. 14.

[8] See below, p. 9.

which in his time included theological topics in addition to canonical subjects.

With the triumphs of al-Ash'arī the prestige of the Mu'tazilite party was
lost. True, now and again one of their partisans got into power and the
name of al-Ash'arī was cursed in the Friday sermon at the mosques and his
disciples were persecuted, but such a recrudescence was of short duration.
Almost a century after al-Ash'arī the atomic philosophy, as sponsored and
established by al-Bāqillānī (d. 403 A.H.), was being developed into one of
the fundamentals of scholastic theology. The earlier orthodox theologians
down to and including the period of al-Bāqillānī and his followers are undoubtedly the Mashāyikh or Early Theologians referred to by al-Taftāzānī.
After some time Muslims used the formal logic of Aristotle as an essential
of their thinking although they rejected philosophy in itself. New proofs
were forthcoming which made use of the physics, metaphysics, and mathematics of the philosophers. This new development was known as the way of
the later scholastics (*ṭarīqat al-muta'akhkhirīn*) as contrasted with the
earlier ones whose methods were largely negative. Al-Ghazzālī (d. 505 A.H.)
and Fakhr al-Dīn al-Rāzī (d. 606 A.H.) are considered as leaders of this
new movement. In the case of the former there seems to be a conversion to the
Aristotelian-Neoplatonic philosophy of matter, form, and emanation, while
some others maintained a noncommittal attitude regarding the atomic explanation of the world processes. However, most of the scholastics in the
centuries that followed held to the atomic theory. This process of the
amalgamation of theology and philosophy went on until they differed little
from one another except that theology concerned itself also with subjects
based on revelation and authority.

Ibn Khaldūn (d. 808 A.H.), writing of the scholastic theology of his time,
bemoaned its decline [9] from its exalted position of the past. It had once been
useful in repulsing heretics and innovators in their attacks on the faith, but
they had passed from the scene of action. During this period of impending
decline philosophy took the brunt of the attack in place of the Mu'tazilite doctrines. However, the writers rehashed the arguments of the past and were
not at all timid about beating the dead horse of Mu'tazilitism.

Already the teachers of dogma, sensing their inability to add anything
original to the mass of dialectic in defense of orthodoxy, had begun to make
commentaries on statements of faith and articles of belief. Rather than go
back to original sources and reconstruct their theology, it was preferable to

[9] See *al-Muqaddima*, III, 43.

reinterpret the articles of belief of someone of the past. This process went on until there were numerous supercommentaries and glosses on commentaries.

It will be necessary to retrace our steps and notice the development of creed-making. The earliest statements which give an epitome of Muslim Belief are to be found in the Qur'ān and the Traditions. Sūra 112, in which Muhammad is commanded to declare the unity of the Deity and that He begets not and is not begotten, and the Throne verse (Qur'ān 2:256), which proclaims that Allah is living, self-subsistent, and knowing, and that to Him belongs what is in the heavens and the earth, are favorite sections of their Holy Book and are often quoted by Muslims as giving the essence of their religion. But in neither of these passages or elsewhere in the Qur'ān do we find in one sentence the exact words of the witnessing formula, "There is no god but Allah and Muhammad is the Messenger of Allah."

Different verses in the Qur'ān admonish men to believe in Allah and His Messengers. Twice at least His angels and His books are added. In Qur'ān 4:135, which reads, "Whoever believeth not in Allah, His Angels, His Books, His Messengers, and the Last Day hath certainly erred a wide error," there appear in the negative form all but one of the elements mentioned in one of the well-known traditions which aims to summarize the principles of the Muslim faith. "Belief . . . is that you believe in Allah, His Angels, His Books, His Messengers, the Last Day, and His decree of good and evil." [10]

But the very simplicity of such statements made them inadequate when party loyalty became heated, when explanation of difficult passages was demanded, and when problems raised by Greek philosophy and Christian theology were encountered and demanded a satisfactory solution.

The late Professor A. J. Wensinck in his *The Muslim Creed* has made all Orientalists his debtors for a thorough study of the statements of Muslim belief.[11] It will thus be necessary to mention here only some of the forms which the creed assumed in the early centuries of Islam.

The first attempts at a confession of faith outside these very brief statements in the Qur'ān and Traditions are striking in things they omit, as in *al-Fiqh al-Akbar* (I) which, even though it is wrongly attributed to Abū Ḥanīfa (d. 150 A.H.), reflects his teaching. Written probably in the early part of the second century of the Hijra, it makes no mention of the attri-

---

[10] *Musnad*, III, 134 ff.
[11] *The Muslim Creed: Its Genesis and Historical Development.*

butes of Allah nor of the Qur'ān as the Speech of Allah, neither is there a discussion of Muhammad and the prophetic office.

A much more detailed statement is that known as the Testament (*Waṣīya*) of Abū Ḥanīfa. This supposed testament of one of the founders of the four orthodox schools of religious practice also is not a systematic outline of Islamic principles but a protest against some of the outstanding heretical opinions that had crept into theological thinking. Again, neither the prophetic office of Muhammad nor the attributes of Allah around which later confessions were built receive consideration.

Another stage in the development of the creed is seen in an early chapter of al-Ash'arī's *Kitāb al-Ibāna 'an Uṣūl al-Diyāna.* Having given the position of innovators and those who have gone astray the author follows with a section setting forth the articles of Belief of the Muslim Community. The first person plural, with expressions like "We believe," "We say," is used throughout. Faith is affirmed in the Unity of Allah, His attributes, His uncreated Speech, His decision and decree regarding the actions of creatures, the Beatific Vision of Allah on the Day of Resurrection. Belief is defined, the Garden and the Fire and other eschatological matters are stated to be realities, and the Imamate is explained as well as other matters over which there had been dispute.[12] In his *Maqālāt al-Islāmiyīn* al-Ash'arī in the chapter dealing with the beliefs of the People of Tradition and the Approved Way again summarizes the Muslim creed, but this time in the third person.[13] As for his own position as revealed in his *Ibāna,* al-Ash'arī not only follows the teaching of Aḥmad b. Ḥanbal, but says, "We hold fast to the Book of our Lord, to the Sunna of our Prophet, to what has been handed down from the Companions and their Followers and the masters of *ḥadīth,* and to what Abū 'Abdallah Aḥmad b. Muḥammad b. Ḥanbal says opposing that which opposes him, for he is the excellent leader and the perfect head, through whom Allah has shown the truth, taken away error, made clear the path, and subdued the innovations of the innovators, the schisms of the schismatics, and the doubt of the doubters."[14] Although al-Ash'arī is usually represented as the theologian who introduced into orthodoxy such methods of logic and interpretations as he had gained from his study with Mu'tazilite teachers, yet both in *al-Ibāna,* where he warmly defends the position of Aḥmad b. Ḥanbal, and *Maqālāt,* where he presents in a detached manner the multifarious views

---

[12] Al-Ash'arī, *Kitāb al-Ibāna 'an Uṣūl al-Diyāna,* pp. 8 ff.; W. C. Klein, *Abu 'l-Ḥasan 'Ali Ibn Ismā'il al-Aš'ari's Al-Ibânah 'an Uṣūl ad-Diyânah,* pp. 49 ff.

[13] Pp. 290 ff.   [14] *Al-Ibāna,* p. 8.

of sectaries and innovators along with those of the People of the Approved Way, there appears to be little of *kalām* in his writings.

Among other writers contemporary with him Abū Ja'far Ahmad al-Tahāwī, an Egyptian who died in 331 A.H., wrote a compendium of Muslim beliefs.[15] A follower of the legal school of Abū Hanīfa, he does not agree with the extreme conclusions of al-Ash'arī, which jeopardize the moral basis for Allah's actions. Al-Māturīdī, another contemporary also of the Hanafite persuasion, has given his name to the rival school of orthodox theology, but no creed by his pen is extant.

From the fourth century of the Hijra the statements of the orthodox creed assumed a more logical form. Al-Ghazzālī (d. 505 A.H.) is credited with having won the day for the Ash'arite position in the west. He wrote at least three treatises on things necessary to Belief. His exposition of the two phrases of the Witnessing formula which appears in the first section of the second book of the *Ihyā'* is the forerunner of a whole group of creeds which center all the articles of Belief around Allah and His attributes and His Messenger Muhammad. This type of creed signified a reversion to the bare essentials of faith and became later very stereotyped in the creeds of al-Sanūsī (d. 895 A.H.) and al-Fadālī (d. 1236 A.H.) where all arguments for Allah's existence rest on the existence of the universe.

By the time, then, of Abū Hafs 'Umar al-Nasafī, who died (537 A.H.) about thirty years after al-Ghazzālī, there had been three distinct stages in the development of creed-making. The Qur'ān verses and Traditions, which briefly stated in a dozen words the objects of faith, gave way to a loosely connected group of sentences which answered heresies that divided the community. The third stage introduced a more logical arrangement of material; considerable space was given to the discussion of Allah's attributes, followed by articles on the prophetic office and on eschatological matters, but much less space was given to subjects on which there had been difference of opinion.

The formal statement of the tenets of Islam made by al-Nasafī is one of the most noted of all the many treatises on the Articles of Belief, which take the place in Islam played by creeds, confessions, and catechisms in Christianity. A canon lawyer of the school of Abū Hanīfa, al-Nasafī gives the viewpoint of the Māturīdites in theology. Made in a period that included both

---

[15] Abu Ja'far Ahmad al-Tahāwī, *Bayân al-Sunna wa 'l-Jamā'a* (Halab, A.H. 1344). English translation by E. E. Elder in *The Macdonald Presentation Volume* (Princeton, 1933), pp. 129–44.

al-Ghazzālī and Fakhr al-Dīn al-Rāzī, his short statement of faith has been the subject of more comment than any of the works of these more famous writers.

With al-Nasafī and others of the fifth and sixth centuries A.H. the accepted arrangement of materials called for an introductory section setting forth the sources or roots of knowledge. Al-Baghdādī (d. 429 A.H.) is credited with being among the earliest to adopt this method, although the Jewish author Sa'adya al-Fayyūmī had already given the sources as three, namely, the knowledge of the Perception, the knowledge of Reason, and intuitive or necessary knowledge.[16]

Following the introduction in al-Nasafī, the world as something consisting of substances and accidents is examined. From this al-Nasafī proceeds to enumerate the attributes of Allah who is the Creator and Originator of the world. The questions next discussed are the possibility of the Beatific Vision of Allah and whether or not all the actions of creatures are brought into existence from nonexistence by Allah alone. Following a description of many of the eschatological elements of Islam, the subjects of the great and small sins and their relation to Unbelief are examined. Next there is a section defining the meaning of Belief. The Messengers, Prophets, and Angels through whom Allah has communicated with the world are investigated, and then follows a study of the gracious acts or wonders of the so-called saints or Walīs. After a full inquiry into the Imamate or sovereignty in the state the treatise closes with a series of conclusions reached concerning various and sundry matters of faith.

The outstanding commentary on al-Nasafī's Articles of Muslim Belief, which has had a remarkable reputation over a period of half a millennium, is that of al-Taftāzānī.

Although Sa'd al-Dīn al-Taftāzānī is in no sense an original writer, his treatise is a standard textbook on Muslim theology and in turn has been the subject of many supercommentaries. Because it was written just after the subject matter of theology had been precipitated into the form it was to retain for five hundred years without perceptible change, this book of al-Taftāzānī has remained for scholars a compendium of the various views regarding the great doctrines of Islam. There is little indeed in his comment that is not found elsewhere. One needs only to read al-Rāzī's discussion of the Beatific Vision of Allah or al-Ījī's explanation of the Reality of Belief to realize that the detailed statements in this commentary on al-Nasafī's Articles

---

[16] *Kitāb al-Amānāt wa 'l-I'tiqādāt* (Leiden, 1881), pp. 12 f.

of Belief (*al-'Aqā'id*) had been used by others before. Al-Jurjānī and al-Taftāzānī must have drawn from common sources, for many of the definitions given in the former's *al-Ta'rīfāt* are identical with those employed by al-Taftāzānī. A glance at the definitions of the five senses given by both is sufficient proof of this.

Lest his work as a compiler give an unfavorable impression of al-Taftāzānī the reader should turn to an illuminating paragraph in Ibn Khaldūn. He says, "I found in Egypt numerous works on the intellectual sciences composed by the well-known person Sa'd al-Dīn al-Taftāzānī, a native of Harat, one of the villages of Khurāsān. Some of them are on *kalām* and the foundations of *fiqh* and rhetoric, which show that he had a profound knowledge of these sciences. Their contents demonstrate that he was well versed in the philosophical sciences and far advanced in the rest of the sciences which deal with Reason."[17]

There are some interesting facts to be noted in connection with this statement. Ibn Khaldūn died in the year 808 A.H., while al-Taftāzānī's death preceded his by only a few years. It did not take al-Taftāzānī centuries or even scores of years to attain a place of prominence as a theologian. By the time of his death or very shortly afterwards he was being studied and appreciated as a scholar in Cairo, which was in those days some months distant from the regions of Khwarizm and Samarqand, where he taught and wrote. And after five hundred years he is still a celebrated authority studied in the schools of the East.

We know very little indeed regarding his life and environment. The following facts concerning him are mentioned in the *Encyclopaedia of Islam*.[18] He was born in the month of Ṣafar, 722 A.H. (February–March, A.D. 1322), at Taftāzān, a large village near Nasa in Khurāsān. He is said to have been a pupil of 'Aḍud al-Dīn al-Ījī and of Quṭb al-Dīn. His earliest work was completed at the age of sixteen. The *Muṭawwal*, the *Mukhtaṣar al-Ma'ānī*, and the *Talwīḥ* were completed in 748, 756, and 758 respectively, at Harat, Ghujduwān, and Gulistān. The commentary on the *al-'Aqā'id al- Nasafīya* was completed at Khwarizm in 768. According to Ibn 'Arabshāh, al-Taftāzānī, like Quṭb al-Dīn al-Rāzī, was one of the scholars attracted to the court of the Mongols of Western Qipčaq. When Timūr invaded Khwarizm, Malik Muḥammad Sarakhsī b. Malik Mu'izz al-Dīn Ḥusayn Kurt asked his nephew Pīr Muḥammad b. Ghiyāth al-Dīn Pīr 'Alī, who was then in the suite of Timūr, to obtain Timūr's consent to send al-Taftāzānī to Sarakhs.

[17] *Al-Muqaddima*, III, 92 f.   [18] IV, 604 ff.

A comparison of the relative positions of al-Nasafī and al-Taftāzānī in respect to the two schools of orthodoxy is of value.

1. Regarding the sources of knowledge for mankind most Muslims, except the extreme Hanbalites, would admit the sound (that is, not defective) senses, true narratives, and Reason.[20] Al-Nasafī in his creed says, "And Illumination (*al-ilhām*) is not one of the causes of the cognition of the soundness of a thing." This is the position of Abū Ḥanīfa, who was inclined to ignore the claims of mystics to special knowledge because of his leanings towards rationalism. But al-Taftāzānī agrees with al-Ghazzālī and many other Ash'arites by saying that in the way of the mystic there is perfection of Belief and absolute knowledge. In attempting to explain away al-Nasafī's opposition to *ilhām*, al-Taftāzānī says that he must have meant that *ilhām* is not a cause by which knowledge results to people in general, nor by which one can enforce it on another, since there is no doubt that knowledge does result from it.[21]

2. In the matter of the origin of the universe the Qur'ān everywhere teaches that Allah is Creator and Maker. Repeatedly man's nothingness is contrasted with the power and wisdom of Allah who brings all things into existence. Most Muslim philosophers, through the use of an amalgam of the Neoplatonic Chain and the Aristotelian Cosmos, came to look at the world not so much as a creation but an emanation from the Deity. The language of the Qur'ān, because of its implicit pantheism, lent itself to this interpretation. Both al-Ash'arī and al-Māturīdī believed that Allah had created the universe out of nothing. This created world consists of substances and accidents; the former subsist in themselves, the latter only in something else.

But the unique contribution of Islam in the realm of philosophy was an elaborate atomic theory which is a combination of material atoms and time atoms into a complete system to explain the origin and working process of the universe. Maimonides, who gives in *The Guide for the Perplexed* a most systematic summary of the theory, says that Muslims borrowed it from the Greek philosophers but notes that there are fundamental differences between the Muslim position and that of Epicurus and other atomists. Al-Bāqillānī (d. A.D. 1013) has been called the original atomist among the Muslims.

Although al-Nasafī uses the term atom (*jawhar*) and explains it as "the part which is not further divided," this is insufficient basis for believing that

----

[20] See below, p. 16.   [21] See below, p. 27.

he held the interpretation characteristic of the thoroughgoing atomists and which has been maintained by the scholastic theologians of the later days of Islam. On the other hand al-Taftāzānī as well as most Ash'arites accepted this theory in its entirety.

The following is a very brief summary of the twelve propositions of the Mutakallim atomists as given by Maimonides: [22]

(1) The universe is composed of individual atoms (*jawhar fard*) which are all exactly alike. They do not have quantity but when combined the bodies thus compounded do.

(2) A vacuum in which nothing exists provides for the combination, separation, and movement of the atoms.

(3) Time is also made up of atoms which cannot be further subdivided.

(4) There are accidents which are elements in the sense of non-permanent qualities, which are superadded to the substance and which are inseparable from all material things.

(5) Atoms do not occur without accidents nor do accidents occur apart from atoms, even though the atoms do not have quantity.

(6) Accidents do not continue through two atoms of time. There is thus no inherent nature in things. Allah creates a substance and simultaneously its accidents. Immediately after its creation it is destroyed and another takes its place. That which is called natural law is only Allah's customary way of acting.

(7) The absence of a property is itself a property that exists in the body, so death is just as real an accident as life, rest as real as motion.

(8) There exists nothing but substance and accident. All bodies are composed of similar atoms, so the difference in bodies is caused only by their difference in accidents.

(9) One accident cannot exist in another accident. Every accident is directly connected with the substance which is its substratum.

(10) There is unlimited possibility in the world, with the exception of logical contradictions, because the divine will is not limited by natural laws.

(11) The idea of the infinite is inadmissible, whether actual, potential, or accidental. An infinite body, an infinite number of bodies, and an infinite number of causes are all impossible.

(12) The senses are not always to be trusted. Their evidence cannot

----

[22] *The Guide for the Perplexed*, tr. Friedländer, pp. 120 ff.

be accepted in face of rational proof. This last proposition answers those who oppose the preceding as contrary to the perception of the senses.

There were variants of this form of the atomistic philosophy in Islam, but that held by al-Taftāzānī and most other Ash'arites, if analyzed, would agree in practically every detail with this scheme set forth by Maimonides.

Though the system is still taught in Muslim religious colleges like al-Azhar, reform movements in modern Islam like that of Muḥammad 'Abdū tend to go back to Ibn Sīnā, Ibn Rushd, and the Aristotelian system for their interpretation of the cosmos. It has been suggested, however, that modern Western atomic speculation may galvanize the atomic system of strict orthodoxy into a semblance of life, just as the facts regarding microbes are interpreted as being in harmony with the Qur'anic teaching concerning the *jinn*.

3. Orthodox Islam, in opposition to the Mu'tazilites, reached early in its development the position that Allah has attributes (*ṣifāt*), which indicate more than the term "the Necessarily Existent" (*wājib al-wujūd*) connotes and which are from eternity. The disciples of al-Ash'arī posited seven essential attributes or those consisting of ideas (*ṣifāt al-ma'ānī*), namely, Power, Will, Knowledge, Life, Hearing, Seeing, and Speech. To these seven the Matuṛidites, including al-Nasafī, added Creating (*takwīn*), which they say is also an eternal attribute and not an indication of activity in the realm of originated things. Al-Taftāzānī presents in his commentary the Ash'arite objection, which is that there is no proof that Creating is another attribute in addition to Power and Willing. However, he favors the view that the act of Creating is from eternity to eternity and that when anything is created it happens through the creation of the connection with the attribute of Creating, just as in the case of Knowledge and Power. In another place he lists *takwīn* among the attributes of Allah.[23]

4. As to the Eternal Speech, which is an attribute of Allah, al-Ash'arī is credited with holding that it can be heard, but al-Māturīdī denied that it could be. Al-Nasafī says that the Qur'ān, the uncreated speech of Allah, is heard by our ears, but he seems to make a distinction between the attribute of Speech and the Qur'ān. Al-Taftāzānī takes the view that the meaning of the verse in the Qur'ān, "Until he hears the speech of Allah," is that he heard that which indicates it. So also Moses heard a sound which indicated the speech of Allah.[24] This approaches the position of the later Ash'arites, who held that Moses did not hear this speech as an ordinary act of hearing, but spirit-

---

[23] See below, p. 57. Many of the differences between the Ash'arite and the Maturidite theologians which follow are mentioned in Al-Rawḍa al-Bahīya.

[24] See below, pp. 64 f.

ually and as coming from every direction and perceived by every one of his organs.

5. Muslims believe that Allah is the creator of all actions of His creatures whether of Unbelief or Belief, of obedience or disobedience. The Jabrites went so far as to say that no action belongs to the creature at all. Many, however, have realized the moral difficulty of such a position for it contradicts experience. The Mu'tazilites, adopting the teaching of the Qadarites (that is, that man has power for actions), denied that Allah wills wicked and vile things. They had recourse to such Qur'anic verses as, "Allah does not impose upon a soul legal responsibility beyond its capacity. It has that which it has acquired and it owes what it has acquired" (Qur'ān 2:286). The idea of acquisition (*kasb* or *iktisāb*) which appears in this verse (as a verb) became the key word of the Ash'arite explanation of the creature's actions as related to Allah's creative activity. Free will and compulsion are both denied. Allah creates, man acquires. Al-Ash'arī is credited with introducing this technical usage, since in *al-Ibāna* he says, "It is impossible under the authority of Allah that there be any acquisition by creatures of that which He does not will." [25] The term is found in *al-Fiqh al-Akbar* (II), which, if it is by the hand of some immediate follower of Abū Ḥanīfa, would suggest that it antedates al-Ash'arī.[26] In a century's time after his death it was in common use among his disciples. Al-Nasafī, in line with the teaching of the Maturidite school, undertakes to explain the dilemma of the presence of evil and man's freedom alongside Allah's eternal Will by adding, "His creatures have actions of choice (*ikhtiyār*), for which they are rewarded or punished, and the good in these is by the good pleasure (*riḍā*) of Allah and the vile in them is not by His good pleasure." [27]

Al-Taftāzānī states the Ash'arite view in saying, "When the creature expends his power and will in action it is an acquisition, and when Allah brings it into existence as a consequence of that, it is a creating (*khalq*)." He realizes how unsatisfactory this explanation is, but admits that he is unable to do more than this in summarizing the expression used which proves clearly that the creature's action is by Allah's creating and bringing into existence along with what the creature has of power and choice.[28]

6. Closely allied to the creature's acquisition or choice of actions is the problem of whether or not all these actions are by Allah's good pleasure,

---

[25] *Al-Ibāna*, p. 63.

[26] *Al-Fiqh al-Akbar* (II), p. 20. See translation in Wensinck's *The Muslim Creed*, p. 191.

[27] See below, pp. 84 ff.   [28] See below, p. 86.

wish, and command. Al-Nasafī states that the good actions are by the good pleasure of Allah and the vile ones are not. This is the Maturidite position which followed the teaching of Abū Ḥanīfa.[29] The Ash'arites held that actions occurred according to Allah's will and did not make the distinction that the good ones were by his good pleasure while the bad were not. Al-Taftāzānī, although he emphasizes the fact that many actions which we deem vile sometimes have in them wise and beneficial matters, does not dissent from the principle enunciated by al-Nasafī. He goes on to explain, "This means that Willing, Desiring, and Decreeing are connected with all actions, while good pleasure, desire, and command are connected only with the good to the exclusion of the vile."[30] In this he takes his stand with the Maturidites.

7. Another question upon which there was difference of opinion was whether the creature possesses ability for every responsibility or not. Abū Ḥanīfa taught that the ability with which the creature disobeys is the same ability which is good for obedience. Al-Ash'arī permitted the rational possibility that a creature be burdened with responsibility beyond his power because he attributed nothing vile to Allah, neither is Allah limited or influenced by purpose. His school believed that the ability which is sufficient for evil deeds is not sufficient for good ones. The Maturidite teaching is expressed in the words of al-Nasafī, "The creature has no legal responsibility imposed upon him which is not in his capacity."[31] Al-Taftāzānī favors the belief that the creature's responsibility fits his ability, which is essentially the position of al-Nasafī.

8. There are varied opinions in Islam regarding what constitutes Belief (*imān*).[32] Al-Shāfi'ī, the traditionalists, the canon lawyers, and many of the scholastic theologians held that it consisted of three things: assent by the heart, confession by the tongue, and the doing of the *arkān* (such as worship, fasting, and the pilgrimage). Al-Ash'arī said that Belief is in word (*qawl*) and in deed (*'amal*) and that it may increase and decrease. This follows from the inclusion of works in Belief. Al-Nasafī said that Belief is assent to that which the Prophet brought from Allah and confession of it, and that though works increase, Belief neither increases nor decreases. Al-Taftāzānī held along with the Ash'arites in general that Belief is assent. A man may for some reason not confess with his tongue and yet be a Believer in the sight of Allah. This, too, is the position of Abū Manṣūr al-Māturīdī.

In general those who followed Abū Ḥanīfa said that the Belief of a

---

[29] *Al-Fiqh al-Akbar* (II), p. 21; *Kitāb al-Waṣiya*, p. 8. [30] See below, p. 87.
[31] See below, p. 92. [32] See below, pp. 116 ff.

muqallid (one who accepts on the authority of others) was sufficient for salvation.[33] It is taught that when one is in doubt regarding any of the fine points of theology he must hold for the time being that which is right regarding Allah until he finds a scholar and asks him; nor is he allowed to delay. This shows the development of the position adopted by the Ash'arites which required men to give a reason for their faith. This naturally was the Mu'tazilite view, since that school emphasized the use of Reason.

Al-Ash'arī held Islam to be a more general term than *imān* (Belief). Perhaps in this he was influenced by the tradition recorded of the Prophet by Ibn Ḥanbal, "The Messenger of Allah used to say, 'Islam is external. Belief belongs to the heart.' " [34] The terms appear to be synonymous in many Qur'anic passages and are so considered by most Muslims today. An expression of their relationship is seen in the passage, "Language distinguishes between Belief and Islam. Yet there is no Belief without Islam, and Islam without Belief cannot be found." [35] Al-Nasafī says that they are one, and al-Taftāzānī in his commentary takes the same position.[36]

9. Another ground for argument between the two orthodox schools was over the use by a Muslim of the words *"in shā'Allāh"* (if Allah wills) after saying, "I am a Believer." Al-Nasafī, following Abū Ḥanīfa and the position taken by the Maturidites, says that it is right for one to say, "I am a Believer in reality" and not fitting for him to add, "if Allah wills." Many of the Ash'arites held that this phrase was to be added since it may show true humility on the part of the Believer and a longing for perfection, and since the real estimate of one's Belief or Unbelief came at the end of life and the creature did not have the assurance of the outcome. Al-Taftāzānī in his commentary appears to set aside the difference between the two positions by pointing out the different aspects from which each school looks at the matter.[37]

10. The Ash'arites held that there is no change in the destiny of the happy or the miserable one throughout life, but al-Nasafī as a Maturidite says that the happy one sometimes becomes miserable and that the miserable one sometimes becomes happy; however, there is no change in Allah's attributes of making happy and miserable. On this matter al-Taftāzānī favors the position of al-Nasafī.[38]

11. The followers of Muhammad, from the nature of their religion, be-

---

[33] *Al-Fiqh al-Akbar* (II), p. 48.   [34] *Musnad*, III, 134 f. Cf. also I, 27 f., and 51 f.
[35] Abū Ḥanīfa, *al-Fiqh al-Akbar* (II), pp. 35 f.   [36] See below, p. 123.
[37] See below, pp. 125 f.   [38] See below, p. 126.

lieve that Allah has sent Messengers to mankind with good tidings, warning people and explaining to them what they need to know of this world and the Judgment. To what degree prophets might be liable to error in conveying their message and in their conduct receives little consideration in the Qur'ān and Tradition. In these sources the prophets appear quite human. There is no trace of sinlessness, nay rather some are guilty of grave sins. It remained for theological speculation to formulate a doctrine which grew out of the Agreement of the Muslim peoples, even though it goes contrary to written tradition. One of the earliest statements on this subject, if not the earliest, is to be found in the teachings of Abū Ḥanīfa: "All the Prophets are far removed from sins, both small and great, from Unbelief and vile things, although slips and mistakes (*khaṭāya*) may happen on their part. . . . He [Muhammad] never committed a small or great sin." [39] Abū Ḥanīfa is reported as maintaining that a prophet should be preserved from error, whereas al-Ash'arī held that he might commit smaller sins.

The Mu'tazilites held that a great sin is impossible for a prophet, for that would nullify his mission. The Shi'ites deny the appearance in a prophet of great and small sins both before and after revelations are made to him. Nevertheless they permit dissimulation in feigning Unbelief for a pious reason.

It came in time to be accepted as the orthodox position that prophets and especially Muhammad were preserved from error and falsehood. Since it was Fakhr al-Dīn al-Rāzī among the Theologians who first especially emphasized this principle as of primary importance, we are not surprised that al-Nasafī, even though a disciple of the Hanafite school, does not mention it in his Articles of Belief. However, al-Taftāzānī says that in al-Nasafī's statement, "All prophets were narrators veracious and sincere, conveying information from Allah," there is an allusion to the fact that prophets were preserved from falsehood in what is connected with the Law, the conveying of judgments, and the guidance of the people, either from errors committed intentionally or through inadvertence. Agreement is the basis for the first position and as for the second the majority agrees on it.

He concludes his discussion by saying, "What is reported of prophets which marks them as false or disobedient is to be rejected. This is to be done if there are only individual traditions. However, if there are *mutawātir* traditions, it is to be changed from its literal meaning if possible. Other-

---

[39] *Al-Fiqh al-Akbar* (II), pp. 22 f.

wise it is possible to explain it as a case of the preferable of two actions, or as something that happened before his mission." [40]

This tenet of faith became so fixed in orthodox Islam that al-Sanūsī (d. 895 A.H.) deduced from the words of the creed, "Muhammad is the Messenger of Allah," the necessity for the veracity of the apostles and the impossibility of falsehood in them. Otherwise they would not be messengers faithful to our Lord who knows hidden things. "From this may also be deduced," he said, "the impossibility of their doing anything prohibited. For they were sent to teach men by their sayings, by their deeds, and by their silence. So it is necessary that in all of these there should be no deviation from the command of our Lord, who has chosen them above His whole creation and instructed them with his secret revelation." [41]

From this comparison of the points on which the two orthodox schools disagreed it is clear that originally there was a distinct difference in attitude. The harsh, unrelenting fatalism that has characterized much of Muslim thought has found sanction for its conclusions in the Ash'arite teaching. Although the Mu'tazilite position that Allah must do what is best for the creature was rejected by the people of the Approved Way, the attempts of Abū Ḥanīfa, al-Māturīdī, and others to justify Allah's treatment of his creatures and to make the creature share the responsibility of his destiny have not been in vain. Through them orthodoxy has an interpretation of the ever-present problem of free will and predestination that has solved the paradoxes of life for many a perplexed Muslim thinker. In fact this explanation has been taken over in part by Ash'arites such as al-Taftāzānī as well.

It is probably unwise to attempt a prediction of the future of theological thinking in the world of Islam and to prophesy concerning the influence which may yet be exercised by this creed of al-Nasafī and the commentary of al-Taftāzānī with its numerous supercommentaries. It is possible that scholasticism may be increasingly replaced by agnosticism as has happened in Turkey today or by a back-to-Muhammad movement fostered by a spirit of romanticism or by fundamentalism of the Wahhabite type. It is not unlikely that some strange and incongruous teachings may claim in the years to come that they are not incompatible with the basic message of Islam. We must not forget that some doctrines have been accepted by the Muslim community although they are not strictly in accord with the Qur'ān and

[40] See below, p. 134.   [41] *Sharḥ Umm al-Barāhīn*, pp. 173 ff.

Traditions. The Agreement of Muslim thinkers may again furnish a basis for change. So far modernist movements in Islam have failed to supplant the dialectic of its religious schools with a complete and consistent scheme of theology. Conservatism will not surrender its entrenched position without a struggle. It may attempt to meet historical criticism and a new atomic age with radical adaptations of its ancient system to new ideas rather than yield its authority to some other power. In any case this commentary of al-Taftāzānī on the articles of Islamic Belief as stated by al-Nasafī remains a record of what orthodox Islam has thought and taught for more than five hundred years.

A Note on the Translation

In this translation, use has been made of the Cairo text of A.H. 1335 with supercommentaries by Ibrāhīm b. Muḥammad b. 'Arabshāh al-Isfarā'inī 'Iṣām al-Dīn and Aḥmad b. Mūsā al-Khayālī. Further references to this work will be designated 'I.D. The numbers in square brackets in the translation indicate the pages in this edition. The Cairo text of A.H. 1329, which is an encyclopaedic work containing a number of the supercommentaries on al-Taftāzānī and glosses on these, has also been used, especially the first volume, which contains the supercommentary by al-Khayālī mentioned above and also one by Mullā Aḥmad al Jundī, and his own glosses on this work. References to this text will read A.J. The Constantinople text of A.H. 1310, which contains a number of minor omissions and grammatical and typographical errors, has been consulted. It contains a supercommentary by Muṣliḥ al-Dīn Muṣṭafa al-Kastalī, with an appendix containing that of al-Khayālī mentioned above and one of Ramaḍān b. 'Abd al-Muḥsin Bihishtī.

The Cureton text (London, 1843) of al-Nasafī's short creed differs in some respects from that found in the three editions of al-Taftāzānī's commentary which have been mentioned. Where these differences represent additions to the text as found in the commentary, attention will be called to them.

There are no chapters or sections in the text and commentary as published in Arabic. The translator alone is responsible for the chapter divisions and headings as they appear in this translation. Al-Nasafī's creed is printed in bold-face type throughout, and as it is taken up by al-Taftāzānī, sentence by sentence or phrase by phrase, it is separated from the commentary by a solidus. The portion of the creed presented thus in each chapter is also printed as a whole at the beginning of the chapter.

Contents

*A Commentary on the
Creed of Islam*

Preface by al-Taftazani[1]

TO HIS COMMENTARY ON THE ARTICLES OF BELIEF [2] BY AL-NASAFI.[3]

In the name of Allah, the Merciful, Compassionate One (*al-raḥmān*).

PRAISE BE to Allah, who is unique in the majesty of His essence and the perfection of His attributes, and who is separated [4] from blemishes and marks of defect through the qualities that belong to His great Power. Blessings on His Prophet Muhammad, who has been aided by His forceful arguments and clear proofs, and on his family and his Companions, guides and protectors of the path of Reality.

To continue: The basis of the science of laws and judgments and the foundation of the rules concerning the articles of Islamic Belief [5] is the science of the unity of the Deity and His attributes, entitled *al-Kalām*, which is devoid of the darkness of doubts and the obscurities of fancies.

The brief treatise known as the "Articles of Belief" (*al-'aqā'id*) is by the painstaking Imam, 'Umar al-Nasafī, the example of the learned of Islam and the star of our faith and religion. May Allah raise his rank in the abode of Peace. It includes under the headings of this branch of knowledge the most striking gems and pearls of great value [6] which are the fundamental standards of our religion. Running through the text [of the creed] these [gems and pearls] are jewels and precious stones of certainty, yet at the same time the

[1] For the list of the writings of Sa'd al-Dīn Mas'ūd b. 'Umar al-Taftāzānī (A.H. 722–791; A.D. 1322–1389) see Brockelmann, *Geschichte der arabischen Litteratur*, II, 215 f. and also the *Encyclopaedia of Islam*, IV, 604 ff.

[2] A translation of al-Nasafī's Creed is given in Macdonald's *Development*, pp. 308 ff. For the importance of such treatises see *Enc. of Islam*, I, 236 f.; Wensinck, *The Muslim Creed*, pp. 1 ff., 102 f.

[3] A list of the writings of Najm al-Dīn Abū Ḥafṣ 'Umar b. Muḥammad b. Aḥmad al-Nasafī (A.H. 460–537; A.D. 1068–1142) is given in Brockelmann's *Geschichte*, I, 427 f.

acme of conciseness and instruction and the last word in good order and arrangement.

I have tried to explain the brief treatise so as to give the details of its general principles and clarify the intricacies of the subject, to straighten out the involved things and reveal those that are concealed, while at the same time keeping the record concise, clearly calling attention to its purpose. The verification of the problems is a result of the statement of them. The detailed application of the proofs is an effect of their presentation. The interpretation of the doctrines comes after proper introduction. The values of the work are manifold in spite of its conciseness. I achieved this end by ridding my commentary of tautology and wearisomeness, and by striking the happy medium between brevity and tediousness. Allah is the guide to the path of those who are led, and of Him we seek preservation from error and guidance to the goal. He is my sufficiency, and excellent is the Guardian.

Chapter I

THE REAL ESSENCES OF THINGS

The People of Reality say that the real essences of things exist in reality and that the knowledge of them is verifiable as real in contradiction to the Sophists.

[7] KNOW THAT of the legal judgments [1] (*al-aḥkām al-shar'īya*) there are some which are connected with practice and are called derived (*far'īya*) and practical (*'amalīya*); and there are others which are connected with dogma and are called fundamental (*aṣlīya*) and doctrinal (*i'tiqādīya*). The science

[1] *Ḥukm* (a judgment) in Muslim technical use may be either legal (*shar'i*) or non-legal (*ghayr-shar'i*) as a logical judgment, an ordinance or decree, or a rule in grammar, *Enc. of Islam*, II, 332; IV, 320 ff.; *Dict. of Tech. Terms*, I, 372 ff. The legal judgment referred to here is an expression for the judgment of Allah which is related to legally responsible human beings (cf. *al-Ta'rifāt*, p. 97). The whole branch of law known as *al-shar'* or *al-shari'a* is the legal system of duties in Islam resting on an absolute basis. This was originally made up from the Qur'ān and Tradition but Agreement (*ijmā'*) and Analogy (*qiyās*) were added later making four bases for the law. It includes not only as does our criminal law what one should not do and the penalties for transgression but also what is incumbent on the Muslim, what is praiseworthy, and what is allowable, etc. Al-Sanūsī in the commentary on his *Umm al-Barāhīn* (pp. 34 f.) says that a legal judgment is by means of demand or permission or by the laying down of postulates for these two. Four things go to make up demand, (1) obligation (*ijāb*) which is the absolute demand that a thing be done, as for example belief in Allah and His Messengers and the five pillars of Islam, (2) recommendation (*nadb*) which is a demand, though not absolute, that a thing be done, like the prayer at dawn, (3) prohibition (*taḥrīm*) which is the absolute demand for the refraining from an act like ascribing a partner to Allah, adultery, etc., (4) disapproval (*karāha*) which is a demand, though not absolute, for refraining from an act, like the recitation of the Qur'ān during the bowings and prostrations. Between the first two and the last two of these four is permission (*jawāz*) which is the choice between the doing and omitting of a thing, such as marriage or trade. Cf. J. D. Luciani, *Les Prolégomènes théologiques de Senoussi* (Algiers, 1908), pp. 14 f.

All acts of Muslims come under one of these five headings, so when the term The Law (*al-shar'*) is used by al-Taftāzānī, this very broad usage must be kept in mind.

The rational judgment (*al-ḥukm al-'aqlī*) may be any one of three categories, necessity (*wujūb*), impossibility (*istiḥāla*) and possibility (*jawāz* or *imkān*). See Wensinck, *The Muslim Creed*, pp. 273 ff.; *Enc. of Islam*, III, 260; al-Shahrastānī, *Kitāb Nihāyatu 'l-Iqdām*, p. 15.

connected with the first [8] is called the science of canon laws and judgments because these things are not comprehended except from the canon law
(*al-shar'*), and it is only to these that the understanding turns when the
[term] judgment is mentioned without further definition. And the science
connected with the second is the science of the unity (*al-tawḥīd*) and attributes (*al-ṣifāt*) of the Deity, since this [subject of unity] is its most noted investigation and its noblest object.

[9] The earliest of the Companions [2] (*al-ṣaḥāba*) and their Followers [3]
(*al-tābi'īn*)—Allah be pleased with them all [4]—because the articles of their
belief were pure through the blessing of their association with the Prophet—
on him be peace; because the period in which they lived was near to his
time; because there were few occasions of attack and disagreement and because
they were able to go back to absolutely reliable authority; well, because of all
these things they dispensed with putting down in writing the material of the
two sciences and with dividing it into divisions and sections, and they also
dispensed with the statement of their investigations in these two sciences
both as to developments and fundamentals.

This condition continued until controversies arose among the Muslims,
pride prevailed among the leaders of the faith (*al-dīn*), and there appeared a
clashing of opinions and a tendency to innovations (*al-bida'*) [5] and to personal desires (*al-ahwā'*).[6] There was a multiplicity of legal decisions
(*al-fatāwī*) and of occasions from which cases arose, and much referring to
the Learned (*al-'ulamā'*) in important matters. So they busied themselves
with speculation and deduction, with attempting to arrive at a correct opinion

---

[2] A Companion (*ṣāḥib* or *ṣaḥābī*) is one who met the Prophet during his life, believed on him, and died a Muslim. *Dict. of Tech. Terms*, pp. 807 f.; *Enc. of Islam*, I, 477 f.

[3] A Follower (*tābi'* or *tābi'ī*) is one who though he personally did not know the
Prophet knew one of his Companions. *Dict. of Tech. Terms*, pp. 166 f.; *Enc. of Islam*,
IV, 583.

[4] The eulogia throughout the translation are as a rule omitted after the first occurrence.
For the significance of these see Goldziher, "Uber die Eulogien der Muhammedaner," in
Zeitschrift der deutschen morgenländischen Gesellschaft, L (Leipzig, 1896), pp. 97 ff.

[5] *Bid'a* (plur. *bida'*) is some view or practice which is an innovation and is not according to the established usage of Islam. *Enc. of Islam*, I, 712 f.; *al-Ta'rīfāt*, p. 44; *Dict.
of Tech. Terms*, p. 133.

[6] There is a technical usage for the phrase *ahl al-ahwā'* (people of personal desires);
however, the meaning of this term differs. Macdonald (*Development*, pp. 122, 299) calls
them "people of wandering desires." They are said to be people of erroneous opinions,
whose belief is not that of *ahl al-sunna*, but who nevertheless have the same *qibla*. Cf.
Dict. of Tech. Terms, p. 1543; *al-Ta'rīfāt*, p. 41; *Enc. of Islam*, I, 183. But al-Shahrastānī
in *al-Milal wa 'l-Nihal*, (pp. 24 and 201 f.) seems to think that properly speaking they
should be put beyond the pale of the recognized religions. Al-Baghdādī (*al-Farq bayn
al-Firaq*, p. 350 f.) calls them Unbelievers and says that it is not permissible to perform
worship behind them or over their dead.

and to elicit meaning from the texts, with the establishing of rules and fundamentals, with the arrangement of [the material related to them in] divisions and sections, with the multiplying of proofs to problems and stating the matters in which there were ambiguities and their explanations, with determining the conventional usages and the technical terms, and with pointing out the [various] ways of proceeding and the differences. [*10*] They gave the name of *al-fiqh* to that which pertained to the science of the practical judgments derived from their detailed proofs, and "the fundamentals of *al-fiqh*" to the science of the terms of the proofs taken together as a whole in proving the judgments; and the science of the articles of Belief as they come straight from their proofs they called *al-kalām*.[7]

The reasons for this are (1) because the subject of its investigations was their saying, "The discourse (*al-kalām*) about such-and-such"; (2) because the problem of [the meaning of the term] Speech [predicated of Allah] was the most celebrated of its investigations, the most strongly disputed, and the subject of the most controversy, so much so that [*11*] some of the leaders killed many of these People of Reality (*ahl al-ḥaqq*)[8] because they failed to admit the creation of the Qur'ān; (3) because it imparts ability in speech in verifying legal matters and in compelling adversaries to submit just as logic (*al-manṭiq*) imparts ability in philosophy; (4) because it is the first of the sciences which can be known and learned by speech only, so this term [speech] was applied to this science, and then it was exclusively used for it and not applied to any other science for sake of distinction; (5) because it can be verified only by discussion and interchange of speech from two sides, whereas others are sometimes verified by meditation and the perusal of books; (6) because it is the most disputatious and controversial of the sciences, so speech was greatly needed for conversing with those of opposite view and for refuting them; (7) because of the cogency of its arguments it has become, so to speak, "the speech" (*al-kalām*) to the exclusion of all other sciences, just as is said of the stronger of two discourses, "This

---

[7] See *Enc. of Islam*, II, 670 ff., in which there is reference to these eight explanations of al-Taftāzānī. Cf. also *Dict. of Tech. Terms*, pp. 22 ff.; T. J. de Boer, *Philosophy in Islam*, pp. 42 f.; Maimonides (Munk), *Le Guide des égarés*, I, 332 ff.; (Friedländer), *The Guide for the Perplexed*, pp. 107 ff.

[8] Al-Khayālī ('I.D., p. 15) says that the evident meaning of this term throughout the book is the People of the Approved Way and the Community (*ahl al-sunna wa 'l-jamā'a*). However, from al-Taftāzānī's explanation the term means not only that they alone were right and therefore orthodox as some translate the term, but also that they are peculiar in that they believe in the reality of things. Lest they be confused with those realists who believe only in the reality of ideas, the term "People of Reality" has been used. See also *Enc. of Islam*, II, 223.

is 'the discourse' "; (8) and because it is based on decisive proofs (*adilla qaṭ'iya*), most of which are supported by proofs to be believed on authority (*al-sam'iya*),[9] it is consequently the strongest in its influence on and penetration into the heart. So it is called *al-kalām* as though derived from *al-kalm*, that is, "the wound." This is the [understanding of the term] *kalām* [in the mind] of the ancients (*al-qudamā'*).

Most of the controversies about *al-kalām* occurred among the different Islamic sects, especially the Mu'tazilites (*al-Mu'tazila*),[10] because they were the first sect which laid the foundation for both that which contradicts [*12*] the plain teaching of the Approved Way (*al-sunna*) [11] and that which the Community (*al-jamā'a*) of the Companions (*al-ṣaḥāba*)—the approval of Allah on them all—followed in the matter of the articles of Belief. That [beginning of the Mu'tazilites] happened when Wāṣil b. 'Aṭā', their leader,

---

[9] Theology is said to concern itself with three things, *ilāhiyāt, nabawiyāt,* and *sam'iyāt,* i.e., things relating to the Deity, to the prophets, and to those things which are only established by hearing. Under this third head there are included the matters concerning the Garden, the Fire, and the Resurrection, of which one can only learn from the Qur'ān and Tradition. See al-Bayjūrī in his commentary on *Kifāyat al-'Awāmm fī 'Ilm al-Kalām* by al-Faḍālī, p. 75, and al-Ghazzālī, *Iḥyā'* (with the commentary by Sayyid Murtaḍā), II, 213 ff.

[10] The account which follows is the story told in most Muslim books regarding the origin of the Mu'tazilites. Cf. al-Baghdādī, *al-Farq bayn al-Firaq,* p. 98 f.; al-Shahrastānī, *al-Milal,* p. 33; *Dict. of Tech. Terms,* p. 1025; *Enc. of Islam,* III, 787 ff. The number of the sects of the Mu'tazilites is often given as twenty. Al-Baghdādī, *al-Farq bayn al-Firaq,* p. 93; al-Ījī, *al-Mawāqif,* p. 335. Different writers, however, make different groupings (cf. al-Shahrastānī, *al-Milal,* p. 3) and are not entirely agreed on those who are to be called Mu'tazilites. For example al-Shahrastānī finds many Mu'tazilite doctrines among the followers of al-Najjār (*al-Milal,* p. 61 ff.), whereas al-Baghdādī (*al-Farq bayn al-Firaq,* p. 195) puts him, as does al-Ash'arī (*Maqālāt,* pp. 283 ff.), under a separate heading, but he also considers his position on Belief as Murji'ite (*Maqālāt,* pp. 135 f.). The stress laid by the writers on enumerating these sects is undoubtedly due to a tradition of the Prophet that his people would be divided into seventy-three sects—some say seventy-two—only one of which would be in Paradise. See also al-Ījī, *al-Mawāqif,* p. 332; al-Baghdādī, *al-Farq,* pp. 4 f.; Aḥmad b. Ḥanbal, *Musnad,* II, 332 f., III, 120, 145.

[11] *Sunna,* a way, course, or manner of conduct, came to have many meanings in Islam: see *al-Ta'rīfāt,* pp. 127 f.; *Dict. of Tech. Terms,* pp. 703 ff.; *Tāj al-'Arūs,* IX, 244; *Lisān al-'Arab,* XVII, 89 f.; Lane, *Lexicon,* p. 1438. It sometimes means one of the four bases of Islam, that is, that which was the usage in speech or deed or the approved manner of conduct of the Prophet; the other three bases being the Qur'ān, the Agreement (*ijmā'*) of the Muslim Community (*jamā'a*), and Analogy (*qiyās*). The term is also applied in worship and other rites of Islam to those utterances and acts that are praiseworthy but not absolutely prescribed. *Al-sunna* also came to mean the theory and practice of the catholic Muslim community. See *Enc. of Islam,* IV, 555 f. The term *ahl al-sunna wa 'l-jamā'a,* which is implied here in the statement of al-Taftāzānī, means the people of whole orthodox communities who refrain from innovation and deviation from the beaten path. Al-Khayālī ('I.D., p. 14) adds that they are the Ash'arites in Khurāsān, Iraq, Syria, and most countries, but that in the lands beyond the river (Oxus) they are the Maturidites, the followers of Abū Manṣūr al-Māturīdī. Cf. Sayyid Murtaḍā's commentary on the *Iḥyā'* of al-Ghazzālī, II, 6 f., where he quotes this statement of al-Khayālī.

withdrew from the circle of al-Ḥasan al-Baṣrī—Allah have mercy on him—asserting that the one who committed a great sin was neither a Believer nor an Unbeliever and maintaining that he was in an intermediate position. Al-Ḥasan said, "He has withdrawn from us," so they were called *al-Muʿtazila* (the Withdrawers). But they called themselves the Maintainers of Justice and the Divine Unity (*aṣḥāb al-ʿadl wa 'l-tawḥīd*), because they said that the reward of the obedient and the punishment of the disobedient are incumbent on Allah, and they denied that He has eternal attributes. [*13*] Subsequently they went deep into the science of *al-kalām* and added the fringes of the Philosophers to many of their principles.

Their school of thought spread among the people until al-Shaykh Abū 'l-Ḥasan al-Ashʿarī said to his teacher, Abū ʿAlī al-Jubbāʾī, "What have you to say about three brothers, one of whom died obedient, another disobedient, and the third in infancy?" He answered, "The first will be rewarded with the Garden (*al-janna*), the second will be punished with the Fire (*al-nār*), and the third will neither be rewarded nor punished." Al-Ashʿarī answered, "And what if the third should say, 'Lord, why didst Thou make me die in infancy, and not detain me until I grew up and believed on Thee, and obeyed and thus entered the Garden?' What would the Lord—the Exalted—say then?" He answered, "The Lord would say, 'I knew that if thou shouldst grow up thou wouldst disobey and enter the Fire, so it was better for thee to die in infancy.'" Al-Ashʿarī said, "And if the second should say, 'Lord, why didst Thou not cause me to die in infancy so that I should not disobey and enter the Fire?' What would the Lord say then?" Al-Jubbāʾī was confounded and al-Ashʿarī abandoned his school of thought. He and his followers worked from that time at refuting the Muʿtazilite view and maintaining that which the Approved Way had handed down and that which [*14*] the community did. Hence they are called the People of the Approved Way and the Community (*ahl al-sunna wa 'l-jamāʿa*).

Then when philosophy [12] was translated into Arabic and the followers of Islam plunged (*khāḍa*) into it, they attempted to refute the Philosophers on the points in which they differed from the canon law (*al-sharīʿa*). So they mixed up with *kalām* much of philosophy in order to understand thoroughly the goals of philosophy and so to be put into a position to show the unreality

---

[12] The philosophy (*al-falsafa*) referred to here and throughout the treatise is that system which had for its principal sources Aristotelian natural science and Neoplatonic speculation and which taught the eternity of the world, and that what some call creation was an emanation from the Deity. Cf. De Boer, *Philosophy in Islam*, pp. 11–30; *Enc. of Islam*, II, 48 ff.; Macdonald, *Development*, pp. 161 ff., and al-Shahrastānī, *al-Milal*, pp. 251 ff.

of it. This went on until they included in *kalām* most of physics and meta-physics and plunged [18] into mathematics until theology was hardly to be distinguished from philosophy had it not been that it included "things to be believed on authority" (*al-sam'iyāt*). This is the *kalām* of the Later Theologians (*al-muta'akhkhirūn*).

In general *kalām* is the most noble of the sciences, first, because it is the foundation of the legal judgments and the chief of the religious sciences; second, because its subject matter is the articles of Belief of Islam; third, because its aim is the attaining of the happiness of this life and the next; and fourth, because its proofs are the decisive arguments most of which are aided by evidences that are based on authority.

As to what has been reported of the Fathers of the first generations (*al-salaf*) of Islam concerning their attack against *kalām* and their pro-hibition of it, that was only directed against the religious zealot and the one who had failed to attain certainty, and against the one who purposed to destroy the articles of Belief of the Muslims and the one who plunged need-lessly into the obscurities of those who claimed to be philosophers. Otherwise how can one conceive the prohibition of the foundation upon which our obligations rest and the basis of laws regarding practice?

[*15*] Furthermore the basis of *kalām* is that there is deduced from the existence of originated things (*al-muḥdathāt*) the existence of the Maker (*al-ṣāni'*), His unity, His attributes and His actions, and from these things all the rest of the things which are to be believed on authority. For this reason it was suitable to begin the treatise by calling attention to the existence of that which is observed of substances and accidents and to verify the knowledge concerning both of them, that thereby one might attain the understanding of that which is the most important goal of all.

Therefore al-Nasafī said,

The People of Reality (*ahl al-ḥaqq*) say/Reality is the judgment which corresponds with the actual fact. It is applied in a general sense to proposi-tions, to articles of Belief, to religions, and to different schools of practice (*al-madhāhib*) with reference to their inclusion of reality. Its opposite is the unreal (*al-bāṭil*). But as for the term truth (*al-ṣidq*), it is especially applied to propositions; its opposite is falsehood (*al-kadhib*). The distinc-tion that may be made between these two pairs of contrast is that in the case

---

[18] 'I.D. reads *ba'ḍ* (some) for *khāḍu fi*.

of reality (*al-ḥaqq*) the correspondence [*16*] is seen from the standpoint of the actual fact, and in the case of truth (*al-ṣidq*), from the standpoint of judgment. And the meaning of the expression "the truth of a judgment" is the agreement of the judgment with the actual fact, and the meaning of the expression "the reality of a judgment" is the agreement of the actual fact with the judgment.

that the real essences of things exist in reality/The real essence (*al-ḥaqīqa*) of a thing and its quiddity (*al-mahīya*) are that which constitutes the identity of a thing (*mā bihi 'l shay' huwa huwa*), as is exemplified by the application of the term "rational (*nāṭiq*) animal" to man in contrast to the application of the terms "laughing animal" and "writing animal"; [*17*] in which case it is possible to conceive of man as not being described by the terms "laughing" and "writing," inasmuch as they [laughing and writing] are accidents. And it may be said further that that which constitutes the identity of a thing is, with respect to its being verified as having external reality, a real essence; and with respect to its being individualized, it is a certain particular thing (*huwīya*), but without respect to either of these it is a quiddity.

Thus in our opinion the term *shay'* [14] (a thing) is identical with the term *al-mawjūd* (that which exists); and the terms *al-thubūt* (real existence), *al-taḥaqquq* (being verified as having real existence), *al-wujūd* (existence) and *al-kawn* [15] (coming-into-existence) are synonymous, and the meaning of them is immediately perceived (*badīhī al-taṣawwur*).

---

[14] *Al-shay'*. With the Ash'arites the *shay'* was the entity (*mawjūd*) but with the Mu'tazilites it included the non-entity (*ma'dūm*). The Baṣriya and al-Jāḥiẓ of the Mu'tazilites defined it as that which is known (*ma'lūm*); al-Nāshī Abū'l-'Abbās defined it as the eternal (*qadīm*) and in the case of "that which is originated" it is used metaphorically; the Jahmiya said it is that which is originated; Hishām said it is the body. (*Dict. of Tech. Terms*, p. 729; 'I.D., p. 17.)

[15] *Kawn*, which is often translated "being," really has the significance of "coming into being" or "state of coming into being." The *Dict. of Tech. Terms* (p. 1274) quoting the *Commentary on al-Mawāqif* says, "The Mutakallims, although they denied the rest of the categories, admitted that of place (*al-ayn*), and called it *al-kawn*. The majority of them said that the *jawhar* [self-subsistent entity] itself was all that was required for obtaining the boundary (*al-ḥayyiz*) which marked existence, that is there was no quality subsisting in the *jawhar* itself. So there were two things, the *jawhar* itself and the obtaining of a boundary in existence, which they called *kawn*. But those of the Mutakallims who established the states (*al-aḥwāl*) said that this obtaining a boundary on the part of a *jawhar* was caused by a quality which subsisted in it. So they called obtaining a boundary '*al-kā'ina*' and the cause of this obtaining '*al-kawn.*' There are then three things in the process, *al-jawhar*, *al-kā'ina*, and *al-kawn*. There are four species of *al-kawn*: motion, rest, being separated into parts, and aggregation of the parts." See al-Taftāzānī, 'I.D., p. 48; Macdonald, "Atomic Time," *Isis*, IX, 2, p. 329.

But if it is objected that such a logical statement as that the real essences of things exist in reality is tautological in the same way as our stating that really existent things exist in reality, [*18*] to this we answer that what is meant thereby is that what we believe to be the real essences of things and designate by certain terms such as "man," "horse," "sky," and "earth" is something existing in the things themselves. It is analogous to the statement that the necessarily existent being (*wājib al-wujūd*) is existent. This statement conveys some useful information; in fact it may have to be demonstrated by argument. It is not like the statement that the really existent things exist in reality, nor is it like the statement [*19*] that I am Abū 'l-Najm and my poetry is my poetry, in which case the statement is self-evident [and hence conveys no useful information].

And the verification of this is to be found in the fact that a thing may have different aspects, in consequence of which when something is predicated of it the judgment may be useful when the thing is seen in one aspect, and useless when it is seen in another. In the case of man, for instance, when taken with respect to his being a body of some sort, to predicate of him animality conveys useful information, but, when taken with respect to his being a rational animal, then to predicate animality of him is tautological.

and that the knowledge of them/that is, of the real essences, both of that which they are perceived to be (*taṣawwur*) and of that which is affirmed of them or of their modes

is verifiable as real/Some say that what this statement refers to is undoubtedly the knowledge of the reality of the existence of the essences, for to know the essences themselves as a whole is impossible. [*20*] In reply to this it may be said that the reference here is to the genus, in refutation of those who say that there is no real existence to any of the essences and also of those who say that there can be no knowledge of the fact whether an essence has real existence or has no real existence.

in contradiction to the Sophists [18] (*al-sūfasṭā'iya*)/For some of them deny the real essences of things and maintain that they are fancies (*awhām*) and

---

[18] The origin of this word is plainly the Greek σοφιστεία (sophistry). These three schools are defined in *al-Ta'rīfāt* in almost the same words, pp. 163 f., 200. They are more fully explained in the *Dict. of Tech. Terms*, pp. 665 f. Cf. Ibn Ḥazm, *Kitāb al-Fiṣal*, I, 8 f.; Wensinck, *The Muslim Creed*, pp. 251 f.; al-Sa'adya, *Kitāb al-Amānāt*, pp. 65 ff.

vain imaginations (*khayālāt*).[17] These are the Obstinate (*al-'inādīya*). Others deny the real existence of essences, maintaining that essences only follow from what one happens to believe, so that if we believe a thing to be a substance (*jawhar*) [18] it is a substance, but if we believe it to be an accident it is an accident; or if we believe a thing to be eternal (*qadīm*) it is eternal, but if we believe it to be originated (*ḥādith*) [19] it is originated. These are the Opinioners (*al-'indīya*). Still others deny that there can be any knowledge of whether a thing has real existence or not. They assert that they are in doubt and that they are in doubt even of their doubt, and so on. [*21*] These are the Agnostics (*al-lā-adrīya*).

As for us, however, to prove our point of view we first convince ourselves, either by sense perception or by demonstration, of the necessity of establishing that certain things have real existence. Then from this premise we argue that if the negation of those things is not proven, then the real existence of those things has been established. But if, on the other hand, the negation has been proven, then, inasmuch as that negation by virtue of its being a species of judgment is one of the real essences it necessarily follows, again, that something of real essence has been established and that it is not proper to negate it absolutely. It is evident that this argument applies to the Obstinate only.

[As for the Opinioners and the Agnostics], they say, with regard to those types of knowledge described as necessary (*al-ḍarūrīyāt*) that (a) some of them are sense perceptions (*al-ḥissīyāt*), [*22*] but that sense perception may sometimes err, as in the case of the squint-eyed who sees one to be two, and of the bilious who finds the sweet bitter, and (b) some of them are immediate perceptions (*al-badīhīyāt*) but that these are subject to differences of opinion and are open to ambiguities for the solving of which there is need of subtle speculation. (c) Another type of necessary knowledge [they say] is that arrived at by means of syllogistic speculations (*al-naẓarīyāt*) [from major premises which are either sense perceptions or immediate perceptions]; but as

---

[17] *Wahm* and *khayāl*. See Macdonald, "Wahm and Its Cognates," *Journal of the Royal Asiatic Society* (1922), 506 ff., and Wolfson, "The Internal Senses in Latin, Arabic and Hebrew Philosophic Texts," *Harvard Theological Review*, XXVIII (1935), 90 ff.

[18] *Jawhar* is the self-subsistent entity or substance as opposed to the accident (*'araḍ*). The Early Theologians said it was that of which other things were compounded. But with the Atomists it means "atom," especially when the term *al-jawhar al-fard* is used. See *Enc. of Islam*, I, 1027; *Dict. of Tech. Terms*, pp. 203 ff.; Macdonald, "Atomic Time," *Isis*, IX, 2, p. 328; Pines, *Beiträge*, pp. 3 ff.; Maimonides (Munk), *Le Guide des égarés*, I, 385 ff.; (Friedländer), pp. 123 f.

[19] See Ibn Sīnā, *al-Najāt*, pp. 355 ff.; *al-Ta'rīfāt*, pp. 85, 179; *Dict. of Tech. Terms*, p. 1212.

for these [they argue] with the unsoundness of these major premises, there necessarily follows the unsoundness of the conclusions. And it is for this reason [they add] that thinking human beings have many differences of opinion [concerning conclusions arrived at by syllogistic speculations].

To these we reply:

(a) The error that may occur in sense perception by reason of particular causes in certain instances does not negate the validity of the sense perception in other instances where the particular causes of the error are not present.

(b) The differences of opinion that may occur with respect to immediate perceptions by reason of one's lack of acquaintance with the subject or of one's difficulty in forming a clear notion of the subject on account of its abstruseness do not destroy the possibility of forming immediate perceptions.

(c) The many differences of opinion that may occur in conclusions arrived at by syllogistic speculation as a result of the unsoundness which may sometimes occur in the act of speculation do not destroy in other instances the validity of conclusions arrived at by syllogistic speculation.

But the truth is that there is no way to enter into discussion with them, especially the Agnostics, because they do not admit anything known by which [23] an unknown is to be established. Rather the only way is to punish them with the Fire, that they may either confess or be consumed in the Fire.

Sūfaṣṭā is a name given to falsified wisdom and specious knowledge, because *sūfā* means knowledge and wisdom, and *asṭā* means the specious and false. And from this is derived *al-safsaṭa,* just as *falsafa* is derived from *faylāsūfā* (philosopher), which means "the lover of wisdom."

Chapter 2

THE CAUSES OF KNOWLEDGE

The causes of knowledge for all creation are three: the sound senses, true narrative, and Reason. The senses are five, namely, hearing, seeing, smelling, taste, and touch, and by each of these senses one is informed concerning that for which it was appointed.

True narrative is of two kinds: one of them is the *mutawātir* narrative, and it is the narrative established by the tongues of people of whom it is inconceivable that they would agree together on a falsehood. It brings about necessary knowledge such as the knowledge of former kings in past times and of distant countries. The second kind is the narrative of the Messenger aided by an evidentiary miracle, and it brings about deductive knowledge, and the knowledge established by it resembles the knowledge established by necessity in certainty and in fixity.

Then as for Reason: it is a cause of knowledge also; and whatever of it is established by immediate perception is necessary, just as the knowledge that the whole of a thing is greater than the part of it; and whatever is established by deduction is acquired.

Illumination is not one of the causes of the cognition of the soundness of a thing with the People of Reality.

The causes of knowledge [1]/Knowledge is an attribute of the knowing subject by means of which any object referred to becomes revealed (*yatajalla*) to him; that is to say, it becomes clear and evident and capable of being described by words, and this regardless of whether that object is something existing (*mawjūd*) or something non-existing (*ma'dūm*). Knowledge includes both the comprehension (*al-idrāk*) by the senses and the comprehension by Reason (*al-'aql*), and this again both of things conceived

[1] Cf. Wensinck, *The Muslim Creed*, pp. 248 ff., for a discussion of the roots of knowledge.

(*al-taṣawwurāt*) and of things asserted (*al-taṣdīqāt*), the latter of which may be both certainties (*al-yaqīnīya*) [2] and non-certainties (*ghayr al-yaqīnīya*).

This is in opposition to the view of the Sophists that knowledge is an attribute [of the knowing subject by means of] which [he] makes an affirmative judgment of which the contradictory (*al-naqīḍ*) cannot be admitted. This definition of theirs, although it includes the comprehension of the senses, provided only that the thing to be perceived is not inaccessible to the senses; [24] and although it also includes the things conceived [by Reason] provided only, as they claim, that the things to be conceived do not have contradictories; yet it does not include the non-certainties of things asserted. So much for their view. Accordingly the revelation of an object to the knower must be taken to mean a complete unveiling (*al-inkishāf al-tāmm*) [3] [which has been identified with knowledge] and therefore precludes opinion (*al-ẓann*) [4] so that knowledge with them is to be contrasted with opinion.

for all creation (*al-khalq*) [5]/that is, for all created beings, whether angels, men or *jinn*, in contrast to the knowledge of the Creator—who is exalted in and through Himself—for knowledge belongs to His essence and is not due to any cause whatsoever [25]

are three: the sound senses (*al-ḥawāss al-salīma*), **true narrative** (*al-khabar al-ṣādiq*), **and Reason** (*al-ʿaql*) [6]/This is by way of enumerating the particulars (*al-istiqrāʾ*).[7] From the standpoint of classification, if the cause of the knowledge is some other person outside the knower, then it is true narration; [but if the cause of knowledge is within the knower

---

[2] Cf. *Al-Risāla al-Shamsīya*, pp. 33 ff.; *Dict. of Tech. Terms*, p. 1537, and Macdonald, "Wahm and its Cognates," *Jour. Roy. As. Soc.*, 1922, pp. 507 ff.; al-Ghazzālī, *Miʿyār al-ʿIlm*, pp. 125 ff., 159 ff.

[3] Cf. *Enc. of Islam*, II, 787; Horten, *Die spekulative und positive Theologie des Islam*, p. 237; Macdonald, *Development*, pp. 120, 172 f.

[4] *Al-ẓann* is that faculty which produces opinion or belief with the admission that the contrary may be the case. See *al-Taʿrīfāt*, p. 149; *Dict. of Tech. Terms*, pp. 939 f.; Wolfson, "Internal Senses," *Harvard Theological Review*, XXVIII (1935), 93 ff.; Ibn Sīnā, *al-Najāt*, pp. 99 f.; al-Ghazzālī, *Miʿyār al-ʿIlm*, pp. 128 ff.

[5] *Al-khalq*. This use of the verbal noun for the passive participle goes back to the Qurʾān. See Qur. 31:10 (al-Bayḍāwī, *Anwār al-Tanzīl*, II, 112); Qur. 36:79 (*Anwār al-Tanzīl*, II, 165 f.), etc.

[6] See al-Saʿadya, *Kitāb al-Amānāt wa l-Iʿtiqādāt*, p. 12 ff. This threefold classification of the kinds of knowledge is common to Muslim, Christian, and Jew. Wolfson, *The Philosophy of Spinoza*, II, 133.

[7] *Al-istiqrāʾ* is the judgment concerning a universal based on particulars. See *Dict. of Tech. Terms*, p. 1229; *al-Taʿrīfāt*, p. 18; *al-Risāla al-Shamsīya*, p. 33; Ibn Sīnā, *al-Najāt*, p. 90; al-Ghazzālī, *Miʿyār al-ʿIlm*, pp. 102 ff.

himself] then, if there is an organ distinct from the perceptive faculty (*al-mudrik*), it is sense perception; otherwise, it is Reason.

Objection may be raised that the efficient cause (*al-sabab al-mu'aththir*) in all kinds of knowledge is Allah, since they all exist through His creation and His bringing them into existence without any impression (*ta'thir*) being made by the sensory faculty, true narration, and Reason. Reason only appears to be a cause, as for instance fire in the case of burning; and as for the senses and narration, the former are only instruments and the latter a method of comprehension.

Further objection may be raised that the ultimate cause (*al-sabab al-mufḍi*) —taken as a whole wherein Allah creates within us knowledge according to the customary way (*jary al-'āda*) [8] in order to include the percipient (*al-mudrik*) such as Reason, the instrument such as the sensory faculty, and the method such as narration—is not confined to three things, but there are other things such as sensibility (*al-wijdān*),[9] surmise (*al-ḥads*),[10] experience (*al-tajriba*),[11] and the speculation (*al-naẓar*) of the Reason, meaning the arrangement of principles and premises (*muqaddimāt*).

[26] To this we reply that this [threefold division given] is according to the method of the Early Theologians, who limited themselves to the aims pursued and shunned the minute precisions of the Philosophers. When these theologians discerned that some of the things perceived came as the result of the use of the external senses, about which there is no doubt, whether in rational beings or non-rational beings, they, therefore, made the senses one of the causes; and since most of the things known about religion are derived from true narrative, they made it another cause. Since they were not positive about the internal senses (*al-ḥawāss al-bāṭina*),[12] which are called the common sense (*al-ḥiss al-mushtarak*) [13] or the estimative faculty (*al-wahm*) or something else; and because they did not attach much im-

---

[8] *Jary al-'āda*. This term is one of the key phrases of the Atomistic theologians. Macdonald, "Atomic Time," *Isis*, IX, 2, p. 332. Cf. Maimonides (Munk), *Le Guide des égarés*, I, 388 ff.; (Friedländer), *The Guide for the Perplexed*, pp. 124 ff.; Pines, *Beiträge*, pp. 26 ff.

[9] See *Dict. of Tech. Terms*, p. 1455.

[10] See *al-Risāla al-Shamsīya*, p. 34; *al-Ta'rifāt*, p. 86; *Dict. of Tech. Terms*, pp. 300 f.

[11] See *al-Risāla al-Shamsīya*, p. 34; *Dict. of Tech. Terms*, pp. 189 f.; Ibn Sīnā, *al-Najāt*, pp. 94 f.

[12] See Wolfson, "Internal Senses," *Harv. Theol. Rev.*, XXVIII (1935), 69 ff.; Ibn Sīnā, *al-Najāt*, pp. 264 ff.; al-Ghazzālī, *Maqāṣid al-Falāsifa*, III, 46 ff.

[13] See Macdonald, "Wahm and its Cognates," *Jour. Roy. As. Soc.*, 1922, pp. 512 f.; *Dict. of Tech. Terms*, p. 304; Wolfson, "Internal Senses," *Harv. Theol. Rev.*, XXVIII (1935), 100 ff.; al-Ghazzālī, *Maqāṣid al-Falāsifa*, III, 46 ff.

portance to the details of surmises (*al-ḥadsīyāt*), experiences (*al-tajribīyāt*), immediate perceptions (*al-badīhiyāt*) and speculations (*al-naẓarīyāt*), and because all these go back to Reason, they made Reason a third cause which ultimately arrives at knowledge by merely giving attention to or by drawing to itself a surmise or an experience or the arrangement of premises. So they made Reason the cause of knowledge in that we have hunger and thirst, that the whole is greater than the part, that the light of the moon is derived from the sun, that scammony is a laxative, and that the world is originated, although in some matters Reason is aided by sense perception.

The senses (*al-ḥawāss*)/The word is the plural of a sense (*ḥāssa*), meaning the sensory faculty.

are five/meaning that of necessity Reason determines their existence. But the proofs for the internal senses, which the Philosophers maintain, are incomplete according to the fundamentals of Islam.

namely, hearing (*al-sam'*)/It is a faculty (*qūwa*) placed in the nerves spread out in the cavity of the ear hole, by which sounds are perceived. This is by way of connecting with the ear hole the air which has assumed the quality of the sounds, meaning that [27] Allah then creates perception in the soul (*al-nafs*).

seeing (*al-baṣar*)/It is a faculty placed in the two hollow nerves which meet each other in the brain, thence they separate and go to the two eyes; by this faculty are perceived rays of light, colors, shapes, measures, motions, the beautiful and the ugly, and other things, the perception of which Allah creates in the soul whenever the creature uses this faculty.

smelling (*al-shamm*)/It is a faculty placed in the two protruding lumps on the front of the brain, which are like the two nipples of the breasts; by this faculty odors are perceived by way of connecting with the cartilage of the nose the air which has assumed the quality of the odors.

taste (*al-dhawq*)/It is a faculty spread out in the nerves situated on the organ of the tongue; by this faculty flavors are perceived through the mixing of the saliva which is in the mouth with the thing tasted, and through its reaching to the nerves.

and touch (*al-lams*)/ It is a faculty spread out into all the body by which heat and cold, moisture and dryness, and the like are perceived at the time of touching and **contact.**

[*28*] **and by each of these senses**/that is, the five senses

one is informed/that is, is given knowledge

concerning that for which it was appointed/that is, that particular sense. This means that Allah has created each one of these senses to perceive certain things peculiar to it, such as hearing for sounds, taste for that which is flavored, and smelling for odors. Nothing is perceived by one sense which is perceived by another sense, but as to whether that is possible or not there is a difference of opinion. However, the correct position is that it is possible, because it is by a purely creative act of Allah without any impression on the part of the senses. So it is not impossible that Allah create after the loss of sight an added perception of sounds, for example. If the question is raised whether the sweetness and heat of a thing are not both together perceived by the tasting faculty, we reply in the negative; rather the sweetness is perceived by taste and the heat by the sense of touch which is present in the mouth and the tongue.

True narrative/that is, that which is in agreement with the fact, for narrative is [a form of] speech in relation to which there is something external with which the relationship agrees, so it is true; or the relationship does not agree with it, and it is then false. So truth and falsehood are descriptives of narrative. They therefore may be used with the sense of giving information about a thing according to what is or what is not. This means [that narration is] the making [of something] known by a complete relationship which agrees [*29*] or does not agree with the fact, so truth and falsehood are among the attributes applied to the narrator. And for this reason in some books the term "the true" is used as an attribute of "narrative" (*al-khabar al-ṣādiq*), and in others it is placed in annexation, "the narrative of the truthful one" (*khabar al-ṣādiq*).

is of two kinds: one of them is the *mutawātir* [14] **narrative**/It is so called because it does not occur just once, but in sequence and continuity.

[14] In the science of Muslim traditions the *mutawātir* (verbal noun, *tawātur*) is the most trustworthy from the standpoint of the number who attest it. For the technical terms

and it is the narrative established by the tongues of people of whom it is inconceivable that they would agree together/that is, Reason does not permit their concurring together

on a falsehood/The thing that proves it is that knowledge takes place without any doubt.

It/of necessity

brings about necessary knowledge such as the knowledge of former kings in past times and of distant countries/The latter phrase "distant countries" may be joined to "the kings" or to "the times"; the former, namely "the kings," is more likely although further away in position in the sentence.

Here then are two matters to be noted; one of them is that the *mutawātir* narrative brings about [30] knowledge and that of necessity, for we come of ourselves to the knowledge of the existence of Mecca and Baghdad and that such facts are only gained through narratives. The other matter is that the knowledge derived from such *mutawātir* narrative is necessary, and that is because it may be obtained by one who is capable of making a deduction and by others as well, even by children who have not yet been brought up to the right way, by the method of the acquisition of knowledge and of arranging the necessary premises. But as for the narrative of the Christians (*al-Naṣāra*) concerning the killing of Jesus,[15] on whom be peace, and that of the Jews (*al-Yahūd*) concerning the perpetuity of the religion of Moses, on whom be peace—well, such *mutawātir* narrative is absurd.

Objection may be raised that the narrative of each individual only gives an opinion (*ẓann*), and heaping opinion upon opinion does not bring about certainty, and also that the possibility of each individual's falsehood brings about the possibility of the whole group's falsehood, for it is made up of the same individuals.[16] To this we reply that it often happens that in the grouping together of individual cases there is something in them collectively

---

used in classifying the content and authorities, etc., of traditions see Guillaume, *The Traditions of Islam*, pp. 85 ff. and 181 f.; S. de Sacy, in *Notices et extraits des manuscrits*, X (Paris, 1818), 481 ff.

[15] The denial by the Muslims of the killing of Jesus rests on the interpretation of a verse in the Qur'ān (4:156). They take it to mean that someone was crucified in his place. The other references (Qur. 3:37, 48; 5:117; 19:34) to his departure are often interpreted in such a way as to deny his crucifixion and death. See al-Bayḍāwī, al-Rāzī, and al-Ṭabarī in their commentaries on these verses.

[16] A. J. adds, "so the *mutawātir* narrative does not give knowledge."

that was not in them separately, as for instance in the strength of a rope made of hairs.

It may be objected that in the case of necessary types of knowledge there is no irregularity or contradiction; still, we do find in the case of such knowledge that the knowledge that one is half of two is stronger than the affirmation of the existence of Alexander. Furthermore, some of those people who employ Reason in their investigations, such as al-Sumanīya [17] and the Brahmins (*al-Barāhima*),[18] deny that *mutawātir* narrative produces knowledge. [*31*] This argument is inapplicable as an objection, for it is to be admitted that various kinds of necessary knowledge sometimes differ from one another by difference in usage, custom, and practice, and in the occurring to one's mind and conceiving the terms of judgments (*aṭrāf al-aḥkām*). And there may be a contradiction about *mutawātir* narrative because of pride and obstinacy just as the Sophists exhibit in contradicting all types of necessary knowledge.

The second kind is the narrative of the Messenger (*al-rasūl*) aided/that is to say, whose message is established

by an evidentiary miracle (*al-muʿjiza*)/A Messenger is a man sent by Allah to creatures in order to convey His judgments; and the bringing of a book may be stipulated of him, in contrast to a prophet (*al-nabī*), for "prophet" [*32*] is a more general term.[19] An evidentiary miracle [20] is something that annuls the customary way of things (*khāriq lil-ʿāda*), the purpose of which is to demonstrate the truthfulness of the one making the claim to be the Messenger of Allah.

---

[17] Al-Sumanīya were responsible for spreading the knowledge of Indian skepticism in Persia. See *Enc. of Islam*, II, 48; Horten, *Die philosophischen Ansichten von Razi und Tusi*, pp. 14 ff.; and *Phil. Systeme der spek. Theologen im Islam*, pp. 93 ff.; Wensinck, *The Muslim Creed*, p. 256; *Dict. of Tech. Terms*, pp. 702, 1390; ʿI.D., p. 30; A.J., p. 53.

[18] See below, Chap. 14, and also al-Shahrastānī, *al-Milal*, pp. 444 ff.; Horten, *Phil. Systeme der spek. Theologen im Islam*, pp. 90 ff.; *Enc. of Islam*, I, 653.

[19] The Muʿtazilites held that there was no distinction between *rasūl* (messenger) and *nabī* (prophet). *Al-Taʿrīfāt*, p. 115. See also *Dict. of Tech. Terms*, p. 584, and al-Khayālī in ʿI.D., p. 31; A.J., p. 54, and below, Chap. 14.

[20] Seven stipulations have been laid down regarding the evidentiary miracle. It must (1) be from Allah, (2) annul the customary way of things, (3) be impossible for those who contend with Allah's Messenger, (4) appear at the hands of him who claims the prophetic office, (5) be in accordance with that claim, (6) substantiate his veracity, and (7) not happen before the claim to the prophetic office is made. See *Dict. of Tech. Terms*, pp. 975 ff. Cf. al-Ījī, *al-Mawāqif*, pp. 169 ff. Cf. Lane, *Lexicon*, p. 1961; *al-Taʿrīfāt*, p. 234; A.J., pp. 54 f.; ʿI.D. (see also the gloss of al-Khayālī), p. 32, and below, Chap. 14.

and it/that is, the narrative of the Messenger

brings about deductive (*istidlālī*) knowledge/that is, that which is arrived at by deduction (*al-istidlāl*), which is by consideration of proof (*dalīl*). Deduction is (1) that thing by the sound consideration of which one is enabled to attain the knowledge of any subject that has been transmitted by narrative. (2) It has also been said to be a [minor] proposition, composed of judgments, which necessarily demands a [major] proposition.

[*33*] So according to the first definition the proof of the existence of the Maker is the world, and according to the second definition it is our saying that the world is originated and that everything originated has a maker. But their statement that proof is that thing from the knowledge of which the knowledge of something else follows is more suitable to the second definition. But as for its bringing about knowledge, that is because it is absolutely certain that he through whom Allah performs an evidentiary miracle for the purpose of asserting his claim to the office of Messenger is truthful in the judgments which he brings. If he is truthful, then the knowledge concerning the contents of his message absolutely follows.

And as for its being deductive, that is because it depends upon deduction [*34*] and because it brings to the mind the fact that it is the narrative of the one whose office of Messenger is established by evidentiary miracles. Every narrative of this kind is truthful and its contents are according to fact.

and the knowledge established by it/that is, by the narrative of the Messenger

resembles/that is, is like

the knowledge established by necessity/[this means] like the things perceived by the senses, those immediately perceived, and the *mutawātir* narratives.

in certainty/that is, in the impossibility of predicating the contradictory

and in fixity/that is, in the impossibility of predicating the discontinuance of this knowledge by that which is ambiguous (*tashkīk al-mushakkik*).[21] And

---

[21] See *Dict. of Tech. Terms*, p. 780; *al-Risāla al-Shamsīya*, pp. 5 f., and Wolfson, "Amphibolous Terms," *Harvard Theological Review*, XXXI (1938), 151 ff.

it is a kind of knowledge that means the absolute established conviction (*i'tiqād*) which agrees with the fact, else otherwise this knowledge would be a matter of ignorance, or of opinion, or of following tradition (*taqlīd*).[22]

If it is objected that this explanation is applicable to the *mutawātir* only, and therefore goes back to the first section [of true narrative], we reply that the statement is about that narrative which is known to be [35] of the Messenger because it has been heard from his mouth or because that or something else possible has been transmitted of him by *tawātur*. The individual narrative is not useful for knowledge because there may be some doubt of its being the narrative of the Messenger.

An objection may also be made that since the statement is *mutawātir* or heard from the lips of the Messenger of Allah, the knowledge which results is then necessary and consequently not deductive, just as in the case of the rest of knowledge obtained by *tawātur* and sense perception. To this we reply (1) that the necessary knowledge, in the case of the *mutawātir* narrative which is from the Messenger, is the knowledge that the narrative is the narrative of the Messenger of Allah—may blessing and peace be upon him—because this means "that by which the giving of the narrative has become *mutawātir*." (2) In regard to that which is heard from the mouth of the Messenger—may Allah bless him and give him peace—the necessary knowledge [in this case] is the perception of the verbal expressions and that they are the speech of the Messenger. (3) But the deductive knowledge [in this case] is the knowledge as to its content and the establishing of that which it proved. For example, the statement of the Messenger, "It is incumbent on the claimant to produce proof, and the defendant must take an oath," [23] is known by *tawātur* to be the statement of the Messenger. This knowledge is necessary. Further it is known from this statement [of the Messenger] that proof devolves on the claimant. [The knowledge of] this [fact] is deductive.

Further objection may be raised that truthful narrative which gives useful knowledge is not confined to these two kinds, but may be narrative coming from Allah or from the Angel or the People of Agreement (*al-ijmā'*), or narrative coupled with that which removes the possibility of falsehood, like the news of the arrival of Zayd as indicated by his people rushing to his house.

---

[22] Some say that *taqlīd*, the acceptance of a religion without argument or proof, is sufficient to make a man a Believer, others deny this holding that the *muqallid* is an Unbeliever. Macdonald, *Development*, p. 316. Cf. *Enc. of Islam*, IV, 630; *Dict. of Tech. Terms*, p. 1178; *al-Bābu 'l-Hādī 'Ashar*, pp. 5 ff.; al-Faḍālī, *Kifāyat al-'Awāmm*, pp. 15 ff.; al-Sanūsī, *Umm al-Barāhin*, pp. 55 ff.; Wensinck, *The Muslim Creed*, pp. 136, 242, 265.

[23] See al-Tirmidhī, *Ṣaḥīḥ*, "Aḥkām," b. 12; al-Bukhārī, *al-Ṣaḥīḥ*, II, 116.

To this we answer that what is meant by narrative is a narrative which is a means of knowledge to all creatures by merely being a kind of narrative without regard at all to the contexts [36] which give certainty by the evidence of Reason.

So the narrative coming from Allah or from the Angel is able to impart knowledge in relation to all creation only when it comes to them by way of the Messenger. The same judgment applies to the narrative of the Messenger and to that of the People of Agreement in the case of a *mutawātir* judgment. Answer may be made that it has no meaning by itself alone but rather by consideration of the proofs which indicate that Agreement is an argument. We then say that likewise the narrative of the Messenger is of the same class and for that reason was classified as deductive.

Then as for Reason (*al-'aql*) [24]/which is a faculty of the soul (*al-nafs*),[25] by which it is prepared for the reception of things to be known and perceived. That is the meaning of their saying, "It is an innate property (*gharīza*) which, whenever the instruments of perception are sound, is followed by the necessary types of knowledge." [37] Some people define it as the substance (*al-jawhar*) by which the things not perceived by the senses are perceived through means, and by which sense perceptions are perceived through observation.

it is a cause of knowledge also/He made this clear because there is a disagreement about it among the heretics (*al-Malāḥida*) and the Sumaniya in regard to all types of speculation, and among some Philosophers in regard to metaphysical speculations, on the basis of numerous differences and the contradiction of opinions. The reply that this is due to the unsoundness of speculation does not preclude the fact that sound speculation on the part of Reason is useful for giving knowledge, although the very thing you mentioned is a deduction by the speculation of Reason. Thus it establishes that which you have denied, so it is contradictory to itself. And if they assert that this means the opposing of the unsound with the unsound, we answer that either it means something [38] and therefore is not unsound, or it does not

---

[24] *Al-'aql* is the translation by the Arabic writers on philosophy of the Greek νοῦς. See Macdonald, *Rel. Attitude and Life*, pp. 230 f.; *Dict. of Tech. Terms*, II, 1027 ff.; Ibn Sīnā, *Rasā'il fī 'l-Ḥikma wa 'l-Ṭābī'iyāt*, pp. 79 f.; al-Ghazzālī, *Iḥyā'*, VII, 201 ff.

[25] *Al-nafs* is "the animal psyche" or "the appetitive soul." See Macdonald, *Rel. Attitude and Life*, pp. 228 ff.; and "Wahm and its Cognates," *Jour. Roy. As. Soc.*, 1922, p. 509; *Dict. of Tech. Terms*, p. 1398; Ibn Sīnā, *Rasā'il*, pp. 81 f.; al-Ghazzālī, *Iḥyā'*, VII, 201 ff.; *Enc. of Islam*, III, 827 ff.

mean anything at all and therefore there is no opposing [of the unsound with the unsound].

Some may say, "Let us grant that speculation is useful for giving knowledge. Well then, if this knowledge is necessary there is no contradiction about it, for it is just as though we said, 'One is half of two'; and if it is speculative, then it is necessary to establish speculation by speculation and that is circular proof (*al-dawr*)." To this we reply that sometimes there may be a contradiction about necessary knowledge because of obstinacy or the limitation of perception. The people who use Reason are agreed that the reasoning faculties of men are distinctly different according to the nature created (*al-fiṭra*) in them. [This position is reached] by deduction from precedents (*al-athār*) and by the testimony of narratives (*al-akhbār*) [from the Prophet].[26] The speculative type (*al-naẓarī*) of knowledge itself may be established by a special speculation which is not expressed in terms of a [general] speculation. An example of this is our saying, "The world is changing, and everything changing is originated." Of necessity that is useful for giving the knowledge that the world was originated. [39] This [necessity] does not rest upon the special character of the speculation, but because it is sound and accompanied by [that which meets] its conditions. So every sound speculation accompanied by that which meets its conditions has a meaning, and in verifying the answer to this objection there is more detail than is fitting to this book.

and whatever of it is established/that is, of knowledge established by Reason

by immediate perception (*al-badīha*)/that is, at the first glance without the necessity of thought

is necessary, just as the knowledge that the whole of a thing is greater than the part of it/For after conceiving the meaning of "all" and "part" and "greater" it is seen that this [proposition] does not rest on anything; and whoever hesitates about it—so that he asserts that a part of a man, like the hand for example, may sometimes be greater than [40] the whole—does not conceive the meaning of "whole" and "part."

[26] Al-Ghazzālī gives the name *khabar* (plur. *akhbār*) to a tradition that goes back to Muhammad himself, while he distinguishes those that can only be traced back to the Companions as *athār*. See *Enc. of Islam*, II, 859, also al-Ghazzālī's use of the terms in *Ihyā'*. However, this usage is not universal for some use *athār* also for traditions that go back to Muhammad. Cf. *Dict. of Tech. Terms*, p. 65; Lane, *Lexicon*, p. 19.

and whatever is established by deduction (*al-istidlāl*)/that is, by consideration of proof, whether by deduction from cause to effect, as whenever one sees fire and so knows that it has smoke; or from effect to cause, as whenever one sees smoke and so knows that fire is there. The first process may be specified as "assigning the cause" and the second as "deduction."

is acquired (*iktisābī*)/that is to say, obtained by acquisition (*al-kasb*). This is [done by] immediate causality (*mubāsharat al-asbāb*) through choice, as in the application of Reason and in speculation on the matters which pertain to deduction, and by inclining the ear, turning about the pupil of the eye, and so forth, in matters which pertain to the senses. So we see that "acquired" is a more general term than "deductive" because deductive knowledge is that which is obtained by consideration of the proof. Everything deductive then is acquired, but not everything acquired is deductive, as for example the use of the faculty of sight which results from purpose and choice.

As for necessary knowledge: it is sometimes contrasted with acquired knowledge and it is then explained as that the obtaining of which is not within the power (*maqdūr*) of [choice apportioned by Allah to] the creature; and sometimes necessary knowledge is contrasted with deductive knowledge and explained as that which results without thought or speculation regarding proof. And so some termed the knowledge resulting from the use of the senses "acquired," that is, resulting from immediate causality through choice; and others termed it "necessary," that is, resulting without the use of deduction.

[*41*] There does not seem to be a contradiction in the statement of the author of *al-Bidāya* [27] when he says that originated (*al-ḥādith*) knowledge is of two kinds: (1) necessary, which Allah originated in the soul of the creature without his acquisition and choice, like the knowledge of his existence and the change of his states (*aḥwāl*); and (2) acquired, which Allah originates in the creature by means of his acquisition, and this is by immediate causality in respect to knowledge, its causes being three: sound senses, truthful narrative, and the speculation of Reason. Then he went on to say that from the speculation of Reason there result two kinds of knowledge: (1) necessary, which comes at the very beginning of speculation

---

[27] This is evidently the book by Nūr al-Dīn Aḥmad b. Maḥmūd b. Abū Bakr al-Ṣābūnī al-Bukhārī (d. A.D. 1184) referred to in Brockelmann, *Geschichte*, I, 375, and Wilhelm Ahlwardt, *Verzeichniss der arabischen Handschriften der königlichen Bibliothek zu Berlin* (Berlin, 1887–99), No. 1737.

without any cogitation (*tafakkur*), such as the knowledge that the whole is greater than the part; and (2) deductive, in which a kind of cogitation is necessary, as the knowledge of the presence of fire on seeing the smoke.

Illumination (*al-ilhām*)/It it that which is explained as the casting of an idea into the intellect (*al-qalb*) by means of overflowing (*al-fayḍ*).

is not one of the causes of the cognition (*al-maʿrifa*) **of the soundness of a thing with the People of Reality**/This statement was made to answer the objection to confining the causes of knowledge to the above-mentioned three things only. It would have been better if al-Nasafī had said, "One of the causes of the knowledge (*al-ʿilm*) of a thing," unless it was that he tried to call attention to the fact that for us knowledge and cognition are the same, not, as some do, making a technical distinction between them by confining knowledge to compounds (*al-murakkabāt*) or to universals (*al-kullīyāt*), and cognition to simple things (*al-basāʾiṭ*) or to particulars (*al-juzʾīyāt*); otherwise there was no use of his particularizing the statement by saying "the soundness of a thing" [instead of "a thing"].

Then it is clear that he meant that Illumination is not a cause by which knowledge results to creatures in general nor by which it is right for one to force knowledge on another; otherwise there is no doubt that knowledge does result from Illumination. [42] There have been reported statements regarding Illumination in the tradition of the Prophet such as, "My Lord illumined me." [28] And this has been said of many of the Fathers (*al-salaf*) also.

As for the narrative of a single unprejudiced person and the following of the tradition (*taqlīd*) of one who attempts a legal opinion (*al-mujtahid*),[29] they are sometimes useful for opinion and sometimes for strong conviction which is enduring. It appears that al-Nasafī meant by knowledge (*al-ʿilm*) that which does not include these two things mentioned; otherwise there is no reason for confining the causes of knowledge to the three [causes mentioned].

---

[28] A. J., who is careful to mention the sources of traditions, gives no reference to this saying.

[29] This is a technical term which applies to the one learned in the Qurʾān and its meanings and the Sunna who exerts himself to the utmost in forming an opinion on something connected with legal judgments. *Enc. of Islam*, II, 448 f.; *Dict. of Tech. Terms*, p. 198; Ibn Khaldūn, *al-Muqaddima*, III, 6.

Chapter 3

THE WORLD

Further, the world in the totality of its parts is a thing originated, since it consists of substances and accidents. A substance is that which has self-subsistence, and it is either a thing compounded, that is, a body; or not compounded, like the atom, which is the part that is not further divided. And the accident is something that does not subsist in itself but is originated in bodies and atoms, such as colors, states of coming into being, tastes, and odors.

Further, the world (*al-'ālam*)/that is, everything except Allah—of the existent things (*al-mawjūdāt*) by which the Maker is known, is called the world of bodies (*al-ajsām*), the world of accidents (*al-a'rāḍ*), the plant world (*al-nabāt*), the animal world (*al-ḥayawān*), and so on. The attributes of Allah are excluded [from the things making up the world] because they are not other than His essence, just as they are not the essence itself.

in the totality of its parts/that is, of the heavens and what is in them and the earth and what is on it

is a thing originated (*muḥdath*) [1]/This means it is something brought from non-existence into existence, [43] meaning that it was once non-existent (*ma'dūm*) and then it existed. This is in opposition to the Philosophers, inso-

---

[1] At the beginning of Chapter 7 according to our division of the commentary al-Taftāzānī gives a number of synonyms for creating (*al-takwīn*). *Takwīn* is sometimes defined as meaning that a thing comes into material existence, while *iḥdāth* (origination) means that a thing comes into temporal existence. See *Dict. of Tech. Terms,* p. 134. *Ḥudūth* is the opposite of *qidam* (eternity). In order to express the further distinction in meaning *muḥdath* has been translated "originated" and *muḥdith* as "originator" rather than "created" and "creator" which have been used for other words. See below, Chap. 7. For the contrast between the Philosophers and the Atomistic Theologians in theory as to the composition and working process of the universe see Maimonides (Munk), *Le Guide des égarés,* I, 313 ff. and 344 ff.; (Friedländer), *The Guide for the Perplexed,* pp. 102 ff. and 109 ff.; Macdonald, "Atomic Time," *Isis,* IX, 2, 334.

far as they held to the position of the eternity (*qidam*) of the heavens,[2] including their respective matters (*mawādd*), forms (*ṣuwar*), and shapes (*ashkāl*), and the eternity of the sub-lunar elements (*al-ʿanāṣir*) including their respective matters and forms, but these forms are only specific forms, inasmuch as the elements were never without form. Strictly speaking, the Philosophers used the term "being originated" with reference to that which is not Allah, but they used it in the sense of being dependent on something else, not in the sense of being preceded by non-existence.

Then al-Nasafī pointed out the proof for the origin (*ḥudūth*) of the world by his statement:

since it/that is, the world

consists of substances (*aʿyān*) [3] **and accidents** (*aʿrāḍ*)/because whatever of it is self-subsistent (*qāʾim bi dhātihi*) is a substance, and whatever is not is an accident. Both of them are originated, as we shall show. And the author—Allah have mercy on him—did not deal with this, because the discussion of it would be very long and inappropriate to this brief treatise of his, seeing that it is confined to problems without their proofs.

A substance is that which/that is, any possible thing

has self-subsistence (*qiyām bi dhātihi*)/By context this is inferred from their being a part of the world. [44] The meaning of self-subsistence with the Mutakallims is that substance is bounded by itself (*yataḥayyaz bi nafsihi*); its being bounded does not follow from the fact that some other thing is bounded, in contrast to the accident, in which case its being bounded follows from the fact that the atom (*al-jawhar*) is bounded, for the atom is the subject (*al-mawḍūʿ*) or the locus (*al-maḥall*) which gives subsistence to the accident.

The meaning of the existence of the accident in the subject is that its very existence is its existence in the subject, and for that reason it cannot be transferred from the subject. This is in contrast to the existence of a body within a boundary (*al-ḥayyiz*), for its very existence and its existence in a boundary are two different things. For that reason a body may be transferred from a

---

[2] Cf. Plato's *Timaeus, Dialogues of Plato*, ed. Jowett (1874), II, 544, 560.

[3] In scholastic theology *ʿayn* is the term used for "substance." The philosophers used *jawhar* as contrasted with "accident" (*ʿaraḍ*) and with "idea" (*maʿnā*). *Dict. of Tech. Terms*, p. 1073; Lane, *Lexicon*, pp. 2214 ff.; *Enc. of Islam, Supplement*, pp. 13, 16; al-Ghazzālī, *Maqāṣid al-Falāsifa*, II, 7 f.

boundary. According to the Philosophers the meaning of the subsistence of a thing in its essence is its being independent of the locus in which it subsists, and the meaning of its subsistence in something else is its being specified by it, so that the first becomes something descriptive (*na't*) and the second something described (*man'ūt*), whether having boundaries, as in the case of the blackness of a body, or not [having boundaries], as in the case of the attributes (*ṣifāt*) of Allah and the absolutes.[4]

and it/whatever of the world is self-subsistent

is either a thing compounded (*murakkab*)/of two [45] or more parts, according to us.

that is, a body (*jism*) [5]/Some say that there must be three parts so that the three dimensions, length, breadth, and depth may be realized; and others say eight parts, in order that the intersecting of the dimensions at vertical angles may be realized. This is not a dispute over verbal expressions to be used, referring to some technicality [in the matter] that can be settled by saying that each may explain the term technically as he wishes. It is a dispute as to whether or not the conventional idea thus given to body is sufficient if it is compounded of two parts only. The Primitive Theologians (*al-awwalūn*) argued that if one of two bodies exceeds the other by one part, then it is bulkier [*ajsam*, that is, more of body] than the other. And if the mere compounding [of parts] were not sufficient to constitute corporeality, then the body would not increase in corporeality by the mere addition of a part. This is a matter for consideration, for the form *af'al* from the noun *al-jasāma* [that is, *ajsam* as used above] has the meaning of bulk and greatness of amount. It is said that a thing becomes bulky (*jasuma*), that is, it becomes great, so it is said to be bulky (*jasīm*) and corpulent (*jusām*). We speak here of body as a name (*ism*) not as an attribute (*ṣifa*).

or not compounded, like the atom (*jawhar*)/that is, the substance which is not divisible, neither actually, nor in fancy, nor by supposition (*farḍ*) [6]

which is the part that is not further divided/He did not say, "it is the atom," but "like the atom," guarding against introducing a restriction; for

---

[4] *Al-mujarradāt*, the absolute souls, i.e., stripped of all materiality.

[5] For the different definitions of *jism* see al-Ash'arī, *Maqālāt*, pp. 301 ff.; *Dict. of Tech. Terms*, p. 258, also al-Ghazzālī, *Maqāṣid al-Falāsifa*, II, 10 ff.

[6] A.J., p. 72, says "rational supposition."

that which is not compounded is not confined according to Reason to the atom, meaning "the indivisible part" (*al-juz' alladhī la yatajazza'*) [46] since it would have been necessary to abolish primary matter (*hayūlī*),[7] form (*ṣūra*), Intelligences (*'uqūl*), and the absolute souls (*al-nufūs al-mujarrada*) [8] in order to complete the restriction of the indivisibles to the atom.

According to the Philosophers there is no such thing as the pure atom (*al-jawhar al-fard*), that is, the indivisible atom. As for the compounding together of the body, they say that it is composed of primary matter (*al-hayūlī*) and form (*al-ṣūra*) only.

The best proof for establishing the [indivisible] part is that were a real sphere to be placed on a real plane it would make a contact at one indivisible point only, since if it should make a contact with it at two points, there would actually be on the sphere a line, so it would not be a real sphere on a real plane.

The most noted proof [of the pure atom] according to the Early Theologians has two aspects. The first is that if every substance were infinitely divisible the mustard seed would not be smaller than the mountain, since each is made up of infinite parts. But hugeness and smallness consist only in the multiplicity and paucity of parts, but that fact is only conceivable in the finite. The second proof is that the combination (*al-ijtimā'*) of the parts of the body into a whole is not due to its own essence, for were that the case the body would not be capable of being separated into parts (*al-iftirāq*). It is because of this that Allah has the power to create in that body the possibility of being separated into parts which cannot be further divided. Now with reference to this ultimate part, the indivisibility of which is under discussion, if it is possible for it to be further separated into parts it follows that the power of Allah would have to bring it about in order to eliminate the assumption that Allah is powerless [47], but if it is impossible [for it to be further separated] then the contention as to the existence of an absolute atom is established.

All [of these three proofs] are weak. The first is weak because it only points to the existence of the geometrical point, and that does not necessitate the existence of the indivisible part, for the fact that a geometrical point is said to have position (*al-ḥulūl fī maḥall*) does not mean that it occupies place

---

[7] *Hayūlī* (Greek ὕλη), is primary matter, matter as capable of receiving form. For the different meanings applied to the word in Arabic see *Dict. of Tech. Terms*, p. 1534; al-Ghazzālī, *Maqāṣid al-Falāsifa*, II, 19 ff.; Pines, *Beiträge*, pp. 40 ff.

[8] A.J., p. 73, adds *min al-abdān*, "of bodies."

(*ḥulūl al-sarayān*) [9] and consequently it does not mean that the indivisibility of the place follows from the indivisibility of the geometrical point.

The second and third are weak because the Philosophers do not say that the body is actually composed of parts that are infinite; but they say that the body admits of an infinite number of divisions and that there is no combination (*ijtimā'*) of the parts in it at all. Greatness and smallness are only according to the quantity which subsists in a body. And it is possible for the parts to be separated (*iftirāq*) to infinity, so the pure atom is not to be postulated.[10] The proofs for denying this are also somewhat weak. For this reason al-Imām al-Rāzī inclined to be noncommittal on the subject.

If the question is raised whether there is any benefit resulting from this position which is different [from that of the Philosophers], we reply that there is. In establishing the pure atom we escape many of the obscurities of the Philosophers, such as the positing of primary matter (*hayūlī*) and form (*ṣūra*) which leads to the eternity of the world, the denial of the resurrection of the body, and many of the fundamental laws of measurement (*al-handasa*), upon which obscurities rests the continual motion of the heavenly spheres; and also the denial of the rending (*al-kharq*) of them and their being coalesced together again (*al-ilti'ām*).

And the accident is something that does not subsist in itself/but it subsists in something else by being incident (*tābi'*) to it in having its boundaries (*taḥayyuz*), or by being specialized by it, just as something descriptive is specialized by the thing described, as has already been said. This does not mean that it cannot be thought of apart from the locus as has been fancied by some, for that only applies to some of the accidents.

but is originated in bodies and atoms/[48] Some say that this is added to give an exact definition and to avoid including the attributes of Allah.

such as colors/The original colors are said to be black and white; others have said that they are red, green and yellow, the rest being compounded from them.

---

[9] The root *sarā* means "to travel by night, to creep along, to be contagious," and in modern Arabic "to circulate" (of the blood). For its technical use see Horten, *Die spek. und pos. Theologie des Islam*, pp. 154, 178; Lane, *Lexicon*, p. 1355; Dozy, *Supplément*, I, 651. *Al-ḥulūl fi maḥall* reflects the expression used by Aristotle in the definition of a point. See *Metaphysics*, V, 6, 1016b, 26.

[10] Cf. Maimonides (Friedländer), *The Guide for the Perplexed*, p. 134.

states of coming into being (*akwān*)/which are: combination (*al-ijtimā'*), being separated into parts (*al-iftirāq*), motion (*al-haraka*) and rest (*al-sukūn*)

tastes (*al-ṭu'ūm*)/There are nine species of them: bitterness, pungency, saltiness, astringency, acidity, puckeriness, sweetness, greasiness, and insipidity. Through combinations of these there are innumerable species of tastes.

and odors (*al-rawā'iḥ*)/These are of many species without special names. And it is most evident that all accidents except the states of coming into being occur only in bodies. If it is established that the world is made up of substances and accidents, and the substances are bodies and atoms, we then may say that everything is originated.

Some of the accidents are known by observation, as motion following rest, light following darkness, [49] and blackness following whiteness. And others are known by proof, such as the occurrence (*ṭarayān*) [11] of non-existence, as seen from its contraries. For eternity is inconsistent with non-existence because if the eternal is necessarily existent in itself, then it is clear that eternity is inconsistent with non-existence; otherwise eternity must be ascribed to the eternal simply by way of affirmation, since that which proceeds from a thing by purpose and choice is of necessity originated, but an effect which is joined to a necessary eternal cause is itself eternal because it is impossible for a necessary effect to lag behind its cause.[12]

As for substances (*al-a'yān*), [they are among the originated things] because they are not free (*lā takhlū*) from originated things, and whatever is not free from originated things is itself originated. The first premise [that substances are not free from originated things] is so, because they are not free of motion and rest, which are originated. This not being free of motion and rest is due to the fact that the body and the atom are not free from residing within some boundary (*ḥayyiz*). If the substance is preceded by another *kawn* (state of coming into being) in that very same boundary, then it is at rest; and if it is not so preceded by another *kawn* in the very same boundary, then it is in motion. This is what they mean when they say, "Motion is two *kawn*'s at two times (*fī ānayn*) in two places (*fī makānayn*), and rest is two *kawn*'s at two times in one place."

[50] If objection is made that it is possible that there was not at all

---

[11] Cf. Horten, *Die spek. und pos. Theologie des Islam*, pp. 198 f.
[12] A.J., p. 77, adds *al-tāmma*, "complete."

another *kawn* preceding this [*kawn* which has been assumed], as for example at the time of its being originated, so [there was a time that] it was neither in motion nor at rest, we reply that this objection does not impair our argument, since it admits the claim that this statement has been made about bodies in which there were a number of *kawn*'s [one after the other] and in which there was a renewing of seasons and times.

As for our belief that motion and rest are originated, that is based upon the fact that they belong among accidents, which are not continuous. Furthermore the very quiddity of motion is that there is in it a transition from one state (*ḥāl*) to another, which logically requires that something else preceded motion; this would be inconsistent with eternity of motion. Moreover every motion may come to an end and is without permanency, and every rest may cease to exist, inasmuch as every body is subject of necessity to motion. But as you know, whatever may cease to exist cannot be eternal.

The second premise [that whatever is not free of originated things is itself originated] is true, for if that which is not free of originated things were established to be from eternity, then it would be inseparably connected with the establishment from eternity of that which is originated, and that is impossible.

Here then are the investigations [to be made of the objections concerning substances]. The first objection is that there is no proof for confining the [use of the term] "substances" to atoms and bodies, and that this [narrow definition] denies the existence of a self-subsistent possible thing which does not have boundaries at all, such as the Intelligences and the absolute souls [*51*] of which the Philosophers speak. And the answer to this is that the thing which is asserted to be originated is that possible thing the existence of which is established by proof. And this possible thing consists of the substances which have boundaries and accidents. The proofs for the existence of the absolute beings [such as Intelligences and absolute souls] are incomplete, as has been shown in larger treatises.

The second objection is that what has been said does not prove the origin of all accidents, since the origin of some of them is not perceived by observation, nor is the origin of that which is contrary to them such as the accidents which subsist in the heavenly spheres, namely shapes (*ashkāl*), extensions (*imtidādāt*), and lights (*aḍwā'*). The answer is that this does not thwart the purpose of the argument, for the origin of the substances demands of necessity the origin of the accidents since they only subsist in these substances.

The third objection is that eternity (*al-azal*) does not express a special state, so that the existence in that state of originated things is inseparably connected with the existence of the body in that state, but eternity is an expression for non-beginning or for the continuance of existence in times which are reckoned as unending in the past. The meaning of the eternity of originated motions is that there is no motion which did not have another motion preceding it, and so on without a beginning. This is the position of the Philosophers, who although they admit that no particular motion is eternal, yet make this statement rather of absolute motion (*al-ḥaraka al-muṭlaqa*). The answer to this is that the absolute does not have existence except in the particular, so, since each particular is originated, the eternity of the absolute is inconceivable.

The fourth objection is that if each body were in a boundary, that would necessitate the non-limitation of bodies, inasmuch as the boundary (*al-ḥayyiz*) [18] is the inner surface of a container which touches the outer surface of the thing contained. The answer to this is that the boundary according to the Mutakallims is the imaginary space (*al-farāgh*) [52] which the body occupies and in which it extends to its dimensions. And when the fact is established that the world is originated—it being known that anything originated must have an originator (*muḥdith*)—it is then established that the world has an originator, for of necessity it is impossible that there be a preponderance (*al-tarajjuḥ*) in favor of one of the two alternatives of something possible without there being "a determinant to bring about the preponderance" (*murajjiḥ*).

[18] See Lane, *Lexicon*, p. 668; *al-Ta'rifāt*, p. 99; *Dict. of Tech. Terms*, pp. 298 ff.; al-Rāzī, *Muḥaṣṣal*, pp. 65 f.; A.J., p. 82.

Chapter 4

THE ORIGINATOR OF THE WORLD

The Originator of the world is Allah, the One, the Eternal, the Living, the Powerful, the Knowing, the Hearing, the Seeing, the Desiring, and the Willing. He is not an accident, nor a body, nor an atom; nor is He something formed, nor a thing limited, nor a thing numbered, nor a thing portioned or divided, nor a thing compounded; nor does He come to an end in Himself. He is not described by quiddity, nor by quality, nor is He placed in place. Time does not affect Him and nothing resembles Him, and nothing is outside of His Knowledge and Power.

The Originator (*muḥdith*) of the world is Allah/He is the necessarily existent essence (*al-dhāt al-wājib al-wujūd*) whose existence is of His essence. He does not need anything at all, since were His existence only possible He would be a part of the world and not suited to be the Originator of it and the one who caused its beginning, even though "world" (*'ālam*) is a name applied to all that is properly a sign (*'alam*) for the existence of the one who caused its beginning. [53] Closely allied to this is the statement that the cause of the beginning of all possible things must be necessarily existent, since were He a possible only, He would be one of the many possible things and not the cause of their beginning.

It is sometimes fancied that this is a proof for the existence of the Maker without necessarily abolishing the endless chain (*al-tasalsul*).[1] But this is not the case. It is rather a reference to one of the proofs for the unsoundness of the endless chain. And this proof is that if a chain of possibles were arranged to infinity, this chain would still need an [efficient] cause, which must not be the thing itself nor a part of it, because it is impossible for a thing to be the [efficient] cause of itself or of its own causes. But it must be

---

[1] Cf. *al-Bābu 'l-Ḥādī 'Ashar*, pp. 13 f.; Macdonald, "Atomic Time," *Isis*, IX, 2, 336; *Development*, pp. 322 f.; al-Faḍālī, *Kifāyat al-'Awāmm*, pp. 32 f.; and *Dict. of Tech. Terms*, pp. 690 ff.

outside the cause, so the efficient cause would then be necessary and the endless chain would be broken.

[54] Of the noted kinds of proof there is the one of tallying (*al-taṭbīq*). This consists in supposing a series [of effects] from the last effect (*maʿlūl*) to infinity and another series, for example, of just one short of this last effect to infinity. Then we apply the two series so that we make the first of the first series correspond with the first of the second series; the second with the second, and so on. Thus, if there is a unit of the second series for every unit of the first series, then the less is like that which is more than it, and that is impossible. Otherwise there is something in the first series without something to correspond to it in the second, so the second is broken off and comes to an end. This necessitates the finiteness of the first series since it only exceeds the second series by a finite amount; and that which exceeds the finite by a finite amount is of necessity finite. This proof of tallying can only be used of that which comes under the category of existence and not with that which has only to do with the estimative faculty (*wahmī maḥḍ*), for it breaks down with the breaking down of the estimative faculty.

This argument is not to be refuted by the arranging of series of numbers, in which two series are applied to each other, [55] one of them from one to infinity and the second from two to infinity, nor by things pertaining to the Knowledge of Allah and things pertaining to the Power of Allah, for in spite of the fact that they are both infinite, the things pertaining to the Knowledge of Allah are more than the things pertaining to His Power. This is so, since infinity, when applied to numbers and things pertaining to the Knowledge and the Power of Allah, means that they do not end in one definite limit beyond which no other limit can be conceived. This does not mean that whatever possesses infinity comes under the category of existence, inasmuch as that is impossible.

the One/that is to say, the Maker of the World is one. The idea of the Necessarily Existent cannot be true except of one essence. The most noted of the proofs for the unity of Allah among the Mutakallims is that of mutual hindrance (*al-tamānuʿ*),[2] which is referred to in the saying of Allah, "If there were in the two of them [that is, the heavens and the earth] gods other than Allah, these two would have been corrupted (*fasadatā*)" (Qurʾān

---

[2] Cf. Maimonides (Munk), *Le Guide des égarés*, I, 440 ff.; (Friedländer), *The Guide for the Perplexed*, pp. 139 ff.; Müller, *Philosophie*, pp. 47 f. See also al-Rāzī, *Mafātīḥ al-Ghayb*, VI, 105 ff.; Macdonald, *Development*, pp. 326 f.; al-Faḍālī, *Kifāyat al-ʿAwāmm*, pp. 40 ff.; al-Bayḍāwī, *Anwār al-Tanzīl*, II, 11.

21:22). The explanation of this is that if two gods were possible, [56] mutual hindrance of each other would be possible. One of them would will that Zayd move and the other that he remain at rest, since each of the two things is possible in itself. In like manner the connection of the Will with each of them [is possible], since there is no mutual opposition between the two wills, but only [a mutual opposition] between the two things willed. So either the two things occur and the opposites unite [8] [which is impossible], or [if only one of the two things occurs] it follows that one of the two gods is powerless. This powerlessness is an indication of being originated and of possibility, because in it there is the defect of being in need of something.

So plurality necessitates the possibility of mutual hindrance, which [in turn] necessitates the impossible, so it is impossible. [57] This is the detailed explanation of the statement that if one of two is not able to oppose the other, it then follows that he is powerless. And if he is able [to oppose the other], then the other is powerless. What we have just mentioned refutes the proposition that it is possible for the two to agree without mutual hindrance, or that hindering and opposing [in the case of two gods] are impossible because hindering and opposing necessitate the impossible, or that the agreement together of the two wills, as though one should will that Zayd move and remain at rest at the same time, is impossible.

Know that the statement of Allah, "If there were in the two of them gods other than Allah, they would have been corrupted" (Qur'ān 21:22) is a convincing argument (*ḥujja iqnā'īya*). The necessary consequence (*mulāzama*) [of such a statement is the acceptance of the conclusion as] is customary in the case of statements which conform to rhetorical syllogisms (*al-khiṭābīyāt*).[4] For it is customary when there are many exercising the office of governor, that there is mutual hindrance of one another and that one gets the upper hand, as is indicated in the statement of Allah, "Some of them gained the mastery over the others" (Qur'ān 23:93). [Otherwise the argument is incomplete.] Then if actual corruption is meant—that is, the passing away from the present visible order [of the heavens and the earth]—a mere plurality [of gods] does not necessitate that, for it is possible that there be an agreement [by the gods] on the present visible order. If the possibility of corruption is meant, there is nothing to indicate the denial

---

[8] A.J. (p. 87) reads after "and the opposites unite," "or they do not, so the lack of power on the part of both follows, or one attains and it follows that one of them is powerless."

[4] Cf. Macdonald, *Development*, p. 259; *idem*, "The Life of al-Ghazzālī," *Journal of the American Oriental Society*, XX, 128; and *Dict. of Tech. Terms*, pp. 404 f.

of this, since the statutes bear witness to the folding up of the heavens and the removal of the present order. So it is undoubtedly possible.

One does not say that the necessary consequence of such a statement is so absolute that the meaning of the corruption of the heavens and the earth is that they were not created, on the ground that, if two makers were assumed, a mutual hindering of one another in performing acts would be possible, so that one of them would not be a maker nor would anything be made. For we say that the possibility of there being mutual hindrance of one another only requires that there be but one maker and not the negation of that which is made, [58] although it does come to mean the impossibility of the necessary consequence, if non-creation is meant by the act; and it comes to mean the impossibility of the negation of the necessary if by possibility non-creation is meant.

It may be objected that [in the Qur'ān quotation above] the force of the word "if" (*law*) is the negation in past time of the second statement through the negation of the first, so it only indicates the denial of corruption in the past because of the denial of the plurality [of gods]. In answer to this we reply that this is grammatically true, but "if" (*law*) may be used to indicate the negation of the apodosis following the negation of the protasis irrespective of time, just as in the statement, "If the world were eternal from the beginning it would be unchangeable." The verse quoted above is of this kind. One of these uses may seem equivocal to the other according to some minds, and hence the confusion.

the Eternal (*al-qadīm*)/This is in explanation as a necessary consequence of what we already know, [59] inasmuch as the Necessarily Existent [5] can not be other than eternal, that is to say, there is no beginning to His existence. If He were something originated preceded by non-existence, His existence would then of necessity be contingent on something else. For this reason some have made the statement that the Necessarily Existent and the Eternal are synonymous terms. But for the sake of accuracy in differentiating these two terms, that is not quite right. A statement about their being co-extensive terms depends on what is true regarding them. Some say that the term "eternal" is more general [than "necessarily existent"] because it is true of the attributes of the Necessarily Existent that they are eternal in contrast to the term "necessarily existent," which is not true of the attributes. It is not impos-

---

[5] This is the abbreviated form for the Necessarily Existent in His essence (*wājib al-wujūd li dhātihi*), that is, the Necessarily Existent. See *Dict. of Tech. Terms*, p. 1444; al-Rāzī, *Muhaṣṣal*, pp. 44 ff., 108 ff.; Wolfson, *The Philosophy of Spinoza*, I, 67.

sible to say that there is a plurality of eternal attributes, but it is impossible to say that there is a plurality of eternal essences. Some of the later Mutakallims like al-Imām Ḥamīd al-Dīn al-Ḍarīr [6] and his followers explain the point by saying that the Necessarily Existent One in His essence is Allah and His attributes. From the idea that everything which is eternal is necessarily existent in its essence they made their deduction that if the Eternal were not necessarily existent, non-existence would have been possible for Him, and He would have needed a determining principle (*mukhaṣṣiṣ*) [7] [to have specified existence in His case]. Thus He would have been originated (*muḥdath*), since we only mean by originated that thing the existence of which is connected with the fact that something else brings it into existence.

Furthermore, those [who say that "eternal" is a more general term than necessarily existent] objected that the attributes, were they necessarily existent in their essence, would be continuous (*bāqiya*). Continuance (*al-baqā'*) [8] is an Idea (*ma'nā*) itself, so the existence of a real Idea then subsists in another Idea. [60] Reply was made to this that each attribute continues by means of a continuance which is that very attribute itself. This is an extremely difficult concept, for the assertion that the Necessarily Existent in His essence is a plurality is inconsistent with the unity of the Deity, while the assertion that the attributes are only possible [and not necessary] is inconsistent with the statement of those who say that every possible being is originated.

If they assert that the attributes are eternal in time, meaning that there was no time when non-existence preceded them; and that this is not inconsistent with their essential origin, in the sense that they need the essence of the Necessarily Existent, then their position is that of the Philosophers, who divided both Eternity and Being-originated into essential (*dhātī*) and temporal (*zamānī*). In this position there is a denial of many foundations of the faith, so a further verifying of this matter will come later.

[6] Imām Ḥamīd al-Dīn al-Ḍarīr (d. A.H. 666; A.D. 1267). See Brockelmann, *Geschichte*, I, 296.

[7] Cf. Macdonald, *Development*, p. 325; al-Faḍālī, *Kifāyat al-'Awāmm*, p. 36; al-Sanūsī, *Umm al-Barāhīn*, pp. 86 ff.; al-Shahrastānī, *Nihāyatu l-Iqdām*, p. 12.

[8] Al-Imām al-Ḥaramayn and al-Qāḍī Abū Bakr (al-Bāqillānī), who were among the earlier Ash'arites, said that Allah continues by His essence not by the attribute of continuance. This was contrary to the position of al-Ash'arī, who said that He continues by this attribute of continuance which is an eternal attribute subsisting in His essence; just as He knows, decrees, and so on by attributes of Knowledge and Power and the like. *Al-Rawḍa al-Bahīya*, p. 66; al-Rāzī, *Muḥaṣṣal*, p. 126. Later Ash'arites held that Continuance is an attribute; al-Sanūsī, *Umm al-Barāhīn*, pp. 79 f.; al-Faḍālī, *Kifāyat al-'Awāmm*, pp. 33 f.

the Living (*al-ḥayy*), the Powerful (*al-qādir*), the Knowing (*al-'ālim*), the Hearing (*al-samī'*), the Seeing (*al-baṣīr*), the Desiring (*al-shā'ī*), and the Willing (*al-murīd*) [9]/The proof for this is by a decisive immediate inference of logical reasoning, inasmuch as Allah is the Originator of the world according to a definite original plan and preconceived order, as is evidenced by the fact that the world comprises [His] well-ordered works and excellent handicrafts. He is not devoid of those attributes, for the contraries of these attributes signify defects from which Allah is necessarily far removed.

Furthermore these attributes have come down to us in the Law (*al-shar'*) [61], but inasmuch as some of them are those upon which the establishment of the Law is not based, it is proper in a case of this kind of attribute to rely upon the Law itself, as for instance the attribute of the unity of the Deity in contradistinction to the attribute of the existence of the Maker and His Speech, and similar attributes upon which the establishment of the Law is based.

He is not an accident/because an accident does not subsist in itself, but needs a locus (*mahall*) to give it subsistence. So the accident is a possible. And [again He is not an accident] because the continuance [of an accident] is impossible. Otherwise continuance would be an Idea that subsists in the accident, and that would necessitate the subsistence of an Idea in an Idea, which is impossible. For the subsistence of an accident in a thing means that its having boundaries (*taḥayyuz*) follows upon (*tābi'*) the fact that the thing has boundaries. The accident has no boundaries of itself, in the sense that something else may be said to have boundaries by following upon the accident. This is based on the fact that the continuance of a thing is an Idea which is superadded to its existence, and on the fact that the meaning of subsistence [of one thing in something else] is [the thing's] following upon the other thing in having boundaries.

The right position [regarding this] is as follows: First, continuance is the perpetuity of existence and the absence of passing out of existence. Its real essence is its existence with respect to another time. The meaning of our saying, "It existed but did not continue," is that it was originated but its existence did not persevere nor was it established [in reality] for the second

---

[9] These epithets applied to the Deity are usually classed by theologians as attributes of Allah. The abstract ideas such as Power, Willing, Knowledge, etc., are called essential attributes or those consisting of ideas (*ṣifāt al-ma'ānī*), but these which are given here, the Living, the Knowing, the Willing, etc., are called attributes derived from ideas (*ṣifāt ma'nawīya*). See al-Ījī, *al-Mawāqif*, pp. 56 f.; al-Sanūsī, *Umm al-Barāhīn*, pp. 96 ff., 118 f.; al-Faḍālī, *Kifāyat al-'Awāmm*, pp. 55 ff.; Wensinck, *The Muslim Creed*, p. 275; Macdonald, *Development*, pp. 336 f.

time. Second, subsistence is the specializing which describes the thing described just as in the case of the terms predicated of the Creator (*al-bārī*). Third, bodies cease to exist at every moment of time (*fī kull ān*), and what we observe of continuance in them by way of renewal of similars is no less credible than what occurs in accidents. Surely [62] it is incorrect for them to maintain that an accident subsists in an accident, as in the case of the swiftness and slowness of motion. There are not two things here—one, motion; and the other, swiftness and slowness—but we have a certain definite motion which in relation to some other motions is called swift and to others slow. This clearly shows that swiftness and slowness are not two different species of motion, for real species in the true sense of the term do not distinctly differ from one another even though there is a difference in their respective relations to something else.

nor a body (*jism*)/for the body is something compounded and having boundaries, which is a mark of being originated

nor an atom (*jawhar*)/[This is true] from our standpoint, for we say that *jawhar* is the name for a part (*al-juz'*) that cannot be further divided, having boundaries and being a part of a body. Allah is far exalted above such a definition;[10] and [it is true also] from the standpoint of the Philosophers, because they make *jawhar* one of the divisions of the possibles, although they make it to be the name of an existing thing—however, not in a subject—whether absolute or having boundaries. They mean by *jawhar* the possible quiddity which whenever it does exist is not in a subject. But if by body (*jism*) and atom (*jawhar*) is meant the self-subsistent and existing thing which is not in a subject, then these terms must not be applied to the Maker, for they are not mentioned in the Law, along with the fact that the understanding jumps at the conclusion that these terms mean "compounded" and "that which has boundaries." The Corporealizers (*al-Mujassima*)[11] and the Christians (*al-Naṣārā*)[12] took the position that *jism* and *jawhar* may be applied to Him, giving a conception of Allah from which He is necessarily far removed.

[10] Cf. the statement of Maimonides giving the argument of the Mutakallims for the incorporeality of Allah. (Munk), *Le Guide des égarés*, I, 450 ff.; (Friedländer), *The Guide for the Perplexed*, pp. 141 ff.

[11] The Karramites were considered as Corporealizers. *Dict. of Tech. Terms*, p. 261; al-Shahrastānī, *al-Milal*, pp. 79 ff., 171 ff.; al-Baghdādī, *al-Farq bayn al-Firaq*, pp. 202 f.

[12] The Christians, according to Islam, believe that Allah may have a body. See *Dict. of Tech. Terms*, p. 1385; al-Shahrastānī, *al-Milal*, pp. 171 ff.

If it is objected that terms like "the existing being," "the necessarily existent," and "the eternal" cannot properly be applied to Allah since they do not occur in the Law, we reply that the basis is by Agreement (*al-ijmā'*), which is one of the canonical bases. It is sometimes suggested that Allah, the Necessarily Existent, and the Eternal are synonymous terms, and that the term "existent" is inseparable from the Necessarily Existent, so if the Law applies one term of a language [to Him] that fact makes it permissible to apply a synonym of that term or whatever approximates it in that or any other language. [*63*] But this is a matter for consideration.[18]

nor is He something formed (*muṣawwar*)/Formed means having a form (*ṣūra*) or a shape (*shakl*) like the form of a man or of a horse. Form is one of the special characteristics of bodies. It occurs in them by means of quantities (*kammīyāt*) [14] and qualities (*kayfīyāt*) [15] and by setting limits and ends.

nor a thing limited (*maḥdūd*)/Limited means having a limit or an end.

nor a thing numbered (*ma'dūd*)/Numbered means having number and multiplicity; that is, He is not the locus of quantities, either continuous (*muttaṣila*) like magnitudes (*maqādīr*), or discrete (*munfaṣila*) like things counted. This is quite evident.

nor a thing portioned or divided/This means possessing portions and parts.

nor a thing compounded/of these, since they all have that need [for something else] which is inconsistent with necessary existence. That which has parts is called "compounded" when they are in composition together, and "portioned" and "divided" when they are separated.

nor does He come to an end in Himself/because this is one of the characteristics of magnitudes and numbers.

---

[13] A.J. (p. 97) adds "from two standpoints; one is the being synonymous, the other is the combination of the two judgments of the two synonymous terms in being applied to Allah."

[14] See al-Ghazzālī, *Mi'yār al-'Ilm*, pp. 203 f.; Macdonald, *Development*, p. 325; al-Faḍālī, *Kifāyat al-'Awāmm* (also commentary of al-Bayjūrī on al-Faḍālī), pp. 38 f.; *al-Ta'rīfāt*, p. 196.

[15] *Al-kayfīyāt.* See al-Ghazzālī, *Mi'yār al-'Ilm*, pp. 204 f.; *Dict. of Tech. Terms*, p. 1257; *al-Ta'rīfāt*, p. 198; Horten, *Die spek. und pos. Theologie des Islam*, p. 347.

He is not described by quiddity (*al-māʾīya*)/That means He does not share the same genus with other things; for when we say [quiddity, or] "What is it?" we mean, "Of what genus [64] is it?" But sharing the same genus (*al-mujānasa*) requires that the things which share the same genus differ from one another by means of certain divisions which are set up, and that necessitates the existence of composition.

nor by quality (*al-ḳayfīya*)/that is, of color, taste, odor, heat, cold, dampness, dryness, or any other thing predicated of bodies or things which follow upon mixture or composition

nor is He placed in place (*makān*)/for being placed (*al-tamakkun*) is an expression for the penetration of one dimension (*buʿd*) into another, whether real or imagined. This is called place. Dimension is an expression for an extension (*imtidād*) subsisting in a body, or in itself according to those who assert the existence of the vacuum (*al-ḳhalāʾ*).[16] Allah is far removed from extension and magnitude, because this requires His being divided into parts.

Objection may be raised [to this argument] that [65] the pure atom (*al-jawhar al-fard*) has boundaries and yet does not have dimension; for otherwise it could be divided [and thus it would not be a pure atom]. To this we reply that "being placed" is a more special term than "having boundaries," because the boundary (*al-ḥayyiz*) is the imaginary empty space which any thing occupies whether it has extension or not. That which has been mentioned above is a proof of His not being placed in place.

But the proof of His not having boundaries is that if He were bounded, He would either be bounded from eternity—and this would necessitate the eternity of the boundary—or He would not be bounded from eternity, so He would be a locus for originated things. He is also either co-extensive with the boundary or is less than it and so [in either case] is finite; or He is more than it and therefore divisible. If He is not in place, He does not extend in any direction of place, being neither upward nor downward nor in any of the other directions, inasmuch as directions are the limits or extremities of places [by which a thing is surrounded], or they are the places themselves with reference to their relationship to the thing [surrounded by the places].

<hr>

[16] According to Scholastic Theologians *al-ḳhalāʾ* is that void which separates bodies and atoms, and thus permits their separation and combination. See Macdonald, "Atomic Time," *Isis*, IX, 2, p. 329; *al-Taʿrīfāt*, p. 105; *Dict. of Tech. Terms*, pp. 458 f.

Time (*al-zamān*) [17] does not affect Him/With us time is an expression for something renewed by which something else renewed is measured. With the Philosophers it is the measure of motion. Allah is far removed from that. Know then [66] that the mention by al-Nasafī of some of the things from which Allah is far removed makes unnecessary the mention of others of them. However, he attempted here to go into detail and to explain clearly the matter of Allah's being far removed [from created things] in order to give all that the subject of the Necessarily Existent deserves and to answer in the most complete and emphatic way the Comparers (*al-Mushabbiha*) [18] and the Corporealizers (*al-Mujassima*) and all the other parties of error and perverseness. It was of no consequence to the author that [in doing so] he had to repeat synonymous terms and explain that which is well known. This remoteness of Allah [from created things] which I have mentioned is based on the fact that these terms [i.e., of the Comparers, Corporealizers, and so on] are inconsistent with the term Necessary Existence, since in them there is that defect which comes from their implying that He is originated and possible, as we have pointed out.

This is not the way which the Early Theologians took [to explain this] for they said that the meaning of accident (*al-'araḍ*) according to etymology is that which cannot continue; that the meaning of atom (*al-jawhar*) is that from which other things are composed; and that the meaning of body (*al-jism*) is that which is composed of other things, as is indicated in their saying, "This is bulkier (*ajsam*) than that." And they said that if the Necessarily Existent were compounded, then the parts of which He is composed would be described by attributes of perfection (*al-kamāl*), and that would require a plurality of necessarily existents; or the parts would not have these attributes and would therefore be lacking in something and have been originated.

Also the Necessarily Existent [according to them either] must be of all forms, shapes, qualities and magnitudes—but if this were the case it would have to follow that He would unite in Himself things contradictory to each other—or else He must be of only some of these forms, shapes, qualities, and magnitudes; and these will have to be of the same order both in conveying equally the idea of either praise or blame, and in the absence of any evidence

---

[17] Cf. *Enc. of Islam*, IV, 1207; *Dict. of Tech. Terms*, p. 619; *al-Ta'rīfāt*, p. 119; al-Rāzī, *Muḥaṣṣal*, p. 61; Ibn Sīnā, *al-Najāt*, pp. 186 ff.; Pines, *Beiträge*, pp. 49 ff.

[18] See al-Baghdādī, *al-Farq bayn al-Firaq*, pp. 214 f.; al-Shahrastānī, *al-Milal*, pp. 75 ff.; al-Ijī, *al-Mawāqif*, pp. 362 ff.

that originated things apply to Allah. But if this were the case, then Allah would need a determining principle (*mukhaṣṣiṣ*) [to make a selection among the things which are assumed not to convey any idea of either praise or blame], and thus He would come under the power of something outside Himself and consequently would be originated. Furthermore [if there were no evidence in originated things that these attributes apply to Allah, then] He would be in contrast to such attributes, for example, as Knowledge and Power, which are attributes of perfection and concerning which there is evidence in originated things that they do apply to Allah; but the opposites of these attributes of perfection are those attributes of imperfection (*al-nuqṣān*) concerning which there is no evidence in originated things that they apply to Allah.

These opinions of the Early Theologians rest on weak foundations, which cause damage to the beliefs of those who seek after truth, and give currency to the effusions of the vilifiers of religion, who in their arguments try to show that all these lofty problems of theology are based on nothing but frail ambiguities like these.

[67] The one who disagrees with this position [regarding Allah's being far removed from created things] [19] cites the statutes (*al-nuṣūṣ*) [20] that plainly teach, regarding Allah, that He extends in a direction, has a body, form, and bodily members. He says further that each of two existing things is by supposition either continuous and contiguous to the other, or is discrete and cut off from the other in some direction. Now Allah is neither residing [in the world] nor a locus for the world, so He is cut off from it in some direction. He therefore has boundaries and is a body or a part of a body, formed and finite.

The answer to this is that here is a case of pure fancy (*wahm*) and a judgment concerning objects not perceived by the senses according to judgments that apply to objects perceived by the senses. The decisive proofs rest on such matters as remove Allah far from any such thing. So the science [dealing with the interpretation] of the statutes must be committed to Allah according to the custom of the Fathers (*al-salaf*), who [committed such things to Allah because they] preferred to follow the safer method. Or the statutes may be interpreted, as the Later Theologians (*al-muta'akhkhirūn*) chose to do, by sound interpretations (*ta'wīlāt ṣaḥīḥa*) in order to refute the thrusts of the

---

[19] See al-Ïjï, *al-Mawāqif*, pp. 12 ff.; Müller, *Philosophie*, pp. 58 ff.; al-Rāzī, *Muhaṣṣal*, pp. 111 ff.; Wensinck, *The Muslim Creed*, pp. 207 ff.

[20] See Chapter 18, where the reference is to the Qur'ān and the Sunna. Cf. *Dict. of Tech. Terms*, p. 1406.

ignorant, to incline [towards the truth] the disposition of those who are immature, and to follow the wiser path.

and nothing resembles Him/that is to say, nothing is like Him. If it is understood that by similarity [to something] there is a being united [to it] in reality, it is clear that He is not like anything. And if similarity means that one of two things may take the place of the other—that is, each is good for what the other is—then no existing thing can take His place in any of the things predicated of Him, for what is predicated of Him in the way of Knowledge, Power, and so on is so much more majestic and exalted than what is found in creatures that there is no basis for comparison between Allah and His creatures.

The author of *al-Bidāya* [21] said that the knowledge which we [creatures] have is something existing, an accident, originated, possible of existence, and renewed every [moment of] time. So if we establish knowledge as an attribute of Allah, it is something existing, an attribute, eternal (*qadīm*), necessarily existent, everlasting from eternity (*al-azal*) to eternity (*al-abad*). Thus the knowledge of creatures is not in any respect similar to His knowledge. [68] This is the statement of the author of *al-Bidāya;* when he explained that the similarity of two things to each other according to our view is established by their sharing together all things predicated of them, so that if the two differ in one thing predicated the similarity breaks down.

Al-Shaykh Abū 'l-Mu'īn said in *al-Tabṣira* [22] that the lexicographers do not preclude the statement that Zayd is similar to 'Amr in knowing *fiqh*, if he equals him in it and can take his place in this matter, although there may be many points of difference between them. The statement of the Ash'arites that similarity does not exist except in equality in all respects is unsound, for the Prophet said, "Wheat for wheat, like for like." [23] He meant by this equality in measure only, for wheat differs as well in weight, in number of grains [to a measure], and in hardness and tenderness. It is clear that there is no disagreement between the two positions, for al-Ash'arī meant equality in all respects where there is a similarity, as in measure, for example. Therefore it is not necessary that the statement in *al-Bidāya* be understood as meaning complete equality; otherwise when two things have in common all things

---

[21] See above, Chapter 2, note 27.

[22] Abū 'l-Mu'īn Maymūn b. Muḥammad al-Nasafī (d. A.H. 508; A.D. 1114) was the author of *Kitāb Tabṣirat al-Adilla* and other books on scholastic theology. Brockelmann, *Geschichte*, I, 426.

[23] See Muslim, *al-Ṣaḥīḥ*, I, 632; *Musnad*, II, 232.

predicated of them and are equal in all respects, that prevents there being a plurality of things, for how is similarity conceivable [if they are exactly alike]?

and nothing is outside of His Knowledge and Power/This is true, for ignorance or inability in a part is a lack and a need which call for a determining principle, whereas the decisive statutes speak of universal Knowledge and all-embracing Power. So then He is Omniscient and Omnipotent. This is unlike the position of the Philosophers, who assert that Allah does not know particulars and that there is only in Him power to do one thing, [since they make Allah's will to do the act necessary] there is no possible choice on His part between doing and abstaining from the act; and unlike the Dahrites (*al-dahrīya*),[24] who claim that Allah does not know His essence; and unlike al-Naẓẓām,[25] who asserted that He is unable to create ignorance and the vile thing; [69] and unlike al-Balkhī,[26] who asserted that He is unable to do anything similar to that which is in the power of the creature [to do]; and unlike the Muʿtazilites in general, who asserted that He is unable to do that which is in the power of the creature to do.

[24] Cf. *Enc. of Islam*, I, 894; Horten, *Die phil. Systeme der spek. Theologen im Islam*, see Index; *Dict. of Tech. Terms*, p. 480; De Boer, *History of Philosophy in Islam*, p. 80.

[25] Al-Naẓẓām (d. A.H. 231; A.D. 847) was a Muʿtazilite who is credited with having been a student of the doctrines of Greek philosophy. He held that Allah could only do that which is just and for the creature's good. Macdonald, *Development*, pp. 140 ff.; Horten, *Die phil. Systeme der spek. Theologen im Islam*, see Index; al-Shahrastānī, *al-Milal*, pp. 37 ff.; al-Baghdādī, *al-Farq bayn al-Firaq*, pp. 113 ff.; al-Ījī, *al-Mawāqif*, p. 337; al-Ashʿarī, *Maqālāt*, p. 486 f.

[26] A.J. (p. 104) says that he is Abū 'l-Qāsim al-Balkhī, who is known as al-Kaʿbī, according to the commentary on *al-Maqāṣid*. However, in the commentary on *al-Mawāqif* and in *Abkār al-Afkār* the two names seem to apply to different persons. Horten (*Die phil. Systeme der spek. Theologen im Islam*, p. 637) considers them as one individual. For al-Kaʿbī (d. A.D. 929) see 'I.D. pp. 77, 109; *Enc. of Islam*, II, 48; al-Ījī, *al-Mawāqif*, p. 342; al-Baghdādī, *al-Farq bayn al-Firaq*, pp. 165 ff.

Chapter 5

SOME ATTRIBUTES OF ALLAH

He has attributes from all eternity subsistent in His essence. They are not He nor are they other than He. And they are Knowledge and Power and Life and Might and Hearing and Seeing and Willing and Desiring and Doing and Creating and Sustaining.

He has attributes/inasmuch as it has been established that He is Knowing, Living, Powerful, and so on. It is known that each of these attributes points to an Idea superadded to what is understood by the term "the Necessarily Existent," nor are these attributes to be taken as synonymous terms. Furthermore if a derivative term can be properly predicated of a thing, that thing necessarily possesses the source from which that term is derived. And thus it has been established that Allah possesses the attributes of Knowledge, Power, Life, and so on.[1] This is unlike the view of the Mu'tazilites, who assert that He is Knowing without possessing Knowledge; He is Powerful without possessing Power, and so on.[2] But this view of theirs is self-evidently impossible, for it is analogous to our saying, "A thing is black but there is no blackness in it." And furthermore it has already been established in the statutes (*al-nuṣūṣ*) that Allah possesses Knowledge, Power, and other attributes. Finally the procession from Allah of acts of which He has perfect understanding points to the existence of Knowledge and Power in Him, not merely to the fact that He can be described as Knowing and Powerful.[3]

[1] Cf. al-Rāzī, *Muḥaṣṣal*, pp. 130 ff.; al-Ijī, *al-Mawāqif*, pp. 29 f.; al-Faḍālī, *Kifāyat al-ʿAwāmm*, pp. 43 ff.; al-Sanūsī, *Umm al-Barāhin*, pp. 96 ff.

[2] The Shi'ites also maintain that Allah is Powerful by His essence and deny to him attributes that consist of ideas (*maʿāni*) and states of being (*aḥwāl*). Cf. *al-Bābu 'l-Ḥādi ʿAshar*, pp. 38 f.; al-Ijī, *al-Mawāqif*, p. 30.

[3] Neither al-Nasafī in his creed nor al-Taftāzānī in his commentary gives the minute classification of the attributes of Allah that is to be found in the works of al-Sanūsī or al-Faḍālī for example, or even of al-Ijī in *al-Mawāqif*.

Al-Sanūsī (see his *Umm al-Barāhin*, pp. 72 ff. and Wensinck, *The Muslim Creed*, p. 275) classifies the attributes as follows: there are twenty that are necessary; twenty that

The question at issue is not regarding that [transient kind of] knowledge and power which is generally included under the qualities (*al-kayfīyāt*) and habits (*al-malakāt*),[4] for our Early Theologians have explicitly stated that just as Allah is Living and has Life from eternity, which is not an accident, nor is it impossible that it continue forever, so [also in the case of Knowledge] they say that Allah is Knowing, that His Knowledge is from eternity, that it is all-embracing, that it is not an accident, that it can continue forever, and that it is not necessitated nor acquired. And they affirm the same of the remainder of the attributes.

[*70*] The question at issue is rather regarding that [eternal] Knowledge of the Maker of the World—and in like manner all the other attributes— whether it is an attribute from eternity subsisting in Him, something super-added to Him, and is analogous to that [transient] knowledge of any one of us who knows, which knowledge is an accident, subsisting in him, some-thing superadded to him and originated.

The Philosophers and the Muʿtazilites denied this and asserted that the attributes are the very essence itself. This means that His essence with respect to its connection with things known (*al-maʿlūmāt*) is described by the term "Knowing" and with respect to things over which He has Power (*al-maqdūrāt*) is described by the term "Powerful," and so on. This, they say, does not imply any plurality in the essence [of Allah] nor does it imply the existence of numerous eternal and necessarily existent beings. The answer to this is to be found in what has already been said, namely, that [even according to us] the existence of numerous eternal essences [outside of Allah]

---

are impossible, which are the opposites of the first twenty; and one that is possible, namely, the doing or not doing of possible things. Of the necessary attributes the first is existence, which is a personal attribute (*ṣifa nafsīya*). Then there are five called the privative attri-butes (*ṣifāt salbīya*), namely, Eternity, Continuance, Difference from originated beings, Self-Subsistence, and Unity. Following these are seven essential attributes of those consist-ing of Ideas (*ṣifāt al-maʿāni*) which are Power, Will, Knowledge, Life, Hearing, Sight and Speech. There are then seven other attributes which are inseparable from these. They are called attributes derived from ideas (*ṣifāt maʿnawīya*). They are Allah's being the one who is Powerful, Willing, Knowing, Living, Hearing, Seeing, and Speaking. Again, the attributes were divided by writers before al-Sanūsī into positive (*thubūtīya*) and priva-tive (*salbīya*) attributes; the former being subdivided into personal (*nafsīya*) and those connected with ideas (*maʿnawīya*) which include both the classes above concerned with ideas. Cf. al-Faḍālī, *Kifāyat al-ʿAwāmm*, pp. 24 ff.; Macdonald, *Development,* pp. 318 ff.; Müller, *Philosophie*, pp. 51, 56.

Yet the Shiʿites who use the term "positive" and "privative" do not posit attributes consisting of ideas. *Dict. of Tech. Terms*, pp. 1490 f.; *al-Bābu 'l-Ḥādi 'Ashar*, pp. 15–39; al-Rāzī, *Muḥaṣṣal*, pp. 111 ff. Al-Ījī (see *al-Mawāqif*, pp. 29 ff.) seems to use the term *wujūdīya* in the sense of *thubūtīya*.

[4] See Wolfson, "Aristotelian Predicables," *Essays and Studies in Memory of Linda R. Miller*, pp. 219 f.; *Enc. of Islam*, II, 227; Ibn Khaldūn, *Muqaddima*, III, 32.

is an impossibility. Furthermore, their contention [that our belief in the existence of eternal attributes within Allah implies a belief in the existence of eternal essences outside of Allah] does not follow. Finally, the Mu'tazilite view would lead to the absurd conclusion, namely, that Knowledge, for instance, would be identical with Power and Life, and that it also would be identical with the Knowing One, the Living One, and the Powerful One; and furthermore it would also lead to the conclusion that He who is of necessary existence would not subsist in His own essence; and so on to many other similar absurdities.

from all eternity (*azalīya*)/This is unlike the Karramites, who assert that Allah has attributes but that those attributes must be originated, inasmuch as it is impossible for things which are originated to subsist in His essence.

subsistent in His essence/Of necessity nothing can be said to be an attribute of something unless it subsists in that something. This is unlike the Mu'tazilites, who assert that Allah speaks with a kind of Speech which subsists in something outside Himself. The purpose of this statement of theirs is to deny the existence of Speech as an attribute of Allah, and not to affirm that Speech does exist as an attribute of Him but without subsistence in His essence. The Mu'tazilites maintained the position that establishing the attributes destroyed the unity of Allah, inasmuch as they are eternally existent and distinctly different from the essence of Allah, so it follows that something other than Allah is eternal and that there are numerous eternal beings, nay rather, there are numerous necessarily existent beings, as seen in references which appear in the statements of the Earlier Theologians (*al-mutaqaddimūn*). The clear explicit statement of the position that the one who is Necessarily Existent in His essence is Allah and His attributes came from the Later Theologians (*al-muta'akhkhirūn*). The Christians (*al-Naṣāra*) have become Unbelievers [so say the Mu'tazilites] in establishing three eternal beings, so what is to be said of one who establishes eight or more?

Al-Nasafī referred to the answer to this question by saying,

They are not He nor are they other than He/that is, [*71*] the attributes of Allah are not His essence itself nor are they other than it. This implies neither the eternity of that which is other than He nor the plurality of eternals. Although the Christians do not expressly state that there are distinctly different eternal beings, yet this position compelled them to posit the three persons of the Godhead (*aqānim*),[5] namely Existence, Knowledge, and Life,[6] calling them the Father, the Son and the Holy Spirit (*rūḥ al-qudus*). They claim that the person (*uqnūm*) of Knowledge transferred himself into the body of Jesus—on him be peace—so they permit the separation and transference of the persons, inasmuch as they are distinctly different essences.

Some say that it is impossible to make plurality and multiplicity depend upon distinct entities being made (*al-taghāyur*),[7] this term meaning that it is possible to separate them absolutely so that series of numbers from one, two, three and so on are many and numerous, [72] yet some are a part of others and the part is not distinctly different from the whole.

It is also inconceivable that there be a dispute among the People of the Approved Way and the Community on the question of the multiplicity and plurality of the attributes of the Deity as to whether they are distinctly separate or not. However, it is preferable to say that the plurality of eternal essences but not the plurality of an essence and attributes is impossible. It is also better not to say boldly that the attributes are necessarily existent in themselves but rather [to say] that they are not necessarily existent in anything else but in that which is not themselves nor other than themselves; I mean by that the Essence of Allah—Exalted of Himself and Extolled.

This is what one means when he says that the Necessarily Existent in His essence is Allah and His attributes, the idea being that these are necessarily existent in the essence of the Necessarily Existent. But in themselves they are possibles. There is no absurdity in the eternity of the possible if this eternity subsists in the essence of the Eternal, is necessarily existent in Him, and is not separated (*munfaṣil*) from Him. Not every eternal is a god, so the existence of a number of gods is not to be implied from the existence of eternals. We must rather say that Allah taken with His attributes (*bi ṣifātihi*) is eternal. The term "eternals" should not be used lest the estimative faculty (*al-wahm*) go so far as to think that each of the eternals subsists in itself and that divine attributes are predicated of it.

[5] J. G. Hava, in *Arabic-English Dictionary* (Beirut, 1921), p. 907, gives the origin of this as from the Greek γνώμη, a means of knowing, the mind, a judgment, but see R. Payne Smith, *Thesaurus Syriacus* (Oxford, 1879–1901), p. 3667: *qnūmā*, hypostasis, substance.

[6] These terms, Existence, Knowledge, and Life, as applied to the persons of the Trinity are also given in al-Shahrastānī, *al-Milal*, p. 172; *Dict. of Tech. Terms*, p. 1225; Müller, *Philosophie*, p. 56, and by A.J., p. 108, who quotes the *Sharḥ al-Maqāṣid*.

[7] Cf. *Dict. of Tech. Terms*, p. 1093; Horten, *Die spek. und pos. Theologie des Islam*,

Because of the difficulty of this question the Mu'tazilites and the Philosophers denied the attributes, the Karramites [8] denied their eternity, and the Ash'arites [9] denied both that the attributes are other than He and that they are His essence.

Objection may be made that this, which appears to be a denial, takes away the force of the two contradictories and is in reality a uniting of them; for the explicit denial that the attributes are other than He, for example, establishes inclusively their identity with Him; and the establishing of them as other than He along with an explicit denial of their identity with Him is a uniting of the two contradictories. So also the explicit denial of identity is a uniting of them for that which is understood by ⌊73⌋ a thing; if it is not that which is understood by any other thing—that is, other than the first thing—then it is identical with the first thing, and there is no third intermediate thing conceivable between the two.

We reply to all this that they have interpreted "otherness" (*al-ghayriya*) to be the state of coming-into-being on the part of two existent things so that the existence of one is determined and conceived along with the non-existence of the other; that is to say, it is possible to separate them from one another. They have interpreted "identity" (*al-'ayniya*) to be the uniting together of that which is understood in such a way that there is no distinction of difference at all, and thus there are not two things contradictory to each other. But an intermediate thing is conceivable to the extent that what is understood by one thing is not that which is understood by the other. Yet it does not exist without the other thing, as the part along with the whole, the attribute along with the essence, and some of the attributes along with other attributes. This is true, for the essence and attributes of Allah are eternal from the beginning, and the non-existence of such an eternal is impossible.

It is impossible for one as a part of ten to continue without the ten, and for ten to continue without the one, inasmuch as one is a part of ten. The non-existence of the ten means the non-existence of the one, and the existence

---

[8] The Karramites were the followers of Abū 'Abd Allāh Muḥammad b. Karrām (d. A.H. 256) who was a literalist holding that Allah had a body with flesh, blood, and limbs. See Macdonald, *Development*, pp. 170 ff.; *Enc. of Islam*, II, 773; al-Shahrastānī, *al-Milal*, pp. 79 ff.; al-Baghdādī, *al-Farq bayn al-Firaq*, pp. 202 ff.; Horten, *Die phil. Systeme der spek. Theologen im Islam*, pp. 340 ff.; 'I.D., pp. 70, 72, 90, 128, 147; *al-Bābu 'l-Ḥādī 'Ashar*, p. 35.

[9] This is the position of the earlier Ash'arites, the later ones maintaining that the attributes were other than the essence, and that they were possible, and yet absolutely denying the multiplicity of Eternals and that possibility requires origination (A.J., p. 109).

of the ten means the existence of the one. This, however, is distinctly unlike the originated attributes, for it is conceivable that the essence subsist [in itself] without these attributes which are originated, so they are other than His essence. Thus did the Early Theologians argue.

But this calls for consideration, for if they mean that from the standpoint of each of the two entities a real separation in existence is valid, this is to be contradicted in the case of the world, which must be taken along with its Maker, and the accident, which follows its locus, inasmuch as the existence of the world is inconceivable if the Maker of the world were non-existent, because His non-existence is impossible; nor is the existence of an accident—such as blackness, for example—conceivable without its locus. All this is quite evident; besides, it is certain that there must be a distinct difference [between the two entities] in order that they may be made to agree. And if they consider the matter from one standpoint only, nevertheless there must be a distinct difference between the part and the whole, [74] and so also between the essence and the attribute; so that it is really possible for a part to exist without the whole and for the essence to exist without the attribute.

What the Early Theologians have said about the impossibility of the one [of ten] continuing without the ten appears to be unsound. One must not say that this means that it is possible then to conceive of the existence of each of them along with the non-existence of the other, even as a mere supposition. Even if it is impossible, the world may be conceived of as existing, and then later the establishing by proof of a Maker is to be sought for. This is different from the question of the part and the whole; for just as the existence of ten is impossible without a unit, so the existence of a unit of ten is impossible without the ten, since were it to exist alone it would not be one of the ten. The result is that some consideration must be given to this explanation of the relationship [between the two entities]; and it is quite evident that the complete separation [of essence and attributes] is impossible.

For we say that the Early Theologians have clearly stated that the attributes are not distinctly different from one another on the basis that their non-existence is inconceivable because they are from eternity. Yet it is certain that we may conceive the existence of some of them like Knowledge, for example, and then establish the existence of others by proof. It is known that they did not have this idea in mind even though it does not apply to the example of an accident and its locus. If consideration were to be given to explaining the relationship between the two entities, there would be no distinct difference between the things related, as between father and son, or between two brothers, or as between cause and effect; rather there would be no distinct difference between two different things (*ghayrayn*), for *ghayr* is a term for showing relationship. But no one holds this.

It may be suggested that it is possible that the idea of the Early Theologians was that the attributes are not He according to what is usually understood, nor are they other than He as far as existence is concerned, as is the case of all predicates in relation to their subjects; for there must be some stipulation of unity between them insofar as existence is concerned, in order that a predication may be valid; and there must be a distinct difference insofar as there is something to be understood about them so that the predication may mean something. This is just as we say, "Man is a writer" and not "Man is a stone," which is unsound, or "Man is a man," which means nothing.

We say that this suggested argument is sound in the case of the attributes "Knowing" and "Powerful" in relation to the essence [of Allah], but not sound in the case of the attributes "Knowledge" and "Power," even though the statement regarding these latter attributes refers to Him. Nor does the argument apply to parts which are other than those which are predicated, such as a unit of ten or the hand of Zayd. In *al-Tabsira* there is mention of the argument that a unit of ten is something other than ten and that the hand of Zayd is something other than Zayd. None of the Mutakallims said this except Ja'far b. Ḥārith.[10] In this he differed from all the Mu'tazilites. This was reckoned a bit of ignorance on his part, because ten is the term which is applied to all the individual units [75] and which includes each individual of the units along with the others. So if one were other than ten, it would be other than itself, for it is one of ten, although ten is formed from something else besides. So also if the hand of Zayd were other than Zayd, then the hand of Zayd would be other than itself. This is what Ja'far says, and what it implies is evident.

And they/that is, the attributes from all eternity

are Knowledge (*al-'ilm*)/which is an attribute from eternity. The things that have to do with Knowledge are unveiled when connected with this attribute.

---

[10] This is possibly the Ja'far b. Ḥarb spoken of by al-Baghdādī (*al-Farq bayn al-Firaq*, pp. 153 ff.) where his position regarding the part of the whole as different from the whole is mentioned.

and Power (*al-qudra*)/which is an attribute from eternity. It makes an impression on things over which He has power on their being connected with it.

and Life (*al-ḥayāt*)/which is an attribute from eternity bringing about the validity of Knowledge

[76] **and Might** (*al-qūwa*)/which has the meaning of Power

and Hearing (*al-sam'*)/which is an attribute connected with things heard

and Seeing (*al-baṣar*)/which is an attribute connected with things seen. It comprehends completely [11] neither by the use of the imagination (*al-takhayyul*) nor of the estimative faculty (*al-tawahhum*) nor by an impression being made on some sense organ and a current of air reaching it. The eternity of these two attributes of Hearing and Seeing does not require the eternity of the things heard and seen, just as the eternity of Knowledge and Power does not require the eternity of the things which are known and in His Power, because they are all eternal attributes, and connections with originated things are originated for them.

and Willing (*al-irāda*) **and Desiring** (*al-mashī'a*)/These terms are expressions for an attribute in the Living One [77] which brings it about that one of two alternatives among the things over which He has power is specified and actually comes into being at a certain time, even though His Power maintains an equal relationship to each of them and even though the connection of Knowledge with it is a consequence of its actually coming into being. In this statement attention is drawn to the answer made in refuting the one who asserts that Desiring is eternal and that Willing is originated and subsistent in the essence of Allah, and also in refuting the one who asserts that the meaning of Allah's Willing His own action is that He is not compelled nor heedless nor overcome, and that the meaning of His Willing the action of others is that He commands them. How can this be the meaning of it, when He has commanded every legally responsible person (*mukallaf*) [12] to believe and perform all the rest of the duties? Had He desired that, it would have happened.

[11] A.J., p. 116, reads "there is comprehended completely by both of them."
[12] See *Enc. of Islam*, I, 239; *Dict. of Tech. Terms*, p. 1255; *al-Bābu 'l-Hādī 'Ashar*, pp. 3 ff., 46 ff., and 82 ff.; also below Chapter 10.

and Doing (*al-fiʿl*) **and Creating** (*al-takhlīq*) [18]/These are expressions for an attribute existing from eternity which is called *al-takwīn* (bringing-into-being). Its verification comes later. Al-Nasafī avoided using the word *al-khalq* (the creation) inasmuch as it is often used in place of *al-makhlūq* (the thing created).

and Sustaining (*al-tarzīq*)/It is a special kind of bringing-into-being which al-Nasafī explained thus in order to point out that things like creating, sustaining, forming, bringing to life and death, and other things as well which are ascribed to Allah are traced back to a real attribute existing from eternity and subsistent in the essence of Allah which is bringing-into-being (*al-takwīn*). This is unlike the position of al-Ashʿarī, for he asserted that these things are relationships (*iḍāfāt*) and attributes of actions.

[18] See below, Chaps. 7, 9, and 10.

Chapter 6

THE ATTRIBUTE OF SPEECH

And Speech.

He speaks with a kind of Speech which is one of His attributes, from all eternity, not of the genus of letters and sounds. It is an attribute incompatible with silence and defect. Allah speaks with this attribute, commanding, prohibiting, and narrating. The Qur'ān, the Speech of Allah, is uncreated and it is written in our volumes, preserved in our hearts, recited by our tongues, heard by our ears, [yet] is not a thing residing in them.

And Speech (*kalām*)/It is an attribute from eternity which is an expression for that context composed of letters called the Qur'ān. [78] [This is similar to] any one of us [who] whenever he commands, prohibits, and narrates finds of himself an idea and then indicates it by an expression or by writing or by a gesture. This attribute is something other than the attribute of Knowledge, since a man may narrate something which he knows not [to be a fact], but rather knows the contrary to it. This attribute is an attribute different from Willing, for one may command something he does not will, like the person who commands his slave to do something in order to reveal his disobedience and insubordination. This kind of speech is called "speech of the mind" (*kalām nafsī*).[1] Al-Akhṭal [2] referred to this kind of speech in saying,

> Verily speech is in the heart,
>
> And the tongue has been made only as a guide to the heart.

[1] *Kalām nafsī*, or *hadīth nafsī*, is the ideas of the mind which do not need letters or words to express them. *Enc. of Islam*, II, 671; *Dict. of Tech. Terms*, p. 1270; al-Faḍālī, *Kifāyat al-'Awāmm*, p. 54; al-Ījī, *al-Mawāqif*, pp. 63 ff.; A.J., pp. 120 f.

[2] Al-Akhṭal, an Arabian Christian poet, born about A.D. 640. A eulogy of the Umayyad regime, under which he flourished, is considered his masterpiece. He is remembered especially for his refusal of the *khalīfa's* offer that he become a Muslim, and for the golden cross which he wore about his neck after the manner of the Arabian Christians. *Enc. of Islam*, I, 234 ff.; Nicholson, *A Literary History of the Arabs*, pp. 240 ff.; Brockelmann, *Geschichte*, I, 49 ff.

And 'Umar—may Allah be well pleased with him—said, "Verily, I made a saying right and sound in myself." And often you say to your friend, "Verily there is speech within me, which I wish to relate to you." The proof for the establishment of the attribute of Speech is the Agreement (*ijmā'*) of the Muslim people [79] and *mutawātir* traditions from the prophets, which assert that Allah is a Speaker since it is certain that speaking is impossible without the attribute of Speech being established. It has been established that Allah has eight [3] attributes: Knowledge, Power, Life, Hearing, Seeing, Willing, Creating, and Speech. And since the last three are more open to dispute and more obscure, he again referred to their being established as sure and eternal and went into some detail in his statement of the fact that they are firmly established.

So al-Nasafī said,

He/that is, Allah

speaks with a kind of Speech which is one of His attributes/Of necessity it is impossible to affirm the derivative of any thing without affirming the subsistence in that thing of the source of its derivation. In this way al-Nasafī refuted the Mu'tazilites,[4] inasmuch as they took the position that Allah is a Speaker of Speech which subsists in something other than Himself, and is not one of His attributes.

from all eternity/Of necessity it is impossible that originated things subsist in His essence.

not of the genus of letters and sounds/Of necessity letters and sounds are originated accidents, the occurrence of some of which is conditioned on the fact that others have been finished. By immediate perception we know that it is impossible to pronounce the second letter [of a word] without finishing off the first letter. This is a refutation of the Ḥanbalites [5] and the Karramites, who say that the Speech of Allah is an accident of the genus of sounds and letters, and yet in spite of that it is eternal.

---

[3] This is the Maturidite position, since the Ash'arites omit Creating (*takwīn*). See al-Rāzī, *Muḥaṣṣal*, pp. 135 ff.; al-Ījī, *al-Mawāqif*, pp. 71 ff.

[4] This position of the Mu'tazilites regarding the Speech of Allah is also that of the Shi'ites. The Kharijites like the Mu'tazilites said that the Qur'ān was created. The Murji'ites differed among themselves in the matter. Al-Ash'arī, *Maqālāt*, pp. 124, 153; al-Bābu 'l-Hādī 'Ashar, pp. 25 ff.

[5] Cf. *Enc. of Islam*, I, 188 ff., II, 670 ff.; Ibn Khallikān, *Biographical Dictionary*, I, 44 ff.; Macdonald, *Development*, pp. 157 f.

It/that is, Speech

is an attribute/that is, an idea subsistent in the essence

incompatible with silence/which is the leaving off of speech while yet having the power to speak

and defect/This is the lack of fitness in the organs of speech either because of the nature created within one, as in the case of dumbness, [*80*] or because of weakness and immaturity, as in infancy. Objection may be made that this definition applies to uttered speech only, in contrast to speech of the mind, since silence and dumbness are incompatible with verbal utterance only. To this we answer that the meaning here is internal silence and internal defect, so that one neither desires utterance within himself nor is capable of it. So just as Speech is of both kinds, uttered and in the mind, so also is its contrary; I mean by that silence and dumbness.

Allah speaks with this attribute, commanding, prohibiting, and narrating/ This means that Speech is a single attribute [6] with a variety of forms for commanding, prohibiting, and narrating that differ according to the matters with which Speech is connected.[7] In this, Speech is analogous to Knowledge, Power, and the rest of the attributes. Each of them is a single eternal attribute, but variety and origination occur only in making connections and adding relationships, inasmuch as that is more fitting to the perfection of the unity of Allah. And there is no proof that each attribute has variety within itself. Objection may be raised that these things [such as commanding, prohibiting, and narrating] are divisions of Speech, without which it is unreasonable to think of the existence of Speech. We reply that this is impossible, nay rather, that Speech becomes one of these divisions only when the

---

[6] This is the orthodox position, which denies that speech should be divided into a variety of attributes corresponding to the various kinds of speech. See al-Rāzī, *Muḥaṣṣal*, p. 134; al-Ijī, *al-Mawāqif*, p. 68; 'I.D., p. 80.

[7] These are the connections which according to the Mutakallims are the relationships between the Knower and the thing known, the Decreeing One and the thing decreed, etc. Because of the difficulty of explaining the real nature of the connection between Allah, the Eternal and Infinite One, and the originated things which exist through his Power and Will the Scholastic Theologians went more and more into great detail. Al-Faḍālī, for example, enumerates seven distinct varieties of connections for the attribute of Power, and al-Bayjūrī in his commentary says that al-Faḍālī omitted one and there should be eight connections for this one attribute. Al-Faḍālī, *Kifāyat al-'Awāmm*, p. 44; *Dict. of Tech. Terms*, pp. 1014, 1061 f.; See Wensinck, *The Muslim Creed*, pp. 127, 189. Al-Ash'arī, *al-Ibāna*, pp. 23 f. (Klein, *al-Aš'arī's Al-Ibānah*, pp. 66 ff.).

connections [with originated things] are made. This is true of Speech which does not pass away, but in the beginning from all eternity there was no division whatsoever.

[*81*] And some took the position that from all eternity Speech was narrative (*khabar*) and that all other kinds of Speech go back to it. They say that the result of the command is to give the information (*al-ikhbār*) that performing the act deserves reward and failure to do it deserves punishment; and that prohibition is just the opposite of this; and the result of asking for information (*al-istikhbār*) is the narrative which comes from seeking to be instructed; and the result of summoning is the narrative which comes from seeking a response. Answer may be made that of necessity we know there are differences in these meanings, and the fact that some of them require the others does not demand their being united into one.

Objection may be raised that command and prohibition without someone who is commanded or who is prohibited is a bit of foolishness and unreality, and that to say that from eternity there is on the part of Allah narration which assumes the past time is a pure falsehood from which Allah must be far removed. To this we reply that no difficulty results if His Speech is not made from eternity to be command, prohibition, and narrative. If we do make His Speech to be command, prohibition, and narrative, then the command from eternity is to compel the one commanded thereby to obtain it at the time he comes into existence and to make him fit to obtain it. It is sufficient then that there be in the knowledge of the one commanding the existence of the one to be commanded, which is analogous to a man's taking it for granted that he had a son, and then commanding him to do something after he should come into existence. Narration that refers to eternity is not described by any time at all, since with Allah there is no past, future, nor present, because He is far removed from all time, just as His Knowledge is eternal and is unchanged by the changing of times.

And when al-Nasafī spoke explicitly of Speech as being from eternity, he wanted to call our attention to the fact that this term "al-Qur'ān" is sometimes applied to the eternal Speech of the mind just as it is applied to the originated context (*al-naẓm*) which is read, so he said,

The Qur'ān, the Speech of Allah, is uncreated (*ghayr makhlūq*)/He followed the term "al-Qur'ān" with the words "the speech of Allah" because of what the Early Theologians had stated saying that the Qur'ān is the uncreated Speech of Allah and not that the Qur'ān is said to be uncreated.

[*82*] This distinction is made lest the mind jump to the conclusion that the thing composed of sounds and letters is eternal. This is just the position that the Ḥanbalites took out of ignorance and obstinacy. And al-Nasafī used "uncreated" instead of "unoriginated" in order, first, to call attention to their oneness in meaning; second, to make his statement agree with the tradition in which the Prophet—may Allah bless and give him peace—said, "The Qur'ān is the uncreated Speech of Allah, and whoever says that it is created is not a Believer in Allah the Majestic One," and, third, to take into account the dispute between the two parties on the well-known subject of whether the Qur'ān is created or uncreated.[8] So the whole question is to be interpreted as the question of the creation of the Qur'ān. The verifying of this matter on which they and we differ goes back to whether or not the Speech of the mind can be established. However, we do not say that the verbal expressions (*al-alfāẓ*) and letters are eternal, and they do not say that the Speech of the mind is originated.

The proof for our position has already been stated, namely, that it is established by Agreement and *mutawātir* tradition of the prophets—may the blessing of Allah be on them—that Allah is a Speaker, the only meaning of which is that He has the attribute of Speech and that, since the subsistence in the essence of Allah of the verbal Speech which is described as originated is impossible, the Speech which is described as eternal and in the mind is designated as the attribute of Allah.

The Muʿtazilites have inferred that the Qur'ān is to be described by attributes which pertain to a created being and by marks which show its origination: that is, such things as its composition and arrangement, its having been brought down as a whole and then revealed bit by bit,[9] its being in the Arabic language, its being heard by the ear of man, and its being rhetorical and inimitable and so on. All this only raises an argument against the position of the Ḥanbalites and not against us, for we admit that the arrangement of the Qur'ān is originated. Our statement [about the Qur'ān being uncreated] has only to do with the Eternal Idea.

---

[8] For the history of the conflict over the significance of the non-creation of the Speech of Allah, see *Enc. of Islam*, II, 670 ff.; Macdonald, *Development*, pp. 146 ff.; Wensinck, *The Muslim Creed*, pp. 149 ff.; Ibn Khaldūn, *Muqaddima*, III, 50 ff.; Ibn Ḥazm, *Kitāb al-Fiṣal*, III, 4 ff.

[9] *Inzāl, tanzīl*, verbal nouns of the IV and II stems of *nazala*: the former means "sending down at one time or in general," the latter is used for "sending down by degrees, or in actuality." The former is probably, says A.J. (p. 124), the sending down of the Qur'ān from the Preserved Tablet (see note 10) to the lowest heaven, the latter from there to the Prophet. Cf. *Enc. of Islam*, II, 1064 ff.; al-Kastalī (Constantinople text), p. 92; *al-Taʿrīfāt*, p. 72; al-Bayḍāwī, *Anwār al-Tanzīl*, I, 17 f.

Since the Mu'tazilites were unable to deny that Allah speaks, they held that when He speaks it means that He brings into existence the sounds and letters in their places or He brings into existence the written characters of the Preserved Tablet (*al-lawḥ al-maḥfūẓ*),[10] which may or may not be read. They differed about this last point. You are well aware that the one who is moved is the one in whom the motion subsists and not the one who brings the motion into existence. Otherwise it would be sound for the Creator to be described with accidents which are created of Him. And Allah is far exalted above anything like that.

[*83*] One of the greatest ambiguities [regarding the Qur'ān] according to the Mu'tazilites is stated by them as follows. You [orthodox people] are agreed that the Qur'ān is the name for that which has been transmitted to us between the two covers of the volumes by *tawātur*. Believing this requires that the Qur'ān be written in the volumes, recited by the tongues of men, and heard by their ears. All these things are of necessity marks which indicate that the Qur'ān was originated. So al-Nasafī pointed out the answer to this by saying,

and it/that is, the Qur'ān, which is the speech of Allah

is written in our volumes/that is, with written characters and with forms of letters which indicate it

preserved in our hearts/that is, by verbal expressions which are imagined

recited by our tongues/with letters which are pronounced and heard

heard by our ears/and with these also

[yet] is not a thing residing (*ḥāll*) in them/He means to say that in spite of all this the Qur'ān, the Speech of Allah, does not reside in the volumes, nor in the hearts, nor in the tongues, nor in the ears; but it is an Eternal Idea subsisting in the essence of Allah. This Idea is expressed and heard

[10] The Preserved Tablet, according to the Multitude of the People of the Law, is a body (*jism*) above the seventh heaven in which is written all that has been and will be until the Day of Resurrection. With the Wise Men it is the Active Intelligence and with the Philosophers it is the Universal Soul; and with the Sufis it is the Divine Light. The Tablet is very often identified, however, with the original copy of the Qur'ān and is then identical with *umm al-kitāb*. *Dict. of Tech. Terms*, p. 1291; *Enc. of Islam*, III, 19; T. P. Hughes, *The Dictionary of Islam*, p. 285; al-Bayḍāwī, *Anwār al-Tanzil*, II, 396.

by means of the context which indicates it, and preserved by the context which is imagined in the mind and is written by marks, by forms, and by characters which are used conventionally for the letters that indicate the Qur'ān. This is analogous to our saying that fire is a burning substance, which is recalled to mind by a verbal expression and is written down with a pen, but it does not follow that the real essence of fire is a sound and a letter.

The verifying of this fact is that a thing has a kind of existence in substances (*al-a'yān*), another kind of existence in minds (*al-adhhān*), another in an expression (*al-'ibāra*), and still another in writing (*al-kitāba*). The writing indicates the expression, the expression indicates what is in the mind, and it in turn indicates what is in the substance. So whenever the Qur'ān is described as one of the things inseparably connected (*lawāzim*) with the Eternal, as when we say that the Qur'ān is uncreated, the meaning is its true existential essence in external reality. Whenever it is described as that which is inseparably connected with things created and originated, the verbal expressions which are spoken and heard are meant, as when we say, "I have recited half the Qur'ān," or the expression imagined in the mind as when we say, [*84*] "I have memorized the Qur'ān," or the characters that are written down are meant as when we say, "It is unlawful for one who is defiled to touch the Qur'ān."

And since that which is indicated in the legal judgments by the term "Qur'ān" is the verbal utterance (*al-lafẓ*) and not the Eternal Idea, the Imams in fundamental matters of dogma defined it as that which is written in the volumes and transmitted by *tawātur*. And they applied the name [Qur'ān] both to the context and the Idea; that is, they applied it not only to the Idea, but to the context as well, in so far as it indicates the Idea. In regard to the Eternal Speech which is an attribute of Allah, al-Ash'arī took the position that it was possible for it to be heard; and al-Ustādh Abū Ishāq al-Isfarā'inī [11] denied it. Abū Mansūr [al-Māturīdī] [12] also chose this [latter] position. The meaning of the saying of Allah, "Until he hear the speech of Allah" (Qur'ān 9:6) is that he heard that which indicates it, which is

---

[11] See *Enc. of Islam*, II, 48; Horten, *Die phil. Systeme der spek. Theologen im Islam*, pp. 556 f.

[12] Abū Mansūr Muhammad b. Mahmūd al-Māturīdī, who came from a village in Samarqand called Māturīd, was the leader of a reform in theology in the lands of the Trans-Oxus. Dying in A.H. 333 (A.D. 944), he was a contemporary of al-Ash'arī, who died in A.H. 324 (A.D. 935). Brockelmann, *Geschichte*, I, 195; 'I.D., p. 14. The differences between his position in dogmatic theology and that of al-Ash'arī have been well summarized in the book *al-Rawda al-Bahīya* (see Brockelmann, *Geschichte*, I, 195), in Horten, *Die phil. Systeme der spek. Theologen im Islam*, pp. 531 ff., and also in Sayyid Murtadā's commentary on the *Ihyā'* of al-Ghazzālī, II, 86 ff.; *Enc. of Islam*, I, 309, and III, 414 f.

analogous to one's saying, "I hear the knowledge of So-and-so." So Moses [13] heard a sound which indicated the Speech of Allah, but since it was without the means of a book or an angel, Moses was given the special name of "interlocutor" (*al-kalīm*).[14]

Objection may be raised that were the Speech of Allah really in an Eternal Idea and metaphorically in a constructed context, then it would be sound to deny Speech of Allah, by saying that the inimitable (*al-mu'jiz*) context which was sent down from above bit by bit and divided into suras and verses is not the Speech of Allah. But the Agreement [of the Muslim people] opposes this last statement. Also it may be objected that if the inimitable thing which was an object of contention [15] in recitation were in reality the Speech of Allah, it would be positively certain that this can only be conceived of the context which was composed and divided into suras, since there would have been no meaning to their opposing the Eternal attribute of Speech. To this we reply that the verifying of this is to be found in the fact that the Speech of Allah is a name common to two things. In the first place it applies to the Eternal Speech of the mind—the idea conveyed by the relationship here in the phrase "Speech of Allah" is that it is an attribute of Allah—and in the second place it applies to the Speech which is originated and to verbal utterance, composed of suras and verses—the idea conveyed by the relationship [of Speech to Allah] here is that it is created by Allah and not one of the compositions of His creatures. So denial of the Eternal Speech as suggested above is not at all sound. That which is inimitable and over which they contended can only be the Speech of Allah.

The claim made by some of the Early Theologians that this expression is metaphorical does not mean that it is the conventional usage applied to the context which has been composed, but rather it means that in being verified as a reality and in essence the Speech is the name of the Idea [85] which subsists in the mind. Giving the verbal utterance the name ["Speech of Allah"] and making it the conventional usage for this Idea are only results of its indicating the Idea. So there is no dispute with them about the conventional usage of the word and giving it this name.

Some of the Verifiers (*al-muḥaqqiqūn*) [16] maintained that the Early Theologians used the term "the Speech of Allah" as an eternal Idea. It was

---

[13] See Qur. 4:162; al-Bayḍāwī, *Anwār al-Tanzil*, I, 130, 241; al-Ṭabarī, *Annales*, I, 463 ff.; al-Thaʻlabī, *Qiṣaṣ al-Anbiyā'*, pp. 174 ff.; Macdonald, *Development*, p. 149.

[14] Cf. *Enc. of Islam*, II, 699; Fleischer, *Kleinere Schriften*, II, 772.

[15] See Qur. 2:21; al-Bayḍāwī, *Anwār al-Tanzil*, I, 36.

[16] A "verifier" was a term sometimes applied to many of the later Scholastic Theologians like al-Rāzī, al-Ṭūsī, al-Ījī, and al-Taftāzānī himself. Cf. *Dict. of Tech. Terms*, p. 336.

not something that was contrasted with the verbal utterance so that it meant
that which is indicated and understood by the verbal utterance, but it was
something in contrast to the substance itself. The meaning of the term was:
that which does not subsist in itself like the rest of the attributes. They meant
that the Qur'ān, being eternal, is the name which is used for both the verbal
utterance and the Idea and includes them both. This is not the position held
by the Ḥanbalites, who maintained that the context [17] which was composed
and arranged in parts is eternal. We know by immediate perception that it
is positively impossible for one to pronounce the "s" (*sīn*) of *bism 'illāhi* without first pronouncing the "b" (*bā'*). But they mean that the verbal expression
which subsists in the mind is not arranged in parts [one after the other] in
His mind like that which subsists in the mind of the one who has memorized
it, without any arrangement of parts and without some of it preceding other
parts. The arrangement takes place only when one gives expression to it in
utterance or when one reads without using the organ [of speech]. This is the
explanation of their statement, "That which is read is eternal, but the reading
is originated." But that Speech which subsists in the essence of Allah has no
arrangement of parts, so that whoever hears His Speech hears it without
any arrangement of parts, for He needs no organ [of speech].

This is the conclusion to be reached from the statement of the Verifiers. It is
well for one then to conceive the Speech of Allah as verbal expression, subsistent in the mind, not composed of letters either uttered or imagined, since
it is stipulated of these that the presence of some precludes the presence of
others; nor is it composed of the characters which are arranged in order and
which indicate it. And we do not conceive the speech which subsists in the
mind of the one who has memorized it except as forms of letters which are
stored up and inscribed in his imagination (*khayāl*), so that if he turns to
them, it becomes speech constructed of verbal expressions which are
imagined, or of marks which are so arranged that whenever he gives utterance to them they become [86] speech which is heard.

[17] A.J. (p. 128) reads *lafẓ*, "verbal expression," instead of *naẓm*.

Chapter 7

THE ATTRIBUTES OF CREATING AND WILLING

And Creating is an attribute of Allah from all eternity. And it is Allah's creating the world and every one of its parts, not in eternity, but rather at the time of its becoming existent, according to His Knowledge and Willing. And it [that is, the attribute of Creating] is not the thing created, according to our opinion.

And Willing is an attribute of Allah from all eternity, subsistent in His essence.

And Creating (*al-takwīn*) [1]/It is the idea expressed by such words as *al-fiʿl* (doing), *al-khalq* (creation), *al-takhlīq* (producing), *al-ijād* (bringing-into-existence), *al-iḥdāth* (originating), and *al-ikhtirāʿ* (inventing). It is explained as the bringing of the non-existent (*al-maʿdūm*) from non-existence into existence.

is an attribute of Allah/because both Reason and Tradition agree that He is the Producer (*al-khāliq*) and the Creator (*al-mukawwin*) of the world, and because it is impossible to apply a derivative term to a thing without the source of the derivative being a descriptive of it and subsistent in it.

from all eternity (*azalīya*)/because of certain reasons. The first is that originated things cannot subsist in Allah, as we have seen. The second is that Allah in His Speech, which is from eternity, described His essence by the term *al-khāliq,* so were He not from all eternity Creator, that would either necessitate falsehood [on His part] or a resorting to metaphorical language,

---

[1] *Takwīn* is used here in the special sense of *creatio ex nihilo* so it has been translated "creating," and *mukawwin*, "Creator," rather than by the more elaborate and cumbersome terminology "causing to come into being" and "the one who causes the coming into being" which the terms really signify. *Dict. of Tech. Terms,* p. 1276.

by interpreting it to mean that He is the Creator in the future or that He is able to create without difficulty. The real fact is that were it permissible to apply the term "the Creator" to Allah as meaning "the One who is able to create," it would then be permissible to apply to Him all of the terms having to do with the accidents over which He has power. The third reason is that were He originated (*ḥādith*), there would be two alternative absurdities. (a) If He were originated by another creation, that would necessitate the Endless Chain, which is impossible. It would necessarily follow then that it is impossible for the world to be created, in spite of the fact that we see that it is. (b) Or if He were originated He would be so without another creation, and thus that which is originated dispenses both with the originator and the act of origination. This statement does away with the Maker [of the world although the fact of His existence has already been proved]. The fourth reason is that were He originated, He would have been originated: (a) either in His essence and therefore He would be the locus of things originated; (b) or in something else, [*87*] just as Abū al-Hudhayl [2] maintained, saying that the creating of each body (*jism*) is something subsistent in it, so each body is the producer and creator of itself. Clearly this is impossible.

These [four] proofs are based on the fact that Creating is a real attribute [3] like Knowledge and Power. But the Verifiers among the Mutakallims say that Creating is one of the relationships (*al-iḍāfāt*) and rational expressions (*al-iʿtibārāt al-ʿaqlīya*), like the statement, for example, that the Maker is before everything and with everything and after everything; His name is on our tongues. He is the object of our homage, He causes us to die and to live, and so on. The conclusion to be drawn from this is that from eternity He is the beginning of the acts of producing and sustaining, the giving of life and of death, and so on.

There is no proof for the position that Creating is another attribute in addition to Power and Willing, for although Power has a relationship equal to the existence or non-existence of a thing created, it is only when Willing

---

[2] Muḥammad b. al-Hudhayl, al-ʿAbdī al-ʿAllāf (A.H. 135–226; A.D. 752–841), one of the outstanding Muʿtazilites, taught that the attributes of Allah were his essence. For the remainder of his doctrines see al-Shahrastānī, *al-Milal*, pp. 35 ff.; al-Baghdādī, *al-Farq bayn al-Firaq*, pp. 102 ff.; Macdonald, *Development*, pp. 136 ff.; Horten, *Die phil. Systeme der spek. Theologen im Islam*, pp. 246 ff.; *Enc. of Islam*, I, 93.

[3] This is one of the points of difference between the Ashʿarites and the Maturidites (those from beyond the River Oxus) the former denying that *takwīn* was an attribute of Allah, the latter asserting that it was. Cf. *al-Rawḍa al-Bahīya*, pp. 39 ff.; al-Rāzī, *Muḥaṣṣal*, p. 135; al-Faḍālī, *Kifāyat al-ʿAwāmm*, pp. 57 ff.; Macdonald, *Development*, pp. 337 f.; al-Ījī, *al-Mawāqif*, pp. 77 f.

embraces one of the two potentialities that this one is specified [and becomes actual].

Those who assert that Creating is originated make the deduction that we can not conceive of it without there being that which is created, just as the act of striking is inconceivable without there being the one who is struck. So were Creating eternal, the eternity of things created must be posited; but that is impossible.

Al-Nasafī pointed out the answer to them by saying,

And it/that is, Creating

is Allah's creating the world and every one of its parts, not in eternity, but rather at the time of its becoming existent, according to His Knowledge and Willing/

So Creating continues from eternity to eternity (*azalan wa abadan*) [88] and the thing created is originated by the origination of the connection [between Creating and that which is created], just as in the case of Knowledge and Power and other eternal attributes, the eternity of whose connections does not follow from their own eternity, inasmuch as their connections are originated. In this there is the verifying, first, of the proposition that if the existence of the world is not connected with the essence of Allah or with one of His attributes, then it follows that the Maker [of the world] has been deprived of His function and also that there is no need for verifying the fact that originated things come from one who brings them into existence, but these conclusions are impossible [so the existence of the world must be connected with the essence of Allah or one of His attributes]; and, second, of the proposition that if the existence of the world is connected with the essence of Allah then this (a) either requires the eternity of that with which its existence is connected, and that necessitates the eternity of the world, which is unsound, or (b) it does not necessitate it; so Creating then is eternal also, even though the thing created which is connected with Creating is originated. In this there is also the verifying of what is to be said of the proposition that the connection of the existence of the thing created with Creating is just as much as saying that it is originated, inasmuch as "the Eternal" is defined as that the existence of which is not connected with anything else, and "the originated" is defined as that the existence of which is connected with something else.

This is a matter for consideration, inasmuch as this is the meaning of "eternal" and of "originated" according to what the Philosophers say. But "the originated" is defined by the Mutakallims as that thing the existence of which had a beginning, meaning that its existence was preceded by non-existence; and "the eternal" is the contrary of this. The mere connection of the originated thing with something else does not require, according to this meaning, that it be originated, but mere connection permits it to be in need of something else, proceeding from it and lasting as long as it lasts, which is just what the Philosophers held in claiming that its eternity is one of the possibles, just like primary matter (*al-hayūlī*), for example. Certainly whenever we establish, by means of a proof that does not rest on the origination of the world, that the world proceeded from the Maker by [His] choice rather than of necessity, then the proposition that its existence is connected with the Creating of Allah is a proposition that it is originated. And from this one may go on to say that it applies to every part of the world, thereby answering the one who asserts that some parts, like primary matter, are eternal. Or the Philosophers maintain that some parts are eternal, meaning that they were not preceded by non-existence, which, however, does not mean [*89*] that the world was not created by something outside itself.

The conclusion to be drawn from this is that we do not admit that Creating is inconceivable without the existence of the created thing, and that Creating has the same relation to the thing created as the act of striking has to the one struck. Striking is an attribute showing relationship which is inconceivable without the two things related, namely, the striker and the one struck, but Creating is a real attribute that is the basis for the relationship, which is the bringing of the non-existent out from non-existence into existence, but not the relationship itself. Yet even were it the relationship itself, according to the terminology used by the Early Theologians, then the proposition, which verifies this relationship as true without there being a thing which was actually created, would be a contention and a denial of that which is necessary. And this [proposition that Creating bears the relation to the thing created that striking does to the thing struck] is not to be rejected by saying that striking is an accident the continuance of which is impossible; for [even if it is an accident] it must be connected with the thing acted upon, and pain must pass on to the thing acted upon, inasmuch as it exists at the same time as the action, since were it delayed [until another time] it would become non-existent. This is unlike the action of the Creator. His action is from eternity and of necessity endures, continuing until the time of the existence of the thing acted upon.

And it [that is, the attribute of Creating] is not the thing created (*al-muḳaw-wan*), according to our opinion/This is true because of necessity the action is distinctly different from the thing acted upon, just as striking differs from the one struck and eating from the thing eaten; and also because certain absurd things would follow were Creating the thing which is itself created. First, the created thing would of necessity be a thing created and produced by itself, since it is created by a creating which is the thing itself, so it would be eternal and independent of the Maker. This is impossible. Second, the Creator would of necessity have no connection with the world, except that He is before it in eternity and exercises His power over it, yet without having made it or without making an impression on it, this being a necessary consequence of its being created by itself. This does not require Him to be a Creator nor the world to be created by Him, consequently it is not valid to say that He is the Creator and the Maker of the world. This is false. Third, it would require that Allah not be a creator [90] of things, since of necessity the only idea that the Creator conveys is that He is the one in whom Creating subsists. But whenever creating is identical with the thing created then it is not subsistent in the essence of Allah. Fourth, it would require one to admit the validity of such a proposition as that the creator of blackness in a given rock, for example, is black, and that the rock is the creator of the blackness, inasmuch as the only meaning of creator and blackness is the one in whom creating and blackness subsists. They are one and the same thing, and their locus is one and the same.

All of this calls attention to the fact that it is necessary to make a clear distinction between the deed and the thing done. However, the one who uses Reason must ponder such investigations as these and not ascribe to the well grounded among those learned in the principles of the faith something which is known by immediate perception to be impossible by anyone who has the least discernment. Rather let him seek valid ground for the statement which they make which serves as a basis for dispute among the Learned and for controversy among those who use Reason.

For whoever says that creating is identical with the thing created means that if the doer does anything, then there is nothing in this but the doer and the thing done. But the idea denoted by terms like "creating" and "bringing into existence" is an expression for that which takes place in Reason, since there is a relation between the doer and thing done. It is not something verified as distinctly different from the thing done in the world of reality. He does not mean that what is understood by creating is identical with

Chapter 8

THE BEATIFIC VISION OF ALLAH

That there is a Vision of Allah is allowed by Reason and necessary by Tradition. A proof on authority has come down affirming that Believers have a vision of Allah in the abode of the next World. And He is seen [unlike any material being] not in place nor in a direction so far as being confronted, nor by the conjunction of the rays of light, nor by a certain definite distance between the one who sees and Allah.

That there is a Vision (*ru'ya*)[1] of Allah/This means the complete unveiling (*inkishāf*) through the [sense of] sight, which is defined as the comprehension[2] of a thing as it really is by means of the sense of sight. That is to say that whenever we look at the full moon and then close the eyes, it is clear that, though we see the moon unveiled both when the eyes are open and when they are closed, its being unveiled is more complete and perfect in gazing at it. So we have in relation to the object seen a special state called Vision.

is allowed by Reason/This means that Reason when acting by itself does not decide that the Vision is impossible so long as there is no proof brought against it, in spite of the fact that at first there was no Vision [before it was

---

[1] This matter of the Beatific Vision was one of the principal points on which the orthodox Muslims differed from the Mu'tazilites. Strange to say, al-Taftāzānī does not mention the Mu'tazilites. The Philosophers and the Shi'ites also denied the possibility of the ocular vision. The Comparers, the Corporealizers and the Karramites because of their extreme anthropomorphic ideas held in a very real sense to the possibility of the vision. See *al-Bābu 'l-Hādi 'Ashar*, pp. 35 ff.; al-Ash'arī, *Maqālāt*, pp. 213 ff., 433 f.; al-Ash'arī, *al-Ibāna*, pp. 13 ff. (Klein, *al-Aš'arī's Al-Ibānah*, pp. 56 ff.); al-Shahrastānī, *Nihāyatu 'l-Iqdām*, pp. 356 ff.; al-Rāzī, *Muhaṣṣal*, pp. 136 ff.; Müller, *Philosophie*, pp. 73 ff.; al-Faḍālī, *Kifāyat al-'Awāmm* (also the commentary of al-Bayjūrī), pp. 66 f.; al-Ijī, *al-Mawāqif*, pp. 78 ff.; A.J., p. 141; Macdonald, *Development*, pp. 145, 296, 344; Wensinck, *The Muslim Creed*, pp. 63 ff., 88 f., 179.

[2] A.J., p. 136, and al-Kastalī, Constantinople text of A.H. 1310, p. 103, read *ithbāt*, "affirmation" or "establishing," instead of *idrāk*.

mentioned in revelation]. This is a necessary ruling, so whosoever claims that the Vision of Allah is impossible must produce his proof.

The People of Reality [3] demonstrated the possibility of the Vision in two ways, one based on rational argument (*'aqlī*) and the other based on traditional authority (*sam'ī*). The establishment of the first proof is as follows. Undoubtedly various [bodily] substances and various accidents are seen by us, inasmuch as we of necessity distinguish by the faculty of sight between one body and another body and one accident and another accident. Now the common designation inevitably implies a common cause; this cause is either existence or origination or possibility, inasmuch as there is no fourth alternative which is common to both substances and accidents.[4] Origination is a term explicatory of the fact that the existence took place after non-existence; and possibility is a term explicatory of the fact that both existence and non-existence are not the result of the necessity of their own nature. But as for non-existence, it cannot enter at all into consideration of causality [for non-existence cannot be the cause of anything]. Consequently [whichever of the three alternatives is taken] existence has been established [inasmuch as origination and possibility also imply existence]; and this existence is common both to the Maker and to that which is made by Him. Thus it has been established that it is possible for Allah to be seen by reason of the fact that the cause for such a possibility, namely existence, has been demonstrated as being true concerning Him.

[92] That sometimes a thing is not seen [even though it exists] is due to the fact that it is of the nature of that kind of possible which depends for its realization on the presence of a certain condition; or as may be said the absence of such a condition acts as something which of necessity is a preventer [of its being seen]. Therefore it would be proper to say that other existent things such as sounds, flavors, odors, and their like may be seen; and the fact that they are not seen is only because Allah did not create in the creature the vision of them in the customary way, and not because they cannot be seen.

It may be objected that it is not proper [for us to say that sounds, flavors, and odors may be seen], so no cause [5] is required. And even if this fact were

---

[3] A.J. (p. 137) explains this term to mean here the early theologians of the People of the Approved Way (*ahl al-sunna*).

[4] That is to say the existence or the origination or the possibility of these things is the cause of their being seen. These three, existence, origination or possibility are common to both substances and accidents, but non-existence cannot be considered as being common to them inasmuch as we see that some of them do exist at some time.

[5] A.J. (p. 138) adds *mushtaraka,* "in which there is partnership."

to be admitted, one specific thing may be caused by different things, just as heat is caused by the sun and by fire. So in this instance the one specific thing did not require a cause that is common [to it and other things that have a common designation]; and even were this fact admitted, the non-existent is suitable as a cause for the non-existent; and were this fact to be admitted, existence in general is not admitted to be a common cause, but rather the existence of each separate thing in itself. To all this it may be answered that the meaning of cause in this case is that which is connected (*muta'alliq*) with the Vision and the one receiving the Vision. It is quite clear that this connection must be something having existence. But then it must not be that which pertains especially to body or accident, for when we first see a shape approaching from afar we comprehend of it only a sort of "itness" (*huwīya*) rather than anything which specifies it as substance or accident or man or horse and so on. After first seeing it as connected with the "itness" of the shape, we may be able to distinguish what substances and accidents there are in it, and sometimes we may not be able. So that which is connected with the Vision is the fact that we may be able to distinguish what substances and accidents there are in it, and that sometimes we may not be able. So that which is connected with a Vision is the fact that the thing has some sort of "itness." [93] This is what is meant by existence, and it is necessary that existence be common to all things seen. This calls for consideration, because the thing which is connected with the Vision may be the fact that it possesses body and whatever there are of accidents accompanying it without considering its particular characteristic (*khuṣūṣīya*).

The statement of proof from the second standpoint [that is, from authority] is first, that Moses requested a vision, saying, "O my Lord, make me see, let me look unto Thee" [6] (Qur'ān 7:139); so had the vision not been possible, the request for it would have been something of ignorance on his part as to what is permissible and not permissible in regard to the essence of Allah, or it would have been some sort of foolishness, or trifling, or a request for the impossible, but the prophets (*al-anbiyā'*) are far removed from anything like that; and second, that Allah connected the vision of Moses with

[6] The remainder of this verse in the Qur'ān reads, "He said, 'Thou shalt never see me, but look towards the mountain, then if it abides in its place, thou shalt see me.' And when his Lord manifested Himself to the mountain, He made it a level place, and Moses fell down in a swoon." Al-Bayḍāwī (*Anwār al-Tanzīl*, I, 343) maintains that the answer "thou shalt never see me" instead of "I am never seen, etc." calls attention to the fact that the vision depends on the preparation of the person seeing. It is a proof that the vision in general is permissible. See al-Rāzī, *Mafātīḥ al-Ghayb*, IV, 292 ff. for a much more detailed statement.

the abiding of the mountain firm in its place, which is something possible in itself. That which is connected with the possible is possible—the idea in this statement being to give the information that the establishing of a thing connected [with something else] goes along with the establishing of the thing with which it is connected—and the impossible is not to be established on the basis of any of those things the determination of which is possible [so the vision requested by Moses and connected with the mountain's abiding firm, is something possible].

Different objections have sometimes been made to this view. The strongest objection is that this request of Moses was made on behalf of his people when they said, "We will never believe in thee, until we see Allah openly" [7] (Qur'ān 2:52). So he asked that they might know that it was impossible, just as he knew that it was. Then some objectors say, "We do not admit that the thing to which it was connected is possible; no, indeed, for it was the abiding of the mountain firm in its place at the very time that it was moving and that is impossible." Answer may be made that each of these two statements is contrary to the literal meaning of the verse. There was no necessity for Moses to commit a fault [like this] because if the people were Believers, it was sufficient for Moses to tell them that the Vision was impossible; and if they were Unbelievers, they would not have believed him in saying that Allah had ruled that the Vision was impossible. In any case the request would have been [under such circumstances] a sort of trifling. The abiding of the mountain firm in its place at the time of motion is also possible [if the verse means] that rest occurs in place of motion, for the only thing that is impossible is the joining together of motion [94] and rest.

and necessary by Tradition. A proof on authority has come down affirming that Believers have a vision of Allah in the abode of the next World/ First, there is the Book, which gives the statement of Allah, "On that day beaming faces to their Lord shall be looking" (Qur'ān 75:22). Second, Tradition (*al-sunna*) gives the statement of the Prophet,[8] "Verily you will see your Lord just as you see the moon on the night when it is full." This is a well-known (*mashhūr*) tradition reported by twenty-one of the principal

---

[7] Al-Bayḍāwī (*Anwār al-Tanzil*, I, 61) in commenting on this verse says that it is possible for Allah to be seen in a vision that is far removed from modality, and that the vision is for Believers in the next world and for individuals from among the Prophets in this.

[8] See al-Bukhārī, *al-Ṣaḥīḥ*, I, 153; Muslim, *al-Ṣaḥīḥ*, I, 85 f.; *Musnad*, II, 368 f.; al-Ghazzālī, *Iḥyā'*, IX, 585. For other traditions concerning the vision see Goldsack, *Muhammadan Traditions*, pp. 279 f.; Wensinck, *Handbook*, p. 17.

Companions. Third, as for Agreement, it states that the Muslim people were agreed that the Vision of Allah occurs in the abode of the next World and that the verses which have come down regarding it are to be taken literally.

Later there appeared the statement of those who differed [from this], and their equivocations and interpretations spread. Their greatest equivocation is the rational one, that it is a stipulation of a person seen in a vision that he must be in place, in a direction and [in a position] confronting the one who sees; that there be a certain definite distance between the two, so that he who is seen is neither extremely near nor extremely far away; and that there be a conjunction of the rays of light from the eye with the one seen. All this, they say, is impossible in the case of Allah. The answer is to make this stipulation impossible. Al-Nasafī referred to it in saying,

And He is seen [unlike any material being] not in place or in a direction so far as being confronted, nor by the conjunction of the rays of light, nor by a certain definite distance between the one who sees and Allah/To draw analogy for the Unseen (*al-ghā'ib*) from the Seen (*al-shāhid*) is unsound. The fact that it is not stipulated that Allah see us [with the sense of sight] is sometimes adduced as a proof [that Allah is not seen in a place, and so on]. This is a matter for consideration, [95] for the statement concerning the Vision says that it is by the sense of sight.

Objection may be made that were the Vision a possibility, were the senses sound and all the other stipulations existent, of necessity He would be seen; otherwise it would be possible for lofty mountains to be in front of us and yet we should not see them, but this is sophistry. We reply that this is impossible, for the Vision according to us is by the creating of Allah; and it does not necessarily follow when all the stipulations are met.

The objectors say that among the authoritative proofs [against it] there is the statement of Allah, "Eyes do not perceive Him, although He perceives the eyes" (Qur'ān 6:103). Now although we admit that the meaning of eyes in the verse is inclusive [without any exception being made]; and that the purport of the verse is a general negation and not a negation of perceiving in general [to which there might have been a particular case as an exception]; and that perception here is absolute vision, not vision from the standpoint of encircling all sides of the one seen; yet our answer is that there is no indication regarding perception that this is a general statement covering all times and states.

It may be deduced from the verse quoted that the Vision of Allah is allowable; since were it impossible there would be no reason for commending the negation of it, just as the non-existent being is not commended for its non-vision, for the Vision itself [in this supposition] is impossible. But rather the commendation appears in the fact that though the Vision of Him is possible, yet He is not seen because of its being made impossible and unattainable by the veil of Majesty.

If we make perception an expression for vision from the standpoint of encircling one from all sides and boundaries, then the verse indicates that the Vision is allowable, nay rather it is verified even more clearly as real, for the meaning is that Allah although seen, is not perceived by the eyes because He is exalted of Himself above being limited and described by boundaries and sides.

Also objectors say that the verses of the Qur'ān expressing a desire for the Vision are joined up with a desire for magnifying [Allah] and disapprobation [of the people of Moses]. The answer to this is that it was for the purpose of distressing the people of Moses and opposing them in asking for the Vision, not because it was impossible. Otherwise Moses would have prevented them from doing it, just as he did when they asked him to make gods for them. And he said, "Nay rather you are an ignorant people" [9] (Qur'ān 27:56). And this is a mark of the possibility of the Vision in this world (al-dunyā). For this reason the Companions of the Prophet differed as to whether the Prophet [10] saw his Lord on the night of the Ascension (al-mi'rāj) or not. And the differing about its occurrence is a proof [96] of its possibility. But [the occurrence of] the Vision in sleep has been recorded of many of the Fathers. Doubtless it is a species of observation by the heart (al-qalb) rather than the eye.

9 Here al-Taftāzānī has quoted from the Qur'ān Lot's statement to his people (*bal antum qawmun tajhalūn*), whereas Moses' words (*innakum qawmun tajhalūn*) are given in Qur. 7:134.

10 Traditions denying that Muhammad ever saw his Lord are to be found in al-Bukhārī, *al-Ṣaḥiḥ*, III, 339 f., IV, 447; *Musnad*, VI, 49 f.; some affirming it are in *Musnad*, I, 285, V, 170 f. See also below, Chap. 15.

Chapter 9

THE CREATOR AND THE ACTIONS
OF HIS CREATURES

Allah is the creator of all the actions of His creatures whether of Unbelief or of Belief, of obedience or of disobedience. And they are all of them by His Will and Desire, by His judgment, by His ruling, and by His decreeing. His creatures have actions of choice for which they are rewarded or punished. And the good in these is by the good pleasure of Allah and the vile in them is not by His good pleasure.

Allah is the creator (*khāliq*) of all the actions of His creatures whether of Unbelief (*al-kufr*) or of Belief (*al-īmān*), of obedience (*al-ṭā'a*) or of disobedience (*al-'iṣyān*)/This is unlike the Mu'tazilites, who asserted that the creature is the creator of his own actions. The early Mu'tazilites refrained from using the expression "creator" when speaking of the creature (*al-'abd*), and only used expressions like "bringer into existence" (*mūjid*), "inventor" (*mukhtari'*), and so on. But when al-Jubbā'ī and his followers saw that the terms all meant the same, namely "the one who brings out of non-existence into existence" (*al-mukhrij min al-'adam 'ilā 'l-wujūd*) they became bold and used the expression "creator" (*al-khāliq*).[1]

The People of Reality objected for certain reasons. The first is that the creature, were he the creator of his actions, would know all the particulars of these actions, since of necessity the bringing a thing into existence through power and choice cannot be anything but that. And the obligation [to know all the particulars] is unsound, for walking from place to place may comprise a series of interrupted rests and of motions, some swifter and some slower than others, yet all the while the person walking has no feeling of this. This is not because he is diverted from the knowledge of it, nay rather, were he asked about the actions he would not know. Yet this happens with the most

---

[1] Some of the Shi'ites hold the same position regarding a creature's acts. See *al-Bābu 'l-Hādi 'Ashar*, pp. 42 ff.; Ibn Ḥazm, *Kitāb al-Fiṣal*, III, 54 ff.; al-Ash'arī, *Maqālāt*, pp. 72 f.

evident of actions. But when you consider the motions of the members of his body in walking, grasping, seizing, and so on, and what he needs for moving his muscles and straining his nerves and so on, the matter is clearer still [that is, that he does not know all their particulars]. The second reason is that there are the statutes (*al-nuṣūṣ*) which have come down regarding this subject, such as the statement of Allah, "And Allah has created you and what you do" (Qur'ān 37:94). This means "your doing," [2] the *mā* (what) being *maṣdarīya* (related to a verbal noun) so that there is no necessity for omitting the pronoun; or it means "your deed," the *mā* being *mawṣūla* (relatival), and this comprises actions. [97] For if we say the actions of the creatures are created by Allah or by the creatures, we do not mean by the action the *maṣdarīya* meaning, which is the bringing into existence and the bringing to pass, but the result of the *maṣdar* (verbal noun) which is connected with the bringing into existence and the bringing to pass, I mean what we observe of motions and rests, for example. The fine point that may be forgotten is that one may fancy that the citation of the verse depends on the *mā* being *maṣdarīya*. And there is the statement of Allah, "Allah is the creator of everything" (Qur'ān 39:63, 13:17). This by rational proof means everything possible, and the action of the creature is a possible thing. There is also the statement of Allah, "Is the one who creates as the one who does not?" (Qur'ān 16:17). This commends the office of creator, and connects it up with being worthy of receiving adoration (*al-ʿibāda*).

But it must not be said that he who asserts that the creature creates his action is a polytheist (*mushrik*) rather than a monotheist (*muwaḥḥid*), for we say that polytheism is positing a partner for the Deity, meaning a necessarily existent partner just as the Magians (*al-Majūs*) [3] assert, or a partner deserving such adoration as the idolaters render their idols. The Muʿtazilites do not assert that, and moreover they do not make the office of creator in the creature like that of Allah, because the creature lacks causes and instruments which are [given to him] by the creation of Allah. However, the Early Theologians of the Trans-Oxus went so far in attributing error to them as to say that the Magians were in a happier state than the Muʿtazilites since the Magians only posited of the Deity one partner, whereas the Muʿtazilites posited innumerable partners. The Muʿtazilites argued that of necessity we distinguish between the motion of one who is walking and of

---

[2] See William Wright, *Arabic Grammar* (Cambridge, 1896–98), I, 270, 273; II, 267, for relative *mā*; I, 277; II, 220, 252, for infinitive *mā*; al-Zamakhsharī, *al-Mufaṣṣal*, pp. 57 f., 147, 160; al-Bayḍāwī, *Anwār al-Tanzīl*, II, 174, al-Zamakhsharī, *al-Kashshāf*, II, 1211.

[3] See Qur. 22:17; *Enc. of Islam*, III, 97 ff.; al-Shahrastānī, *al-Milal*, pp. 179 f.; *Dict. of Tech. Terms*, p. 1330.

one who is trembling, for the first movement is by choice, but the second is not. They also said that if everything were by the creative act of Allah, the imposing [on the creature] of a legal responsibility (*taklīf*) would be unsound, as would also praise and blame, reward and punishment [of him]. [98] And this [according to them] is quite clear. The answer is that this argument should be addressed to the Jabrites (*al-Jabrīya*) [4] who deny absolutely to him, that is the creature, the power of acquisition and choice.

But we shall establish this point on grounds which we shall verify, if Allah wills. It is sometimes maintained that if Allah were the creator of the actions of the creatures, He would then be the one who stands, sits, eats and drinks, and the adulterer and the thief and so on. But this is a bit of stupendous ignorance, for the one of whom something is predicated (*al-muttaṣif*) is that one in whom it subsists, not the one who brought it into existence. Do they not see that Allah is the creator of blackness and whiteness and all the other things predicated of bodies, but they are not predicated of Him? Or perhaps it is maintained [that the creature creates] because of the sayings of Allah, "And Allah the best of creators is blessed" (Qur'ān 23:14), "Since thou dost create [5] from clay as it were in the shape of birds" (Qur'ān 5:110). The answer is that creating here means decreeing (*al-taqdīr*).

And they/that is, the actions of creatures

are all of them by His Will and Desire [6]/It has been shown that we hold these [two terms] to be an expression for the same idea.

by His judgment (*ḥukm*)/It is not unlikely that the reference here is to the direct command (*khiṭāb*) [of Allah] in creating.

by His ruling (*qaḍīya*)/that is, His decision (*qaḍā'*). [7] This is an expression for the action taken together with the judgments in addition [to it]. Objec-

----

[4] The Jabrites were the believers in absolute predestination. See *Enc. of Islam*, II, 605; Wensinck, *The Muslim Creed*, pp. 106, 157, 213; al-Faḍālī, *Kifāyat al-'Awāmm*, pp. 67 f.; al-Shahrastānī, *al-Milal*, pp. 59 f.; *Dict. of Tech. Terms*, p. 200.

[5] Al-Bayḍāwī, *Anwār al-Tanzīl*, I, 156, also explains *khalq* when used by al-Masīḥ as *taqdīr*.

[6] Cf. *al-Rawḍa al-Bahīya*, p. 19; al-Rāzī, *Muḥaṣṣal*, pp. 140 ff.; al-Ījī, *al-Mawāqif*, pp. 105 ff.; al-Faḍālī, *Kifāyat al-'Awāmm*, p. 64.

[7] "The accepted position in Islam is that *al-qaḍā'* means the universal, general and eternal decree and *al-qadar* the individual development or application of that in time." *Enc. of Islam*, II, 603 ff.; cf. *Dict. of Tech. Terms*, pp. 1179 f., 1234 f.; *al-Ta'rīfāt*, pp. 181, 185; Abū Ḥanīfa, *al-Waṣīya*, p. 8.

tion is not to be made that were Unbelief by the decision of Allah, it would be necessary to be well pleased with it, for it is incumbent on us to submit to Allah's decision. The obligation [suggested here] is unsound, for being well pleased with Unbelief is Unbelief, for we say that Unbelief is not a decision but something decided, and that being well pleased is with the decision and not with the thing decided.

and by His decreeing (*taqdīr*)/This is the limiting of each creature to the limit within which he exists whether of goodness or vileness, of use or harm, and to what he occupies of time and place and to what results thereby of reward and punishment. The purpose is to make a general statement concerning the Will and Power of Allah because of what has already been said about everything being by the creation of Allah. This [creation] calls for Power and Will [in Allah] since there is no coercion or compulsion [of Him].

[99] Objection may be raised that the Unbeliever (*al-kāfir*) is made an object of compulsion in His Unbelief (*kufr*) and the evil-doer (*al-fāsiq*)[8] in his evil-doing (*fisq*), so it is not sound to make them legally responsible for Belief and obedience. To this we reply that Allah willed for them Unbelief and evil-doing by their own choice, so there is no compulsion. For just as He knew that on their part they would choose Unbelief and evil-doing, so He did not make them legally responsible for the impossible [because they had choice].

The Mu'tazilites denied that Allah wills wicked and vile things, even to the extent that they said that He wills of the Unbeliever and the evil-doer that they believe and obey, and not that they disbelieve and disobey, because they [that is, the Mu'tazilites] asserted that willing the vile is vile, just as is the creating of it and bringing it into existence. We preclude that by saying that rather the vile is that which is acquired by the vile creature and is predicated of him. So with the Mu'tazilites most of the actions of creatures that occur are contrary to the Will of Allah. That position is indeed abominable. It was said of 'Amr b. 'Ubayd [9] that he said, "No one ever silenced me as did a Magian who was on a ship with me. I said, 'Why dost

---

[8] *Fāsiq*, "one who departs from the right way," "one who has taken upon himself to observe the law and has fallen short." *Ẓālim*, "wrong-doer," "one who acts unjustly" is a more general term. *Fāsiq*, in turn, is more general than *kāfir*. Lane, *Lexicon*, p. 2398; *Enc. of Islam*, II, 81; *Dict. of Tech. Terms*, p. 1132.

[9] 'Amr b. 'Ubayd (d. A.H. 145, A.D. 762) was an early Mu'tazilite. See *Enc. of Islam*, I, 336; Ibn Qutayba, *al-Ma'ārif*, pp. 243 f.; Ibn Khallikān, *Biographical Dictionary*, II, 393 ff.

thou not become a Muslim?' He said, 'Because Allah has not willed my becoming a Muslim; if He wills it, I shall become a Muslim.' So I said to the Magian, 'Allah wills your becoming a Muslim but the Shaytāns do not leave you alone.' So the Magian replied, 'In that case I shall stay with the more victorious partner.' " It is related that al-Qāḍī 'Abd al-Jabbār al-Hamadānī [10] came on a visit to his friend Ibn 'Abbād [11] with whom was al-Ustādh Abū Isḥāq al-Isfarā'inī. When he saw al-Ustādh, he said, "Praise be to Him who is far removed from wickedness (al-faḥshā')." And al-Ustādh immediately replied, "Praise be to Him in whose kingdom nothing transpires but what He wills."

And the Mu'tazilites believed that command (al-amr) requires willing and that prohibition (al-nahy) requires non-willing. So they made the Belief of the Unbeliever the thing willed [by Allah] and his Unbelief that which was not willed. But we know that a thing may sometimes not be willed and yet commanded and may sometimes be willed and yet prohibited because of wise and beneficial matters which are within the knowledge of Allah; or because He is not to be asked concerning that which He does. Do you not perceive that a master whenever he wishes to demonstrate before those present with him the disobedience of his slave commands him to do something, and yet does not will that he do it? [100] Both sides [the orthodox and the Mu'tazilites] may hold fast to verses [which they cite] on the subject, and the door of interpretation is open to both parties.

His creatures have actions of choice for which they are rewarded/if they are actions of obedience

or punished/if they are actions of disobedience. This is unlike the position of the Jabrites, who claimed that no action at all belongs to the creature and that his movements are merely the movements of solid bodies (al-jamādāt), the creature having no power over them, and no purpose or choice. And this is unsound, because of necessity we distinguish between the movement of grasping and that of trembling. We know that the first is by choice and the second is not. It is also unsound because were the creature not to have any part at all in action, it would not be sound to impose responsibility on him or to base his deserving reward and punishment on his actions, nor

[10] Al-Qāḍī Abū 'l-Ḥasan 'Abd al-Jabbār (d. A.H. 415, A.D. 1024), a leading Mu'tazilite and a Shāfi'ite Qāḍī in Ray. See Brockelmann, *Geschichte*, I, 411.

[11] The Ṣāḥib Abū 'l-Qāsim Ismā'īl Ibn 'Abbād al-Tālakānī, was a vizier of the Buwayhids (d. A.H. 385, A.D. 995). See Ibn Khallikān, *Biographical Dictionary*, I, 212 ff.

would it be sound to ascribe to him actions which demand for being real that purpose and choice precede them, that is, such actions as "he worshipped," "he fasted," and "he wrote," which are different from "the boy grew tall" and "his color darkened." The decisive statutes deny the position [of the Jabrites] as seen in the sayings of Allah, "A reward [*101*] for that which they were doing" (Qur'ān 32:17, 46:13, 56:23), "Whoever wills let him believe and whoever wills let him be an Unbeliever" (Qur'ān 18:28). And there are other verses.

Objection may be raised that since the Knowledge and Will of Allah have been rendered universal it is absolutely certain that compulsion [of creatures] follows, for Knowledge and Will are either connected with the existence of the action and so it is necessary, or with the non-existence of the action and then it is impossible; and there can be no choice when there is necessity and impossibility. To this we reply that He knows and wills that the creature will do the action or not do it by his own choice, so there is no confusion about that. Or objection may be made that his act of free choice is either necessary or impossible, which fact is inconsistent with free choice. To this we reply that this position is impossible, for necessity by choice verifies choice as a reality and is not inconsistent with it. Furthermore, the position is contradicted by the actions of the Creator—glorious is the mention of Him—for His knowledge and Will are connected with His actions, so it follows that His action is necessary to Him.

Objection may be raised that there is no meaning to the statement that the creature acts by choice, unless he be the one who brings his actions into existence by purpose and will; and that it has already been shown that Allah is independent in creating actions [*102*] and bringing them into existence; and also that it is a well-known fact that a thing over which someone has power does not come under two independent powers. We reply there is no use discoursing about the force and strength of this statement. We can only say that since it has been established by proof that the Creator is Allah, and that of necessity the power and will of the creature enter into some actions like the movement of grasping, though not into others like the movement of trembling, we needed to escape from this perplexing problem by saying that Allah is the creator (*al-khāliq*) of everything and the creature is an acquirer (*kāsib*).[12]

12 Al-Taftāzānī here introduces the Ash'arite solution, which is the use of the term *kasb*, "acquisition," and its derivatives. The Maturidites emphasized *ikhtiyār*, "choice." See *al-Rawḍa al-Bahīya*, pp. 26 ff.; *Dict. of Tech. Terms*, pp. 419 ff., 1243 f.; *Enc. of Islam*, II, 785 f.

The verification of this position is that when the creature expends his power and will in action it is an acquisition (*kasb*), and when Allah brings it into existence following upon that, it is a creating (*khalq*), so the *maqdūr* (the thing which is subject to power) comes under two powers but from two different standpoints. The act is a *maqdūr* of Allah from the standpoint of being brought into existence (*al-ījād*), and a *maqdūr* of the creature from the standpoint of acquisition (*al-kasb*). This statement is necessary from the meaning of the word "decreeing," even though we are unable to go beyond this in summarizing the expression used which already proves that the creature's action is by Allah's creating and bringing into existence exercised along with what the creature has of power and choice.

There are a number of ways of expressing the difference between the two things [that is, creating and acquisition]. Acquisition is that which occurs by the use of some instrument, but creating does not. Acquisition is a *maqdūr* which occurs in the locus of its power, and creating is a *maqdūr* which does not occur in the locus of its power, and it is not valid to separate acquistion from the one who has power over it; but it is valid to do so with creating.

And someone may object, "You have thereby established a co-partnership (*al-sharika*) [with Allah], the very thing with which you charge the Mu'tazilites." We reply [18] that co-partnership is the coming together of two for a certain thing; then each may detach himself from the other along with that which is his own. [*103*] So that would be like the partners of a village or a place, for example, just as though the creature were made a creator of his own acts and the Maker were made creator of all the rest of the accidents and the bodies. This is quite different from the position that something may be related to two things from two different standpoints; as for example a bit of ground belongs to Allah from the standpoint of creating and to creatures from the standpoint of the establishment of control over it; or just as the act of the creature is ascribed to Allah from the standpoint of creating and to the creature from the standpoint of acquisition.

And someone may object, saying, "How is it that the acquistion of the vile (*al-qabīḥ*) is vile, vulgar, and necessarily deserving of blame and punishment, whereas the creating of it is not?" We reply that it is because it has been established that the Creator is wise, and because he does not create anything unless it has a praiseworthy outcome. Although we do not perceive

---

[18] Cf. the answer of a modern Muslim theologian: Mohammed Abdou, *Rissalat al-Tawhid*, pp. 43 f.

it, we must hold that those actions which we deem vile sometimes have in them wise and beneficial matters,[14] just as in the creation of the base and harmful bodies which give pain, whereas it is not so in the case of acquisition; for sometimes the good may be done and sometimes the vile. So together with the prohibition of that which is vile we make his acquisition of it vile and vulgar and necessarily deserving of blame and punishment.

And the good in these/that is, of the actions of the creatures. And the good is that which is connected with praise now and reward hereafter, or it may be better interpreted as that which is not connected with blame and punishment in order to include that which is permissible (*al-mubāh*).

is by the good pleasure (*riḍā'*) of Allah/that is, by His Will without any objection

and the vile in them/and it is that which is connected with blame now and punishment hereafter

is not by His good pleasure/since there is objection to His having pleasure in it. Allah said, "And He does not take pleasure in the Unbelief of His creatures" (Qur'ān 39:9). This means that Willing, Desiring, and Decreeing are connected with all actions, while good pleasure and desire and command are only connected with the good to the exclusion of the vile.

[14] This is a point much emphasized by Mohammed Abdou (*Rissalat al-Tawhid*, pp. 46 ff.).

Chapter 10

THE CREATURE'S LEGAL RESPONSIBILITY AND ALLAH'S SUSTENANCE AND GUIDANCE

And ability accompanies the action, and it is the real essence of the power by which the action comes into being; and this word applies to the soundness of causes, instruments, and members of the body. And the validity of imposing a legal responsibility depends upon this ability, and the creature has no legal responsibility imposed upon him which is not in his capacity.

And the pain which exists in the one beaten as the consequence of being beaten by some man, or the state of being broken in glass as the consequence of its being broken by some man, and such things—all that is something created by Allah. The creature has no part in the work of its creation, and a slain man is dead at his appointed time. The appointed time is one.

The forbidden thing is still Appointed Sustenance. Everyone receives in full his Appointed Sustenance whether from things permitted or forbidden; and it is inconceivable that a man will not eat his own Appointed Sustenance or that another than he will eat his Appointed Sustenance.

Allah leads astray whom He wills and guides aright whom He wills, and it is not incumbent on Allah to do that which is best for the creature.

And ability (*al-istiṭāʿa*) accompanies the action/This is contrary to the position of the Muʿtazilites.

and it is the real essence of the power by which the action comes into being/ This is a reference to that which was mentioned by the author of *al-Tabṣira*, in that ability is an accident which Allah creates in the animal, whereby he performs actions of choice, the ability being the cause (*ʿilla*) of the action.[1]

---

[1] The majority of the Muʿtazilites said that Power was connected with the action before its existence and that it was impossible for its connection to be at the time of the origina-

The Multitude (*al-jumhūr*) hold that it is a condition (*sharṭ*) for the performance of the action, but not its cause. In general, ability is an attribute which Allah creates [within the creature] following upon the soundness of the causes and the instruments when there is the purpose for acquiring the action. So if the creature purposes a good action Allah creates the power to do good, and if he purposes an evil action Allah creates the power to do evil [*104*] and he thus loses the power to do good and deserves blame and punishment. For this reason Allah blames the Unbelievers because they are lacking [in the ability] to hear.

If ability then is an accident, it is necessary that it be concomitant with the action and not prior to the action, otherwise it would take place without [his having] any ability and power over the action. This rests on what has already been said regarding the impossibility of the continuance of accidents. Objection may be raised as follows, "Suppose the impossibility of the continuance of accidents is admitted, still there is no dispute about the possibility of similar new accidents coming into being following upon the passing away of these; where then is the necessity for saying that the action occurs without there being any power?" In reply we say, "We claim that this is necessary only if the power by which [you say] the action takes place is that power which was there prior to the action; but if you make it a similar new power which is concomitant to the action, you thereby admit that the power by which the action is, can only be one that is concomitant with it. Then if you claim that there must have been similar powers prior to it, you must explain why it was impossible for the action to occur when the power first occurred.

Let us consider then what is to be said were we to suppose that the power which precedes the action continued until the time of the action either by similar new powers coming into being one after the other or by the continuous recurrence of accidents one after the other. If they say that the existence of the action is permissible through similar new powers coming into being one after the other, they abandon their first position whereby they made it permissible for the action to be concomitant with the power. Or if they say that the existence of the action is impossible in this way, then it follows that there was a making of a decision by someone and a preponderance of one thing over another without a determinant (*murajjiḥ*) to make the preponderance, since the power [*105*] remains unchanged in the

---

tion of the action. Wensinck, *The Muslim Creed*, pp. 157 f.; al-Ash'arī, *Maqālāt*, pp. 229 ff.; A.J., p. 150; 'I.D., p. 104.

state in which it was. But this conveys no meaning, for in the case of accidents it is impossible [that a change occur without a determinant].

Why then is the action caused by the power in the second case a necessary action and in the first case an impossible action? This is a matter for consideration, because those who say that ability precedes the action do not say that it is impossible for the power and the action to be concomitant in time; nor do they say that the origination of every action must be through a power absolutely prior to it in time, thus precluding the origination of the action at the same time as the origination of the power—all other conditions having been fulfilled.

This is also a matter for consideration, for it is permissible for the action in the first case to be impossible because of some unfulfilled condition or because of the existence of something that prevents the action, and yet in the second case to be necessary to fulfill the conditions although power is equally an attribute of the one possessing power in each case.

So some took the position [2] that if the power, which gathers to itself all the conditions for making the impression (*al-ta'thīr*), is meant by the word "ability," then the real fact is that it accompanies the action or else it precedes it.

As for the fact that it is impossible for accidents to continue: this is based on certain premises [3] which are hard to explain. These are, first, that the continuance of a thing is something verified as real and superadded to it, second, that it is impossible for an accident to subsist in an accident, and third, that the two accidents cannot subsist together in a locus.

Since those who assert that ability precedes the action have made the deduction that the imposition of legal responsibility (*al-taklīf*) occurs before the action, for of necessity the Unbeliever is legally responsible for Belief, and the one who neglects worship is legally responsible for worship after the time for it arrives; then if ability were not verified as real, it would follow that the one who is powerless is legally responsible, and that is unsound; so al-Nasafī referred to the refutation of this by saying,

and this word/that is, the expression "ability"

---

[2] This is the position of al-Rāzī (A.J., p. 152). Al-Ṭaḥāwī (d. A.H. 321; A.D. 933), a Hanafite and a contemporary of al-Māturīdī, said that there are two sorts of ability, one having to do with the help from Allah which comes along with the action, the other having to do with soundness of instruments, etc., and preceding the action. See his *'Aqīda Ahl al-Sunna wa 'l-Jamā'a* (Kazan, 1902), p. 14.

[3] Cf. al-Rāzī, *Muḥaṣṣal*, pp. 79 ff.; *Dict. of Tech. Terms*, p. 988.

applies to the soundness of causes, instruments, and members of the body (*al-jawāriḥ*)/as in the saying of Allah, "And Allah demands of men Pilgrimage (*ḥajj*) to the House, of him who is able (*istaṭā'a*) to find a way" (Qur'ān 3:91). Objection may be raised that ability is an attribute of the one legally responsible, that the soundness of causes and instruments is not one of his attributes, and that how then is it valid to interpret ability as soundness? We reply that the purpose is the soundness of the causes and instruments which he possesses, so then ability may be predicated of the one who is legally responsible just as is this soundness. Therefore one may say [*106*] that he is the possessor of soundness of causes and instruments. Because this compound expression is used, there is no derived name of the agent (*ism fā'il*) which may be predicated of him, which is not true of the word "ability."

And the validity of imposing a legal responsibility (*al-taklīf*) depends upon this ability/which is the soundness of the causes and the instruments, not ability according to the first definition. If by powerlessness (*al-'ajz*) lack of ability is meant according to the first definition, we do not admit that it is impossible to impose responsibility on the one who is powerless. If it is understood to have the second meaning we do not admit the necessity of it, for it may be that the soundness of the causes and the instruments takes place prior to the action, even though the real essence of the power by which the action takes place has not yet come into being. Answer may be made that power is something potential (*ṣāliḥa*),[4] applicable to [either of] two contraries according to Abū Ḥanīfa,[5] so that the power which is spent in Unbelief is the same power that is spent in Belief. There is no difference between them except in the connection which is made. This does not require a difference in the power itself, for the Unbeliever possesses power to believe, for which Belief he is legally responsible, only he has spent his power in Unbelief and by choice has wasted the opportunity of spending it in Belief, so he deserves blame and punishment. It is evident that in this answer there is an admission that power precedes the action, for one's power to believe while yet in the state of Unbelief is undoubtedly prior to Belief.

And if someone answers that the purpose of this statement is that even though the power is potentially applicable to two contraries, yet from the

---

[4] See Horten, *Die spek. und pos. Theologie des Islam*, p. 193. Cf. use of the term *ṣulūḥi* by al-Faḍālī, *Kifāyat al-'Awāmm*, p. 43.

[5] See *al-Rawḍa al-Bahīya*, pp. 53 ff. for his position on *taklīf*. Cf. Wensinck, *The Muslim Creed*, p. 191.

standpoint of connection it applies to only one of them—so that what must be concomitant to the action is the power connected with the action, and what must be concomitant to refraining from the action is the power connected with this refraining—so the power itself may be something antecedent and connected with the two contraries, we reply that it is inconceivable that there should be a dispute about this, nay rather it is futile. This is a matter which should be taken into consideration.

and the creature has no legal responsibility imposed upon him which is not in his capacity/whether something impossible in itself like the uniting together of contraries, or possible in itself, but not possible for the creature, like the creation of a body. As for what is impossible on the basis that Allah knows something different or wills something different, as in the case of the Belief of the Unbeliever or the obedience of the disobedient, there is no disputing the fact that legal responsibility is imposed upon him, since this is something in the power of the one who is legally responsible when seen from his viewpoint. Then again it is a matter of agreement that there is no imposition of legal responsibility which is not in his capacity, as seen in the statement of Allah, "Allah does not impose upon a soul legal responsibility beyond its capacity" (Qur'ān 2:286). There is also the command in His saying, "Tell me the names of these" (Qur'ān 2:29). This was to baffle them, not to impose a legal responsibility. There is also the statement of Allah in which he spoke of the state of the Believers, "O our Lord, do not burden us beyond our ability"[6] (Qur'ān 2:286). The meaning of "burden" here is not the imposing of legal responsibility but the introduction [*107*] of limiting obstacles beyond their ability. The dispute is whether or not it is permissible [to impose a legal responsibility beyond the creature's ability]. The Mu'tazilites, disapproving of it on rational grounds, said that it was impossible. Al-Ash'arī permitted it because nothing which is from Allah is to be disapproved.

From the saying of Allah, "Allah does not impose upon a soul legal responsibility beyond its capacity" (Qur'ān 2:286), the denial of its being permitted is sometimes inferred. The statement of this is that were it permissible to impose legal responsibility on a creature beyond its capacity, on the supposition that it actually occurred, something impossible would not necessarily follow. For of necessity the impossibility of *al-lāzim* (the necessary) brings about the impossibility of *al-malzūm* (the thing made necessary) in

---

[6] Other verses from the Qur'ān with the same meaning are 2:233, 6:153, 7:40, 23:64. See al-Bayḍāwī, *Anwār al-Tanzīl*, I, 143.

order to verify the meaning of *al-luzūm* (necessity); but were this actually to occur it would necessarily follow that the Word of Allah is false. But that is impossible.

This is a telling point in showing that it is impossible for anything to occur if its non-occurrence is connected with the Knowledge, Will, and Choice of Allah. The solution of this question is that we do not admit in regard to everything possible in itself that, on the supposition that this possible thing occurred, it then follows that there was an impossible [as an alternative], and that this is necessary only were it [that is, the impossible] not precluded by something else which happens to it. Otherwise it would be permissible to say that the impossible is necessary on the basis of its being precluded by something else. Is it not seen that when Allah brought the world into existence by His power and choice, its non-existence was possible in itself, even though on the supposition that it occurred, the thing caused followed necessarily the complete cause? And this is impossible. And the upshot is that because something is possible in itself, then an impossible as an alternative does not necessarily follow on the supposition that the thing occurred. This is when we consider the essence of the thing; but when we consider something superadded to itself, we do not admit that there is no necessity for the impossible [as an alternative].

And the pain which exists in the one beaten as the consequence of being beaten [*108*] by some man, or the state of being broken in glass as the consequence of its being broken by some man/The statement is limited in this way because it is valid that there be a ground for difference as to whether the creature has a part in it or not.

and such things/as death, for example, as the consequence of killing

all that is something created by Allah/because of what has already been said about Allah alone being the Creator and about all possible things being ascribed to Allah without there being any intermediary. The Mu'tazilites, in ascribing some actions to something other than Allah, said that if the action proceeds from the doer without the interposition of another action, then it results by way of immediate causality; otherwise it is by way of mediate causality (*tawlīd*).[7] The meaning of this is that the one action makes it

---

[7] Al-Rāzī uses the term *tawallud, Muḥaṣṣal,* p. 145. Cf. al-Ijī, *al-Mawāqif,* pp. 116 f.; Macdonald, *Development,* p. 142; al-Ash'arī, *Maqālāt,* pp. 400 ff.; Horovitz, *Ueber den*

necessary for him to do another action, as, for example, the motion of the hand necessitates the motion of the key in the hand; so pain is derived from the blow and the state of being broken from breaking. There are not two things created by Allah. We hold that everything is by the creation of Allah.

The creature has no part in the work of its creation/It would have been better not to have limited the statement by saying "creation," for in those acts resulting from mediate causality which they call *mutawallidāt* the creature has no part at all. As for creation, [he has no part in it] because it is impossible for the creature to create; and as for acquirement [of the action, he has no part in it] because it is impossible for the creature to acquire that which does not subsist within the locus of his power. For this reason the creature is not enabled to do anything of this because he has not obtained this power, which is in contrast to actions of choice.

and a slain man is dead at his appointed time (*'ajal*)/That is to say, at the time decreed for his death. This is unlike the assertion of some of the Mu'tazilites, who say that Allah [8] cut short his appointed time. We believe that Allah has decided the appointed times of His creatures according to His knowledge without any changing of His mind, as is to be seen in the verse, "Whenever their appointed time comes, they will neither delay nor outstrip it an hour" (Qur'ān 7:32, 16:62). The Mu'tazilites objected to this, citing traditions [9] which mention the fact that some actions of obedience increase one's age; [*109*] and also saying that if one should die thus at his appointed time, then his slayer would not deserve blame or punishment, nor would the payment of blood-money or chastisement be necessary, since the death of the slain man is neither by the creation of the slayer nor by his acquiring it.

The answer to the first objection is that Allah knew that, were the man not to perform such and such an obedient action, his age would be forty years; but He knew that he would perform it, so his age is seventy years. This increase in his age is related to that action of obedience because Allah knew that were it not for this action there would not have been an increase in his

---

Einfluss der griechischen Philosophie auf die Entwicklung des Kalam (Breslau, 1909), pp. 78 ff.

[8] A.J. (p. 157) suggests that al-Taftāzānī should have said "the killer" instead of "Allah," because with the Mu'tazilites the *"mutawallid"* is one of the creature's actions, not something created by Allah.

[9] Cf. *Musnad*, III, 229.

age. To the second objection the answer is that the necessity for punishing the slayer and making him accountable for his deed is linked up with service to Allah, because the slayer committed a thing forbidden by Allah and thereby acquired the action which resulted in death to the one slain by the customary way of things, for slaying is the action of the slayer by way of acquisition, although it is not his by way of creation.

And death subsists in the dead man and is created by Allah, and the creature has no part in it either in creating it or in acquiring it.[10] This is based on the fact that death is existential (*wujūdī*), in proof of which there is the statement of Allah, "He created death and life" (Qur'ān 67:2). The majority, however, hold that it is non-existential (*'adamī*) [11] and that the meaning of the creation of death is that He ordained it.

The appointed time is one/This is unlike the position of al-Ka'bī,[12] who asserted that the slain man had two appointed times, the one being slain and the other death, so that were he not slain he would live until his appointed time which is his death. This is also unlike the position of the Philosophers, who asserted that an animal has a natural appointed time, which is the time of its death through the dissolution of its moisture and the snuffing out of its heat, both of which are implanted in it, and other appointed times which cut it off contrary to the requirements of its nature through plagues and sicknesses.

The forbidden thing (*al-ḥarām*) **is still Appointed Sustenance** (*rizq*) [13]/ for Appointed Sustenance is that which Allah conveys to the animal so that he eats it. This may sometimes be a lawful thing (*ḥalāl*) and sometimes a thing forbidden (*ḥarām*). This is a better way of defining Appointed Sustenance than by saying that it is that by which the animal is nourished, because such a definition lacks any relating of Appointed Sustenance to Allah, whereas He must be taken into consideration from the very meaning of the term. With the Mu'tazilites the forbidden thing is not Appointed Sustenance, because they explain it sometimes as something possessed which is eaten by the possessor, and sometimes as that by which one may be benefited

---

10 A.J. (p. 157) makes this sentence a part of the text of al-Nasafī. Al-Kastalī (Constantinople text of A.H. 1310, p. 126), puts the words "and death subsists in the dead man" in al-Nasafī's text, and the remainder as the words of al-Taftāzānī. The Cureton text agrees with 'I.D.

11 See *Dict. of Tech. Terms,* p. 1461 f.

12 For al-Ka'bī see above, Chap. 4. n. 25 on al-Balkhī.

13 See *Dict. of Tech. Terms,* pp. 580 ff.; *al-Ta'rīfāt,* p. 115.

and that can only be something lawful. But it follows then according to their first definition that what the beast eats is not Appointed Sustenance. And according to both definitions he who eats what is forbidden throughout his whole life is not sustained by Allah at all.

This difference of opinion rests upon the question of taking into consideration the relationships which Allah bears to Appointed Sustenance. [They reason as follows trying to show the fallacy of our position]: there is no provider of Appointed Sustenance save Allah alone; the creature deserves [110] blame and punishment for eating forbidden things; that which is supported by Allah is not a vile thing, and so [they say that we should hold that] the one who does this is not deserving of blame and punishment. The refutation of this argument is that the creature has made a wrong contact with the causes of the action through his free choice.

Everyone receives in full his Appointed Sustenance whether from things permitted or forbidden/for he obtains nourishment from both of them

and it is inconceivable that a man will not eat his own Appointed Sustenance or that another than he will eat his Appointed Sustenance/for a person must eat what Allah has ordained as nourishment for him, and it is impossible that another than he eat it, but if Appointed Sustenance means possession, then it is not impossible [that one's Appointed Sustenance may be the possession of another].

Allah leads astray (*yudillu***) whom He wills and guides aright (***yahdi***) whom He wills** [14]/meaning that He does so by creating the acts of going astray (*al-dalāla*) and being guided (*al-ihtidā'*), for He alone is Creator. In conditioning [the leading astray and guiding aright] upon His will there is an allusion to the fact that the meaning of guidance is not "to explain the way of Reality," for the explanation of the way of Reality is something general for everyone; nor is leading astray an expression for "finding the creature astray" or his "being called astray," since to connect these things with the will of Allah would mean nothing. Indeed, guidance is figuratively related to the Prophet by way of assigning causation just as it is ascribed to the Qur'ān, and leading astray may be ascribed to Satan figuratively just as it is to idols (*al-aṣnām*) [yet it is Allah who leads astray and guides aright]. Moreover, expressions in the statements of the Early Theologians such as

[14] Cf. al-Rāzī, *Mafātiḥ*, I, 246 ff.

"With us guidance is the creation of being guided" and "Allah guided him but he was not guided" are figurative terms for "indication of the way" (*al-dalāla*) and "the call to be guided."

But with the Mu'tazilites all of these usages are "a declaration of the right way." This position, though, is unsound because of the statement of Allah, [*111*] "Verily thou dost not guide him whom thou lovest" (Qur'ān 28:56), and because of the statement of the Prophet, "O Allah, guide my people." Muhammad said this in spite of the fact that he had declared the way and called them to be rightly guided. It is well known that guidance (*al-hidāya*) with the Mu'tazilites means the indication (*al-dalāla*) of the way, which indication actually reaches the goal; but with us guidance is the indication of a way which reaches the goal, whether it actually is arrived at and one is really guided or not.

and it is not incumbent on Allah to do that which is best for the creature [15]/ otherwise He would not have created the poor Unbeliever who is tormented in this world and the next; nor would He have shown favor to His creatures and deserved thanks for guidance, and poured out all kinds of good things upon them, for these things would be the performance of a duty incumbent upon Him. And [furthermore were this not true] the favor of Allah to the Prophet would not be above that of His favor to Abū Jahl [16]—Allah curse him —since He should go to the limit in doing the best within His power for each of them. And [also were it not true] there would be no meaning to the question of a prophet's being preserved from error (*al-'iṣma*), of succor [in time of trouble], and of the exposure of some to harm and the giving to some abundance of fruitfulness and ease. What Allah failed to do in the case of each one would be for each one something of a cause of corruption from which Allah ought to desist; nor would the power of Allah continue to bear any relation to the welfare of creatures, since He would have performed that which is incumbent on Him.

And I swear that the causes leading to corruption which are found in this principle—I mean, that it is incumbent on Allah to do the best for his creatures—rather, [one might say], in the most of the Mu'tazilite principles, are so clear that they cannot be hidden and are so many that they cannot

---

[15] The Mu'tazilites of Baṣra said that Allah must do what is best for His creatures in the Judgment; those of Baghdād said, "in this world and the Judgment." 'I.D., p. 111; A.J., p. 160; cf. al-Rāzī, *Mafātīḥ*, III, 440; *ibid.*, *Muḥaṣṣal*, pp. 147 f.; al-Ijī, *al-Mawāqif*, pp. 155 ff.; *Ihyā'* (commentary of Sayyid Murtaḍā), II, 186 f.

[16] Abū Jahl, one of the bitterest opponents of Muhammad. See *Enc. of Islam*, I, 83; Ibn Hishām, *Sīrat Rasūl Allah*, pp. 190 f.; al-Ṭabarī, *Annales*, I, 1175 ff., 1187, 1307.

be counted. This fact is because of their limited consideration of the various kinds of knowledge dealing with divine matters and because by temperament they are firmly intent on finding an analogy between the seen and the unseen. The extreme tenacity with which they hold to their position is because of their belief that for Allah to forsake that which is for the creature's best interest means niggardliness and foolishness [on His part].

The refutation of this is that since His generosity, His wisdom, His grace, and His knowledge of the outcome of events have been established by decisive proofs, [*112*] so if there is any denial of good to the creature by the one who has the right to deny, this then is absolute justice and wisdom. Then what, pray, is the meaning of something being incumbent on Allah, since it does not mean in this case that he who forsakes the duty incumbent on him deserves blame and punishment? This is plainly so. There is no need then for even supposing that something contrary to what is incumbent on Him proceeds from Him, since He is not enabled to forsake that which is incumbent on Him—on the basis that this requires something impossible in the way of foolishness, or ignorance, or nonsense, or niggardliness, or something like that. This position of theirs rejects the principle of choice and is a leaning towards that type of philosophy the shame of which is quite evident.

Chapter 11

SOME ESCHATOLOGICAL REALITIES

The punishment of the grave for Unbelievers and for some of the disobedient Believers, and the bliss of the obedient in the grave by that which Allah knows and wills, and the questioning of Munkar and Nakīr are established by proofs based on authority. And the Quickening of the Dead is a Reality, the Weighing is a Reality, the Book is a Reality, the Questioning is a Reality, the Tank is a Reality, and the Bridge is a Reality; the Garden is a Reality and the Fire is a Reality, and they both are created, existing and continuing; they shall not pass away, nor shall their inhabitants pass away.

The punishment (*'adhāb***) of the grave** [1] **for Unbelievers and for some of the disobedient Believers**/Al-Nasafī specified some of the Believers, for there are some of them whom Allah does not will to punish, so they will not be punished.

and the bliss (*tan'īm***) of the obedient in the grave by that which Allah knows and wills**/This statement is better than that of the majority of books, which are confined to establishing the punishment of the grave rather than the bliss, on the ground that there are many more statutes (*nuṣūṣ*) referring to it and that the people of the grave in general are Unbelievers and disobedient, so it is more fitting to mention the punishment.

and the questioning of Munkar and Nakīr/They are two angels who enter the grave and ask the creature concerning his Lord, his religion, and his prophet. Al-Sayyid Abū Shujjā' [2] said that children are questioned, and some say also that the prophets are questioned. [3]

---

[1] The Mu'tazilites and the Kharijites denied the punishment of the grave. See al-Ash'arī, *Maqālāt*, pp. 127, 430.

[2] Abū Shujjā' (b. A.H. 434; A.D. 1042) was the author of a much-used manual of jurisprudence. See *Enc. of Islam*, I, 107; Brockelmann, *Geschichte*, I, 392.

[3] Some say that children, prophets, martyrs, and also the demented are not asked. See A.J., p. 161.

are established/that is, every one of these things

by proofs based on authority (*al-sam'īya*)/because they are possible things which [*113*] the Veracious One has narrated concerning things spoken of by the statutes. Allah said, "The Fire, to which they will be exposed morning and evening, and the day when the Hour shall arise—'Bring in the people of Pharaoh (*Fir'awn*) [4] for the severest torture' " (Qur'ān 40:49), and "They were drowned and made to enter the Fire" (Qur'ān 71:25). The Prophet said, "Avoid contact with urine, for the punishment of the grave in general comes from it." [5] The Prophet also said that the statement of Allah, "Allah will establish those who believe with His established word in this world and the next" (Qur'ān 14:32), was revealed in regard to the punishment of the grave; [6] and that whenever [the occupant of] it is asked, "Who is thy Lord, what is thy religion, and who is thy prophet?" he should reply, "My Lord is Allah, my religion is Islam, and my prophet is Muhammad." [7] The Prophet said, "Whenever a dead man is placed in his grave, two black angels with blue eyes come to him, one being called Munkar and the other Nakīr" [8] and so on to the end of the tradition. The Prophet said, "The grave is either one of the meadows of the Garden or one of the pits of the Fires." [9] In general the traditions [10] which have come down on this subject and on many of the states of the next world are *mutawātir* in meaning, although the individual traditions taken separately do not attain the rank of *tawātur*.

Some of the Mu'tazilites [11] and the Rawāfiḍ [12] denied the punishment of the grave because a dead man is a solid body (*jamād*) devoid of life and comprehension, so punishing him is impossible. The answer to this is that it is possible for Allah to create in all or in some of the parts a kind of life such as

[4] For the story of the torture of Pharaoh and his people see al-Ṭabarī, *Annales*, I, 481, al-Tha'labī, *Qiṣaṣ al-Anbiyā'*, pp. 171 ff., as well as the commentaries on this text.

[5] See al-Bukhārī, *al-Ṣaḥīḥ*, I, 66; Muslim, *al-Ṣaḥīḥ*, I, 127; A.J., p. 162; Wensinck, *The Muslim Creed*, p. 118.

[6] See also al-Bayḍāwī, *Anwār al-Tanzīl*, I, 491.

[7] See *Musnad*, III, 4; al-Nasā'ī, *Sunan* (Cairo, A.H. 1312), "Janā'iz," 114.

[8] See al-Tirmidhī, *Ṣaḥīḥ*, "Janā'iz," 70; Wensinck, *The Muslim Creed*, pp. 164 f.

[9] This is given by al-Tirmidhī, *Ṣaḥīḥ*, "Qiyāma," 26.

[10] See Muslim, *al-Ṣaḥīḥ*, II, 488 ff.; al-Bukhārī, *al-Ṣaḥīḥ*, I, 267 ff.; *Kitāb Aḥwāl al-Qiyāma*, ed. Wolff (Arabic), pp. 40 f., cf. al-Ghazzālī, *Iḥyā'* (commentary of Sayyid Murtaḍā), II, 216 ff.

[11] That is, most of the later Mu'tazilites; many of them, however, like Abū al-Hudhayl, Bishr b. al-Mu'ammar (*sic*), the Jubbā'ites, and al-Ka'bī affirmed it according to al-Ash'arī, *Maqālāt*, p. 430, and A.J., p. 162. Cf. 'I.D., p. 113.

[12] See *Jour. Am. Or. Soc.*, XXIX, 137 ff.; al-Baghdādī, *al-Farq bayn al-Firaq*, p. 22 ff.; Horten, *Die phil. Systeme der spek. Theologen im Islam*, see Index.

would be able to comprehend the pain of punishment or the enjoyment of bliss. This does not require that the spirit (*al-rūḥ*) be returned to the body nor that it move or be troubled or show any mark of punishment; for even the drowned man in water, or the one devoured [and] in the bellies of beasts, or the one [who hangs] crucified in the air is punished, although we do not see it. Whoever ponders the wonders of Allah in the kingdoms of this world (*mulk*) and of Heaven (*malakūt*) and the marvels of His Power and His Might (*jabarūt*) [13] will not consider such things improbable, let alone impossible.

Know then that since the states (*aḥwāl*) of the grave are midway between this world and the next, al-Nasafī put this in a section apart and then went on to explain the Reality of the great Assembly (*al-ḥashr*) and the details connected with the matters of the next world. The proof of all these is that they are possible things about which the Veracious One has informed [us] and of which the Book and the Tradition speak, so they are established facts. He explained the Reality of each of them for the sake of verifying them, for emphasizing them, and in order that their importance may be realized.

[*114*] **And the Quickening of the Dead** (*al-baʻth*)/that is to say that Allah quickens the dead from the grave by gathering their original parts and restoring their spirits to them.

is a Reality/because of the statements of Allah, "Then on the Day of Resurrection (*yawm al-qiyāma*) [14] you will be quickened" (Qurʼān 23:16), and, "Say, 'He who formed them at first will revive them'" (Qurʼān 36:79). And there are many other decisive statutes [15] which speak of the Day when the bodies will be assembled.

The Philosophers denied the Quickening of the Dead on the basis that the restoration of the non-existent thing (*al-maʻdūm*) with its substance is impossible. Although there is no proof worthy of consideration for their

---

[13] For *jabarūt* in contrast with *mulk* and *malakūt* see *al-Taʻrīfāt*, pp. 77, 246; *Dict. of Tech. Terms*, pp. 200, 1339; *Enc. of Islam*, I, 986 f.; Macdonald, in *Jour. Am. Or. Soc.*, XX, 116 ff.

[14] There are about 70 verses in the Qurʼān in which the expression "*yawm al-qiyāma*" occurs. See *Concordantiae Corani Arabicae*, ed. Flügel, p. 159; *Fatḥ al-Raḥmān*, pp. 373 f. See also al-Rāzī, *Muḥaṣṣal* (*Maʻālim*), pp. 128 ff.; al-Ījī, *al-Mawāqif*, pp. 244 ff.; al-Shahrastānī, *Nihāyatu 'l-Iqdām*, pp. 467 f. for *al-baʻth*.

[15] See Muslim, *al-Ṣaḥīḥ*, II, 487 f.; al-Bukhārī, *al-Ṣaḥīḥ*, I, 206 ff., IV, 235 ff.; Goldsack, *Selections*, p. 269; Wensinck, *Handbook*, pp. 205 f.; *Kitāb Aḥwāl al-Qiyāma*, pp. 49 ff.

statement it does not harm the purpose [of the Quickening], for our meaning is that Allah gathers the original parts of man and restores the spirit to him, whether or not that is called the restoring of the non-existent thing with its substance. In this way their supposition falls down, which is that if a man ate a man so that he became part of the one who ate him, then those parts must be restored in both of them, and that is impossible; or in one of them only, and thus the other is not restored with all his parts. This [supposition falls down] because the restored parts are the original parts continuing from the earliest of one's life until its end; and the parts eaten are superfluous in the eater and not original.[16]

Someone may object that this statement admits that there is transmigration (*al-tanāsukh*),[17] for the second body is not the first [*115*] because tradition[18] relates of the people of the Garden that they are without hair on their bodies and beardless, and ornamented with *kuḥl;* and that the molar tooth[19] of one of the people of *jahannam* (Hell) is like the mountain of Uḥud. So from this it is seen that in every school of thought [the idea of] transmigration has a firm footing. But we reply that transmigration would only be necessary were the second body not a creation out of the original parts of the first body. If anything like that is called transmigration the dispute is only in the name; and there is no proof that it is impossible to restore the spirit to such a body; but the proofs rest on the fact of its reality, whether or not this is called transmigration.

the Weighing (*al-wazn*)[20] **is a Reality**/This is based on the statement of Allah, "The Weighing on that day is the Reality" (Qur'ān 7:8). The Balance (*al-mīzān*) is the expression used for that by which the amounts of the deeds are known. Reason falls short of comprehending the manner in which the Balance works. The Mu'tazilites[21] deny the weighing because deeds are accidents and so, even if they were restored, they could not be

---

[16] Cf. al-Ījī, *al-Mawāqif*, pp. 249 ff., and al-Dasūqī's supercommentary on al-Sanūsī, *Umm al-Barāhīn*, p. 220.

[17] Cf. *Dict. of Tech. Terms*, p. 1380; al-Baghdādī, *al-Farq bayn al-Firaq*, pp. 253 ff.; al-Rāzī, *Muḥaṣṣal*, pp. 166 f.; Ibn Ḥazm, *Kitāb al-Fiṣal*, I, 90; Ibn Sīnā, *al-Najāt*, pp. 309 f.

[18] Al-Tirmidhī, *Ṣaḥīḥ*, "Janna," 8 and 12.

[19] This is given by Aḥmad (b. Ḥanbal) from Abū Hurayra. A.J., p. 165.

[20] See *Musnad*, III, 178; *Kitāb Ahwāl al-Qiyāma*, pp. 81 f.; Goldsack, *Selections*, p. 271. Cf. *Iḥyā'* (commentary of Sayyid Murtaḍā), II, 218 ff.

[21] Some of the Mu'tazilites like Abū 'l-Hudhayl and Bishr b. al-Mu'tamir held it possible (A.J., p. 165). Cf. al-Shahrastānī, *al-Milal*, p. 35.

weighed; and since they are known to Allah it is nonsense to weigh them. The answer to them is that it is the books of deeds that are weighed [22] according to what has come down in tradition, so there need be no difficulty. Since we admit that there are purposes in the acts caused by Allah, perchance there is some wisdom in the Weighing which we do not discover, and just because we have not discovered the wisdom of it, it does not necessarily make it to be nonsense.

the Book (*al-kitāb*) [23]/in which are established the acts of obedience and disobedience belonging to creatures. The Believers receive their books in their right hands and the Unbelievers [theirs] in their left hands and behind their backs.

is a Reality/This is based on the saying of Allah, "We shall produce a book for him on the day of Resurrection, offered to him wide open" (Qur'ān 17:14), and His saying, "Whosoever is presented with his book in his right hand, will be easily accounted with" (Qur'ān 84:7). The author did not mention the Accounting (*al-ḥisāb*),[24] considering [the mention] of the Book as sufficient. The Mu'tazilites denied the Book, asserting that it was nonsense. The answer to them has already been given.

the Questioning (*al-su'āl*) is a Reality/This is based on the saying of Allah, "We shall certainly question them all" (Qur'ān 15:92). There is also the statement of the Prophet,[25] "Allah will bring the Believer near and He shall place over him His wing (*kanaf*) and cover him and then say, 'Dost thou know such and such a sin? Dost thou know such and such a sin?' Then he will answer, 'Yes, my Lord.' This goes on until He makes him confess his sins, and see himself lost; then Allah will say, 'I have veiled thy sins over thee in this world, and I will forgive them to thee this Day.' He will be given the Book of his good deeds. But the Unbelievers and the Hypocrites

22 This is by means of *al-baṭāqa*, which is a paper on which is inscribed, "There is no god but Allah," which will outweigh the 99 scrolls recording the sins of a man. Lane, *Lexicon*, p. 218; *Tāj al-'Arūs*, VI, 296; A.J. (p. 165) says that the tradition concerning *al-baṭāqa* is given by al-Tirmidhī and al-Ḥākim.

23 See *Kitāb Ahwāl al-Qiyāma*, pp. 77 ff.

24 Al-Bukhārī, *al-Ṣaḥīḥ*, IV, 238; Muslim, *al-Ṣaḥīḥ*, II, 491 f.

25 This tradition is given by the Two Shaykhs from Ibn 'Umar, A.J., p. 165. A.J. explains away any anthropomorphic interpretation that the saying might have. Cf. al-Bukhārī, *al-Ṣaḥīḥ*, III, 362, where it says that the Lord will uncover His leg and every Believer will prostrate himself before Him; also *Kitāb Ahwāl al-Qiyāma*, pp. 79 f.

(*al-munāfiqūn*) shall be proclaimed above the heads of all creatures, 'These are they who denied their Lord, is not the curse [*116*] of Allah on all wrong-doers?' " (Qur'ān 11:21).

the Tank (*al-ḥawḍ*) [26] is a Reality/This is based on the saying of Allah, "Verily we have given thee *al-kawthar*" [27](Qur'ān 108:1), and also on the saying of the Prophet, "My tank is a month's journey long, and its corners are symmetrical, its water is whiter than milk and more fragrant than musk, and its goblets outnumber the stars of the heavens. Whoever drinks from them never thirsts." There are numerous traditions about the Tank.

and the Bridge (*al-ṣirāṭ*) [28] is a Reality/It is a causeway stretched over the middle of hell (*jahannam*), finer than a hair, sharper than a sword, over which the people of the Garden will pass, while the feet of the people of the Fire will slip on it. Most of the Mu'tazilites deny it on the grounds that it is impossible to cross such a bridge and that were it possible it would be a punishment for the Believers. The answer is that Allah is Powerful to make possible the crossing of the Bridge. And He makes the way easy for the Believers so that some go over as quickly as swift lightning and others as a gust of wind, while others go over like a steed, and so on according to the traditions on this subject.

the Garden (*al-janna*) is a Reality and the Fire (*al-nār*) [29] is a Reality/ for the verses (*al-āyāt*) and the traditions (*al-aḥādīth*) which have come down regarding these two matters are too plain to be hidden and too many

[26] For traditions about *al-ḥawḍ* see al-Bukhārī, *al-Ṣaḥīḥ*, IV, 247; Muslim, *al-Ṣaḥīḥ*, II, 283 ff.; *Musnad*, II, 134, 162 ff., V, 275 ff.; Wensinck, *Handbook*, p. 33; Goldsack, *Selections*, p. 272. Cf. al-Ghazzālī, *Iḥyā'* (commentary of Sayyid Murtaḍā), II, 221.

[27] Among the delights to be enjoyed by the Faithful in the Gardens of Paradise is an abundance of milk, wine, and honey, as well as sweet-smelling water. The tradition of the Prophet describes the Tank and its contents. Many authorities differ from al-Taftāzānī and distinguish between the Tank and *al-kawthar*, which they say is a river in the Garden, A.J., p. 166; al-Faḍālī, *Kifāyat al-'Awāmm*, p. 75; al-Bayḍāwī, *Anwār al-Tanzil*, II, 419; Wensinck, *The Muslim Creed*, pp. 231 f. See also *Enc. of Islam*, II, 834; *Kitāb Aḥwāl al-Qiyāma*, pp. 105 ff.; Ibn Hishām, *Sirat Rasūl Allāh*, p. 261; 'I.D., p. 116.

[28] For traditions about *al-ṣirāṭ* see al-Bukhārī, *al-Ṣaḥīḥ*, IV, 238, 246; *Musnad*, II, 368 f.; Wensinck, *Handbook*, p. 40, *The Muslim Creed*, pp. 232 f.; *Kitāb Aḥwāl al-Qiyāma*, p. 82; cf. *Iḥyā'* (commentary of Sayyid Murtaḍā), II, 220.

[29] *Al-janna, al-nār*. There are many references to these in the Qur'ān. See *Concordantiae* (Flügel), pp. 45, 200. For references in tradition and description of them see also Muslim, *al-Ṣaḥīḥ*, I, 90 ff., II, 464 ff.; Wensinck, *Handbook*, pp. 96, 180; Hughes, *Dict. of Islam*, pp. 170, 449; *Kitāb Aḥwāl al-Qiyāma*, pp. 86 ff.; al-Ījī, *al-Mawāqif*, pp. 254 f.; al-Rāzī, *Muḥaṣṣal* (*Ma'ālim*), pp. 132 ff. The positions taken regarding the creation of the Garden and the Fire are discussed by Ibn Ḥazm, *Kitāb al-Fiṣal*, IV, 81 f.

to be numbered. And those who deny the Garden maintain that since its breadth is described as being the breadth of the heavens and the earth it is therefore an impossibility in the world of elements, and in the world of spheres the insertion of one world into another or into another world outside it necessitates the passing through an opening (*al-kharq*) and its joining together again (*al-ilti'ām*), and that [they say] is unsound. We reply, "This is based on the corrupt foundation of your position," and we have already spoken of that in its proper place.[30]

and they both/that is, the Garden and the Fire

are created/now [31]

existing/He said this for sake of repetition and emphasis. Most of the Mu'tazilites assert that they will only be created on the day of Recompense. To support our position there is the story of Adam and Eve and their being made to live in the Garden.[32] There are also the verses [*117*] which plainly show the preparation of the Garden and the Fire, such as, "prepared for the pious, prepared for the Unbelievers" (Qur'ān 3:126, 127). [They are to be taken according to their evident meaning] since there is no necessity for deviating from what is the plain teaching [of the statutes]. But if this position is opposed by [the citation] of a statement of Allah such as, "This is the final abode we will prepare for those who do not desire an exalted place in the earth nor corruption" (Qur'ān 28:83), we reply that it is possible for the tense of the verb to be present and continuous. If it were admitted [that the reference above is to other than the present continuous tense] the story of Adam remains unaffected by the one who opposes [this position]. They say that if the Garden and the Fire were in existence now, it would not be permissible to speak of the destruction (*halāk*) of the food of the Garden, because of the statement of Allah, "Its food is everlasting (*dā'im*)" (Qur'ān 13:35). They also say that the necessary [conclusion in that case that its food be not destroyed] is unsound because of the statement of Allah, "Everything perishes except His face" (Qur'ān 28:88). But we reply that it is clearly impossible for the food of the Garden in its substance to last forever, but "everlasting" here means that if any of its food passes away something takes its

<hr>

[30] See above, Chap. 3; A.J., p. 75; 'I.D., p. 47.
[31] A.J. makes "now" a part of al-Nasafī's text.
[32] See Qur. 2:33. 7:18; al-Bayḍāwī, *Anwār al-Tanzīl*, I, 52; al-Tha'labī, *Qiṣaṣ al-Anbiyā'*, pp. 26 f.; al-Ṭabarī, *Annales*, I, 115 ff.

place. This is not inconsistent with the destruction momentarily of some of it, although destruction does not require passing away (*al-fanā'*), but merely passing beyond the limit of its being used. Even were it admitted [that everything actually perishes except the face of Allah] it is permissible that the meaning is "every possible thing," for it perishes within the limit of its essence. This means that possible existence when considered from the standpoint of necessary existence ranks as non-existence.

and continuing: they shall not pass away, nor shall their inhabitants pass away (*yafnā*)/That is to say, everlasting; no perpetual non-existence befalls them, because of the statement of Allah in regard to both parties [that is, those of the Garden and those of the Fire], "They abide forever in it" (Qur'ān 4:60, 121, 167). But as for what has been said about the Garden and the Fire being destroyed even though for a moment in order to verify the statement of Allah that "Everything perishes except His face" (Qur'ān 28:88): this meaning is not inconsistent with their abiding. You well know that there is nothing in the verse to indicate passing away.

The Jahmīya [38] took the position that both the Garden and the Fire and their inhabitants with them pass away. This is without doubt an unsound position contrary to the Book, the Sunna, and the Agreement. Beyond the fact that this is an argument [it is of no consequence].

---

[38] These were the followers of Jahm b. Ṣafwān (d. A.H. 128), who was a Persian rebel against the Arab rule. He held that belief is an affair of the heart and denied all anthropomorphic attributes of Allah and the eternity of the Fire and the Garden. Macdonald, *Development*, pp. 126, 138, 146; al-Shahrastānī, *al-Milal*, pp. 60 f.; al-Baghdādī, *al-Farq bayn al-Firaq*, pp. 199 f.; Wensinck, *The Muslim Creed*, p. 119.

Chapter 12

SINS

A great sin does not remove from Belief the creature who believes, nor does it lead him into Unbelief. Allah does not forgive the one who joins another with Himself, but He pardons whomsoever He wills any sin, whether great or small, except this.

The punishment of a small sin is permissible, and also the pardon of a great sin, if it is not of the nature of considering lawful what is forbidden; for that is Unbelief. The intercession of the Messengers is established by narratives in the case of those who commit great sins.

And those of the Believers who commit great sins do not remain forever in the Fire.

A great sin (*al-kabīra*) [1]/The traditions differ about this term. It is related by Ibn 'Umar—Allah be well pleased with both father and son—that the great sins are said to be nine; namely, polytheism (*al-shirk bi 'llāh*), unlawful manslaughter, slandering a chaste woman by a charge of adultery, adultery, fleeing from war against Unbelievers, magic, devouring the property of an orphan, disobedience to Muslim parents, and contravening the ordinances concerning the sacred territory (*al-ilḥād fī'l-ḥaram*). Abū Hurayra added to these usury, and 'Alī added stealing and wine drinking. A great sin has been said to mean anything the corruption of which is like the corruption of the things already mentioned or more than it; or it is that concerning which the Law [2] threatens a punishment; also, every disobedience in which the creature persists is a great sin, and everything for which he asks pardon

---

[1] For other statements of the Muslim doctrine of sin see *Enc. of Islam*, II, 925 ff.; *Enc. of Religion and Ethics*, XI, 567 ff.; al-Ash'arī, *Maqālāt*, p. 475. The number of great sins differed in tradition. See al-Bukhārī, *al-Ṣaḥīḥ*, II, 151 and 193, IV, 269, 313–14; Muslim, *al-Ṣaḥīḥ*, I, 49; al-Bayḍāwī, *Anwār al-Tanzīl*, I, 206; Wensinck, *Handbook*, p. 215; *al-Rawḍa al-Bahiya*, p. 60.

[2] A.J. (p. 168) reads *al-Shāri'*, the Lawgiver.

is a small sin (*ṣaghīra*). The author of *al-Kifāya* [3] said that in reality [*118*]
the two are relative terms, which cannot be defined separately. Thus every
disobedience, if it is compared to that which ranks above it, is small; and
if to that which is below it, is great.[4] The absolutely great sin is Unbelief,
since there is no offence greater than it. In general the meaning of "great
sin" here includes other things besides Unbelief.

does not remove from Belief the creature who believes/because assent, which
is the real essence of Belief, continues.[5] This is unlike the position of the
Muʻtazilites in that they assert that whoever commits a great sin is neither
a Believer nor an Unbeliever. This is the rank which they make between
the two ranks [that of the Believer and that of the Unbeliever] on the
basis, according to them, that works are a part of the real essence of Belief.

nor does it lead him/that is, the creature who believes

into Unbelief/This is unlike the Kharijites, for they took the position
that one who commits a great sin or even a small sin is an Unbeliever and
that there is no middle position between Belief and Unbelief.

We have some points to stress. The first, the statement of which comes
later, is that the real essence of Belief is the assent of the heart (*al-taṣdīq
al-qalbī*). So then the Believer is not removed from being described by
Belief through doing that which is inconsistent with it. And merely per-
severing in a great sin because appetite, or an outburst of anger, or indigna-
tion, or even laziness got the better of him is not inconsistent with Belief
whenever it is joined with the fear of punishment, the hope of forgiveness,
and the resolution to repent. But whenever it is by way of making lawful
the unlawful (*al-istiḥlāl*) or making light of it, it is Unbelief because it is a
sign of denial (*al-takdhīb*). There is no doubt that the Lawgiver made some
disobedient acts an indication of denial. This is known from proofs based
on the Law, as seen in such acts as prostration to an idol, throwing the
Sacred Volume (*al-muṣḥaf*) amidst filthy things, uttering words of Unbelief, and other things which are established by proofs to be Unbelief. And in
this there is the solution of what has been stated, in that if Belief is an ex-

---

[3] The author was Abū Bakr Aḥmad b. ʻAli b. Thābit al-Khaṭīb al Baghdādī, (A.H. 392–
463; A.D. 1002–1071). See Brockelmann, *Geschichte,* I, 329.

[4] Al-Ghazzālī (*Iḥyā',* VI, 511) said that persistence in a small sin becomes a great sin,
and that even the continuance of some thing permissible might become a small sin.

[5] Cf. al-Rāzī, *Muḥaṣṣal,* p. 174; al-Ījī, *al-Mawāqif,* pp. 264 f.

pression for assent and confession, the one who assents and confesses does not become an Unbeliever by committing any of the acts or utterances of Unbelief so long as denial or doubt on his part is not established.

The second point is that the verses and the traditions apply the term "Believer" to the disobedient, as seen in the sayings of Allah. "O ye who believe, retaliation for the slain is prescribed for you" (Qur'ān 2:173). "O ye who believe, turn to Allah in sincere repentence" (Qur'ān 66:8). "If two parties of the Believers are carrying on warfare against one another, etc." (Qur'ān 49:9). The verses on this subject are many.

The third point is the Agreement of the Muslim people (al-umma) from the time of the Prophet till now that worship (al-ṣalā) be performed over any one of the People of the qibla [worshiping in the direction of Mecca] who dies unrepentant. And prayer (al-du'ā) for them and petition for their forgiveness are made with full knowledge of their having committed great sins; although it is understood that this is not permissible in the case of one who is not a Believer.

The Mu'tazilites objected on two grounds. The first was that the Muslim people, after agreeing that he who has committed a great sin is an evil-doer (fāsiq), differed as to whether he is a Believer, which is the position of the people of the Approved Way and the Community; or an Unbeliever, which is the position of the Kharijites; or a hypocrite (munāfiq), which is the position of al-Ḥasan al-Baṣrī. Therefore [say the Mu'tazilites] we hold to the point upon which there is agreement and forego the point in dispute, saying that he is an evil-doer, neither a Believer, nor an Unbeliever, nor a hypocrite. The answer to them is that this position is [only] saying anew that which contradicts the position on which the Fathers agreed, namely that there is no [middle] rank between the two ranks; so it is unsound.

The second [of the Mu'tazilite objections] is that he [who commits a great sin] is not a Believer. They based this on the statement of Allah, "Was the Believer like the evil-doer?" (Qur'ān 32:18)—where the Believer is contrasted with the evil-doer; and on the statement of the Prophet, "The adulterer, when he commits adultery does not commit adultery being a Believer,"[6] and also his statement, "He who is devoid of trustworthiness (amāna) is devoid of Belief (īmān)."[7] They also say that anyone who com-

---

[6] This tradition is capable of an antinomian interpretation, especially in the light of the tradition of the Prophet's statement to Abū Dharr which comes later. Sayyid Murtaḍā on al-Ghazzālī, Ihyā', II, 254 ff., interprets it to mean that one who commits such a deed could not be a Believer. Cf. Ibn Khaldūn, Muqaddima, III, 34.

[7] Musnad, III, 135.

mits a great sin is not an Unbeliever, because of the *mutawātir* tradition that the Muslim people did not kill him, nor did they carry out the judgments in his case regarding apostates, but they buried him in a Muslim cemetery. The answer to this is that the meaning of "evil-doer" in the verse referred to (Qur'ān 32:18) is "Unbeliever" since Unbelief is one of the greatest of evil deeds. [*119*] The tradition that has been handed down in this connection is stated in strong and emphatic language in order to counsel strongly against disobedience. This is by way of proof from the verses and traditions which indicate that the evil-doer is a Believer inasmuch as the Prophet said so to Abū Dharr [8] to his great humiliation [9] when he asked repeatedly in this connection, "And if he commits adultery and steals?"

But the Kharijites objected, citing the statutes which clearly say that the evil-doer is an Unbeliever, such as, "And those who do not judge according to what Allah has sent down, those are the Unbelievers" (Qur'ān 5:48), and the verse, "And those who become Unbelievers after that, those are the evil-doers" (Qur'ān 24:54). They cited also the statement of the Prophet, "Whoever forsakes worship intentionally has become an Unbeliever." They also cite statutes which say that punishment applies to the Unbeliever such as the statements of Allah, "Punishment is for him who denied and turned his back" (Qur'ān 20:50), and, "None shall burn in it except the most wretched, who denied and turned his back" (Qur'ān 92:15–16), and, "Verily this day shame and evil shall be on the Unbelievers" (Qur'ān 16:29). And there are other verses. The answer [to the Kharijites] is that [*120*] the literal meaning is set aside by the statutes, which [definitely] say [10] that he who commits a great sin is not an Unbeliever, and by the settled Agreement which is according to what has already been said. The Kharijites are secessionists from the settled position of Agreement, and therefore no recognition is to be made of them.

Allah does not forgive the one who joins another with Himself/This is by the Agreement of [all] Muslims. However, they disagreed as to whether or not forgiveness of *ishrāk* [that is, the joining of another to Him] is permissible on the basis of Reason. Some took the position that it is permissible on the basis of Reason, but from authoritative proof it is known not to be permissible; while some took the position that it is impossible on the basis

---

[8] *Musnad*, V, 159.

[9] *Raghima 'l-anfu* literally means "The nose touched the dust." See Lane, *Lexicon*, p. 1113; *Tāj-al-'Arūs*, VIII, 314; *Lisān al-'Arab*, XV, 137; A.J., p. 170; 'I.D. and al-Khayālī, p. 119.

[10] A.J. (p. 171) reads *al-ẓawāhir* (plur.) for *al-ẓāhir* (sing.), "literal"; and *al-qāṭi'a*, "decisive," for *al-nāṭiqa*.

of Reason since wisdom demands a distinction between the doer of wickedness and the doer of good. Since Unbelief is the extreme offense, it is impossible to permit the forgiveness of *ishrāk* or to lift the ban from it at all, so
it does not admit of being pardoned and cleared of the damage done. The
Unbeliever also has the conviction that this is a Reality and does not seek
pardon and forgiveness; so it is unwise to pardon him. Also this is a conviction which, in contrast with the rest of the offenses, has to do with
eternity (*al-abad*) so it demands a recompense that shall be to eternity.

but He pardons whomsoever He wills any sin, whether great or small, ex-
cept this/whether accompanied by repentance or not. This is unlike the position of the Mu'tazilites. In the statement of this judgment consideration
is to be given to that type of verse which indicates that this has been
established. The verses and traditions giving this meaning are many. The
Mu'tazilites applied these especially to small sins and to great sins accompanied by repentance. They held firmly to two points. First there are the
verses and traditions which have come down regarding [*121*] the threatening
of the disobedient. And the reply [to the Mu'tazilites] is that these verses
and traditions, on the supposition that they have a general application, indicate only that forgiveness may take place rather than that it necessarily does.
Since there are many statutes that have to do with pardon, there is specified
the sinner who is forgiven in general terms, the being threatened [with
punishment].

Some [11] assert that the non-fulfillment of a threat is a favor permissible
to Allah. However, the Verifiers, who hold to the opposite of this, say,
"How is this possible since it is a changing (*tabdīl*) of Allah's word, and
Allah has said, 'The word which comes from me changes not'?" (Qur'ān
50:28).

In the second place the Mu'tazilites say that should the sinner know that he
was not to be punished for his sin, that would only establish him in his
sin and incite others to sin. This is inconsistent with the wisdom of [Allah
in] sending Messengers. The answer to this is that the mere possibility of
pardon does confirm the opinion [of some] that there is no punishment at
all in addition to the [fact that we have] knowledge [that there is]. How
[do they say this] when being threatened [with punishment] in general is
accompanied by the declaration that punishment will very probably occur
when related to each individual case? For this reason, the author considered it sufficient to give warning.

11 The Ash'arites. See T.D., p. 121; A.J., p. 172.

The punishment of a small sin is permissible/whether or not the one who committed it avoided a great sin, because it comes under the category of the statement of Allah, "And He forgives less than this to whomsoever He wills" (Qur'ān 4:51, 116), and, "He does not pass by a small sin nor a great one without counting them" (Qur'ān 18:47). And counting is only by way of questioning and of giving recompense. There are other statements [in proof of this] in the verses and the traditions. Some of the Mu'tazilites took the position that if one avoided great sins it is not permissible to punish him. This does not mean that it is impossible on the basis of Reason, but that it is not permissible for it to happen, since in proofs based on authority there is ground to believe that it does not happen. There is the statement of Allah for this, "If ye avoid great sins (*kabā'ir*) which are forbidden you, we shall blot out your faults" (Qur'ān 4:35). Answer is made that the great sin which is absolute is Unbelief because it is the perfect sin. The noun is plural [*kabā'ir*, in the verse above] because of the different kinds of Unbelief, [*122*] even though all are of one degree from the standpoint of judgment; or the statement is of individual sins subsisting in the individuals addressed. This is according to what has been fixed by the rule that putting a plural alongside a plural demands the separation of the units into units, just as we say, "The people (*al-qawm*) rode their beasts and wore their clothes."

and also the pardon (*al-'afw*) of a great sin/He has already mentioned this but he repeated it that it might be understood that the neglect to punish sin may be termed "pardon" just as it may be termed "forgiveness" (*al-maghfira*), and that the following statement might be connected to it.

if it is not of the nature of considering lawful what is forbidden; for that is Unbelief/since in it there is a denial that is inconsistent with assent. In this way are interpreted the statutes which indicate that the disobedient are made to remain forever in the Fire and that they are deprived of the term "Belief."

The intercession [12] **of the Messengers is established by narratives** [13] **in the**

---

[12] Cf. al-Rāzī, *Muḥaṣṣal (Ma'ālim)*, pp. 143 f.; al-Shahrastānī, *Nihāyatu 'l-Iqdām*, pp. 470 f.; Ibn Ḥazm, *Kitāb al-Fiṣal*, IV, 63 ff.; al-Ash'arī, *Maqālāt*, p. 474; Wensinck, *The Muslim Creed*, pp. 180 ff.

[13] A.J. (p. 173), al-Kastalī (p. 148) and the Cureton text (p. 3) read *wa lil-akhyār*, "and of the excellent," which suggests the position of the Shi'ites, namely, that others than Messengers have the power of Intercession. See *al-Bābu 'l-Ḥādī 'Ashar*, p. 88.

case of those who commit great sins/by the narratives widely spread abroad [14] (*al-mustafīḍ*).[15] This is unlike the position of the Mu'tazilites. It rests on what has already been stated, namely, that pardon and forgiveness are permissible without intercession, so how much more permissible they would be with it! But the Mu'tazilites held that when pardon is not permissible, neither is intercession. We have on this the statements of Allah, "Ask pardon for thy sin and for the Believers, both men and women" (Qur'ān 47:21), and, "Then the intercession of the intercessors will not avail them" (Qur'ān 74:49). This kind of statement indicates that intercession is established in general; otherwise there would be no meaning in denying the value in it for Unbelievers, when the purpose is to render vile their state and to verify as certain their misfortune; for in such a position there is a demand that they [who are Unbelievers] be stamped in some particular way rather than by something that is a general characteristic of them and others as well. This does not mean that connecting the judgment [regarding intercession for those who commit great sins] with the Unbeliever indicates that it is not connected with anyone else, so that answer might be made that this is raising an argument only against the one who takes the sense to be that Allah does not carry out His threat. There is also [as a proof of intercession for Muslims who have committed great sins] the statement of the Prophet, "My intercession is for those of my people who have committed great sins." [16] This tradition is well known (*mashhūr*); moreover, there are traditions which are *mutawātir* as to meaning on the subject of intercession.

The Mu'tazilites objected [to this conception of intercession], quoting such statements of Allah as, "Dread the day [*123*] when in nothing a soul shall render satisfaction for a soul, nor shall any intercession be received for it" (Qur'ān 2:45), and, "The wicked shall have no friend nor intercessor who shall be obeyed" (Qur'ān 40:19). The answer [to their position] is that although we admit that these verses apply in general to persons, times and states, yet there must be a special application to Unbelievers here to make the proofs consistent (*jam'an bayn al-adilla*). And when the foundation for pardon and intercession became established in Islam by de-

---

[14] The Cureton text makes this a part of al-Nasafī's text whereas A.J. and 'I.D. make it a part of Taftāzānī's commentary. Al-Kastali follows the Cureton text, but reads *akhyār* again for *akhbār*.

[15] *Mustafīḍa* is the equivalent of *mashhūr*, see Guillaume, *The Traditions of Islam*, p. 182; *Notices et extraits*, XX, 1, 484.

[16] Abū Dā'ūd, *Sunan*, "Kitāb al-Sunna," b. 20; al-Tirmidhī, *Ṣaḥīḥ*, "Ṣifāt al-Qiyāma," b. 11.

cisive proofs from the Book, the Sunna, and Agreement, the Mu'tazilites claimed that the small sins were pardoned absolutely and the great sins by repentance and through intercession to augment the reward [of Believers]. Both of these claims are unsound. The first is unsound, because neither he who is repentant nor he who has committed a small sin and abstained from a great sin deserves punishment according to them, so pardon means nothing. The statutes indicate in the second place that intercession has the meaning of asking pardon for an offense.

And those of the Believers who commit great sins do not remain forever in the Fire/although they die without repentance, by reason of the statement of Allah, "Whoever has done an atom's worth of good shall behold it" (Qur'ān 99:8). And Belief itself is a good work, so it is impossible for the Believer to behold the reward of it before entering the Fire and then to enter the Fire to remain there forever. That is unsound by Agreement, so al-Nasafī specified the exit from the Fire. There are also other statements of Allah in support of this. "Allah promised to the Believers, both men and women, Gardens beneath which the rivers flow" (Qur'ān 9:73). "Verily those who believe and do good works [*124*] have the gardens of Paradise (*al-firdaws*) for a resting place" (Qur'ān 18:107). Similar statutes indicate that the Believer [17] is of the people of the Garden, as well as other things which have already been stated, such as that the creature is not removed from Belief because of disobedience and that remaining forever in the Fire is the severest of punishments. Since the Fire has been made the recompense for Unbelief, which is the greatest of offenses, were others than the Unbeliever so recompensed [and remain forever in the Fire] that would be more than their offense deserves and therefore an injustice to them.

The Mu'tazilites took the position that the one who is consigned to the Fire remains in it forever, for he is either an Unbeliever or the unrepentant one who has committed a great sin; since from what we have seen of their principles the person preserved from error (*al-ma'ṣum*), the repentant one, and the one who commits a small sin—if he has avoided great sins—are not of the people of the Fire. The Unbeliever remains forever in the Fire on the basis of Agreement and so also [they say] does the unrepentant who commits a great sin, for two reasons. The first is that he deserves such punishment as a genuine everlasting injury to him, and this punishment is inconsistent with his deserving a reward, which is a genuine, everlasting benefit.

---

[17] A.J., p. 175, reads "Believers."

The answer to this is to preclude the restriction of the meaning of "everlasting," yea rather to preclude the meaning of "deserves" [such punishment] since what they mean to say is that there "necessarily follows" [such punishment]. But reward is only an act of grace from Allah, and punishment an act of justice; if He wills He pardons, and if He wills He punishes for a time and then causes him to enter the Garden. The second reason [for the unrepentant who has committed a great sin remaining in the Fire] is that there are the statutes which indicate that he remains forever in the Fire, like the statements of Allah, "Whoever kills a Believer purposely, his reward is *Jahannam;* forever he remains in it" (Qur'ān 4:95), and, "Whoever disobeys Allah and His Messenger and transgresses His restrictive ordinances, him He makes enter the Fire; forever he remains in it" (Qur'ān 4:18), and, "Whoever acquires an evil, and he whose sin environs him—those are the dwellers of the Fire; forever they remain in it" (Qur'ān 2:75). And the answer [to the Mu'tazilites] is that the one who kills a Believer because he is a Believer can only be an Unbeliever, and so also is anyone who transgresses all the restrictive ordinances and so also the one whom sin environs and surrounds from every side. Even were the Mu'tazilite position to be admitted, the term "abiding forever" is sometimes used to express an extended period, just as they say "perpetual imprisonment." Also were their position admitted [as a rational one] it nevertheless opposes the statutes, which indicate that abiding is not forever as already stated.

Chapter 13

BELIEF

Belief is assent to that which he brought from Allah and confession of it. As for works, they increase in and of themselves, but Belief neither increases nor decreases.

And Belief and Islam are one. And whenever assent and confession are found in the creature, it is right for him to say, "I am a Believer in reality," and it is not fitting that he should say, "I am a Believer, if Allah wills."

The happy one sometimes becomes miserable and the miserable one sometimes becomes happy; and the changing is in happiness and misery, not in making happy and making miserable, for these are both attributes of Allah and there is no alteration in Allah and His attributes.

Belief (*al-īmān*) [1] /linguistically is assent (*al-taṣdīq*) [*125*], that is to say, acknowledging (*al-idh‘ān*) the judgment of a narrator, accepting it, and considering it to be veracious. *Imān* is the noun on the measure of *if‘āl* from *al-amn* (safety, security) as though the real meaning of "he believed in him" were "he rendered him secure from denial and disagreement." The verb takes its object [2] with the preposition *li* as when Allah relates,[3] "And thou art not a Believer on us?" (Qur'ān 12:17). This means "one who assents." Or it takes its object with the preposition *bi* as in the statement of the Prophet, "Belief means that thou believe in Allah, etc.," that is, "that thou assent to."

The real essence of assent does not bear the relation to the heart [4] that

---

[1] Cf. *Dict. of Tech. Terms*, p. 94; al-Shahrastānī, *Nihāyatu 'l-Iqdām*, pp. 470 ff.; Ibn Ḥazm, *Kitāb al-Fiṣal*, III, 188 ff.; al-Sanūsī, *Umm al-Barāhīn*, p. 226; al-Faḍālī, *Kifāyat al-‘Awāmm*, p. 77; *al-Rawḍa al-Bahiya*, p. 24; al-Bayḍāwī, *Anwār al-Tanzil*, I, 15; al-Rāzī, *Mafātīh*, I, 172 f.; Wensinck, *The Muslim Creed*, pp. 22 ff., 131 ff.

[2] See *Tāj al-‘Arūs*, IX, 125.

[3] The text of A.J. (p. 176) adds, "of the brothers of Joseph (Yūsuf)."

[4] Cf. *Dict. of Tech. Terms*, pp. 1170 ff.; Macdonald, *Rel. Att. and Life*, pp. 221 ff.; al-Ghazzālī, *Ihyā'*, VII, 201 ff.

veracity does to the narrative or to the narrator without any acknowledgment or acceptance [of the object], but it is an acknowledgment and an acceptance of that, so that the term "surrender" (*al-taslīm*) may be applied to it as the Imām al-Ghazzālī [5] explained. And in general it has the meaning which is expressed in Persian by the term *girawīdan*.[6] It has the meaning of assertion (*al-taṣdīq*) as contrasted with conception, just as is said in the first principles of the science of logic (*al-mīzān*),[7] "knowledge is either conception (*taṣawwur*) or assertion (*taṣdīq*).[8] The leader of the logicians, Ibn Sīnā,[9] made this clear. For though this meaning [of assertion] were applied to some Unbelievers,[10] the term "Unbeliever" would be used with the idea that the person has some signs of denial and rejection. It is just as though we should suppose that someone assented to all that the Prophet brought and confessed it and practised it and yet girded himself with | *126*] the *zunnār* [11] by choice or bowed to an idol by choice; we should consider him an Unbeliever because the Prophet made such things a sign of denial and rejection.

The verifying of this position according to what I have mentioned simplifies for you the explanation of many of the difficulties which have come down regarding the question of Belief. If you would know the real essence of the idea of assent, then know that Belief according to the Law

is assent to that which he [12] brought from Allah/that is, assent in general to the Prophet with the heart regarding all that his coming from Allah made known; and that it is sufficient to bring one out [13] into the category of Belief. The degree of this kind of Belief is no lower than that of detailed Belief. The Polytheist (*al-mushrik*) who asserts the existence of the Maker and His attributes is only a Believer according to the uses of language, but not ac-

---

[5] See al-Ghazzālī's *Ihyā'*, II, 240.

[6] *Girawīdan*, "to follow, admire, adore, believe, confide in" from the root *giraw* meaning "to wager, pawn, contract." Steingass, *Persian-English Dictionary* (London, 1930), p. 1085.

[7] See *Dict. of Tech. Terms*, p. 33.

[8] Cf. al-Ghazzālī, *Maqāṣid al-Falāsifa*, I, 4 ff.; Ibn Sīnā, *al-Najāt*, pp. 3 ff.; *al-Risāla al-Shamsiya*, p. 1.

[9] Ibn Sīnā, *al-Najāt*, pp. 3 ff.

[10] Cf. *Dict. of Tech. Terms*, pp. 1251 f. for a full statement of the definitions of *kāfir*.

[11] *Zunnār*. This is the belt worn by one who pays the *jizya*, to distinguish him from Believers, in order that the honors due to Muslims only should not be paid to him. See Lane, *Lexicon*, p. 1258; *Enc. of Islam*, IV, 1241 f.; Dozy, *Dictionnaire des noms des vêtements chez les Arabes*, pp. 196 ff.

[12] The text in A.J. (p. 178) inserts "the Prophets."

[13] See Heinrich L. Fleischer, *Kleinere Schriften* (Leipzig, 1885–88), II, 649 f.

cording to the Law, because he falls short of monotheism. Allah alludes to such a one in the statement, "And most of them do not believe in Allah, without being polytheists as well" (Qur'ān 12:106).

and confession of it/that is, by the tongue. It is not permissible at all for one to fall short in the matter of assent, whereas it is permissible for one not to confess as when under compulsion. And if objection is made that assent may not [always] continue as [when one is] in sleep or in a state of unmindfulness, we reply that assent continues in the heart, the neglect [of Belief] only being a neglect of realizing it. Even were we to admit the objection [that assent does not always continue], the Lawgiver considers that the kind of Belief which has been verified is that against which there has not occurred any judgment to the contrary, so that the word "Believer" is applied to the one who believed in the past or present and in whom there appeared no sign of denial.

This position that al-Nasafī mentioned, namely, that Belief is assent and confession, is the position of some of the Learned [14] (*al-'ulamā'*) and it was also chosen by al-Imām Shams al-A'imma [15] and Fakhr al-Islām [16]—Allah have mercy on them both. The Multitude (*al-jumhūr*) of the Verifiers took the position that assent is by the heart but that confession is the condition on which judgments [as to whether one is a Believer or not] are passed in this world (*al-dunyā*), because, since assent is by the heart, it is a hidden thing which must have a sign. So then whoever assents with his heart and does not confess with his tongue is yet a Believer with Allah, even though he is not according to the judgments of this world; but whoever confesses with his tongue and does not assent with his heart like the hypocrite is just the opposite. This is the position chosen by Abū Manṣūr [al-Māturīdī].

The statutes support this position, for Allah said, [*127*] "On the hearts of those He has written Belief" (Qur'ān 58:22), and, "His heart being tranquil in Belief" (Qur'ān 16:108), and, "Belief has not yet entered your hearts"

---

[14] This is the position of Abū Ḥanīfa, A.J., p. 179.

[15] The reference is probably to Shams al-A'imma Abū Bakr Muḥammad b. Aḥmad b. Abī Sahl al-Sarakhsī, or Shams al-A'imma Abū Muḥammad 'Abd-al-'Azīz b. Aḥmad al-Halwānī, both of whom lived in the fifth century of the Hijra and wrote extensively on *Fiqh* from the Hanafite standpoint. See Haji Khalfa, *Lexicon*, ed. Fluegel (London, 1858), VII, 1213; Brockelmann, *Geschichte*, I, 373.

[16] This must be either Fakhr al-Islām Abū 'l-Ḥasan 'Alī b. Muḥammad al-Pazdawī (d. A.H. 482), who was a Hanafite writer on jurisprudence, or Fakhr al-Islām Abū Bakr Muḥammad b. Aḥmad al-Qaffāl (d. A.H. 507) who was a Shafi'ite. See references in Haji Khalfa, *Lexicon*, VII, 1071 and Brockelmann, *Geschichte*, I, 373.

(Qur'ān 49:14). The Prophet said, "Establish, O Allah, my heart in Thy religion and obedience to Thee." [17] He said to Usāma,[18] when Usāma had killed one who said that there is no deity but Allah, "Didst thou not cleave his heart?" [19]

And if you say that Belief is assent, yet the lexicographers know only assent by the tongue, and the Prophet and his Companions were content to have Believers utter the words of the Witnessing Formula (*al-shahāda*) and judged one a Believer without asking for an explanation of what was in his heart; I answer that it is clear that what we express by assent is the work of the heart, so even if we should suppose that assent did not have this conventional usage, or had a usage other than the assent of the heart, none of the lexicographers and the people who know common usage would rule that whoever uttered the words, "I assented [to him]" was [of necessity] one who assents to the Prophet and believes in him. Therefore it is quite sound to deny Belief in the case of some who confess with the tongue. Allah said, "Some people say, 'We believe in Allah and the last day,' but they are not Believers" (Qur'ān 2:7), and, "The desert Arabs say, 'We have believed.' Say thou, 'Ye have not believed, but rather say, We have become Muslims' " (Qur'ān 49:14).

But as for one who confesses with his tongue only, there is no dispute about his being called a Believer from the standpoint of the language, nor about the application to him in outward matters of the laws dealing with Belief. But the dispute is whether he is a Believer when it is a matter between him and Allah. The Prophet and those who came after him, just as they ruled that one was a Believer who uttered the Witnessing Formula, also ruled that a hypocrite was an Unbeliever. Thus the Prophet indicated that the action of the tongue is not sufficient for Belief. Also the Agreement of the Muslim community confirms the Belief of him who assented [*128*] with his heart and purposed to confess with his tongue, but something like dumbness prevented him.

It is evident that the real essence of Belief is not merely the two words of the Witnessing Formula as the Karramites asserted. And since the Multitude of the Mutakallims and the Traditionalists (*al-muḥaddithūn*) and the Canon Lawyers (*al-fuqahā'*) take the position that Belief is the assent of the

---

[17] Al-Tirmidhī, *Ṣaḥīḥ*, "Qadar," b. 7; *Musnad*, III, 112, 257, VI, 251, 294, etc.

[18] See Ibn Qutayba, *Kitāb al-Ma'ārif*, p. 71; Ibn Ḥajar, *A Biographical Dictionary of Persons Who Knew Muḥammad*, I, 55; Wensinck, *Handbook*, p. 239.

[19] See *Musnad*, V, 207, and also Wensinck, *The Muslim Creed*, pp. 29 f.

inner heart (*al-janān*), confession by the tongue and the performance of the pillars (*al-arkān*) of Islam, the author alludes to the denial of this by saying,

As for works [20] /that is, the obedient acts

they increase in and of themselves, but Belief [21] **neither increases nor decreases** [22] /Here then are two matters [for consideration].

The first is that works do not enter into Belief, since we have already seen that the real essence of Belief is assent and because of certain things that have come down to us in the Book and the Sunna. (a) In the first place works are coupled with Belief as in the saying of Allah, "Verily those who believe and do good deeds" [23] (Qur'ān 2:23, 277, etc.), and yet it is quite certain that the conjunction of the two together demands a distinction between them so that the thing joined on does not enter into that to which it is joined. (b) Secondly, Belief was made a condition of the soundness of works as in the statement of Allah, "Whoever does good deeds, whether a male or a female, being a Believer" (Qur'ān 4:123), and yet it is quite certain that the thing conditioned does not enter into the condition, since it is impossible to condition a thing on itself. (c) Thirdly, Belief is affirmed of one who even neglects some of the [required] works as in the saying of Allah, "If two factions of Believers are at war" (Qur'ān 49:9). And yet as has already been said it is quite certain there is no real verification of a thing without that which is its fundamental element. It is clear then that these points only raise an argument against the one who makes obedience a fundamental element of the real essence of Belief, so that, as the Mu'tazilites held, he who omits works is not a Believer. But it is not an argument against those who hold that works are a fundamental element of perfect Belief, so that he who omits them is not outside the real meaning of Belief, as the school of al-Shāfi'ī [24] holds. And the tenets of the Mu'tazilites and the re-

---

[20] Cureton (p. 3) adds in the text of al-Nasafī "and they are obedient acts."

[21] The text of A.J. (p. 181) inserts, as from al-Taftāzānī, "in itself."

[22] See al-Rāzī, *Muḥaṣṣal*, p. 175 f.; al-Ījī, *al-Mawāqif*, p. 282 f.; al-Ghazzālī, *Iḥyā'* (commentary of Sayyid Murtaḍā), II, 256 ff.

[23] This expression occurs about sixty times in the Qur'ān, see *Concordantiae*, pp. 17, 110; *Fatḥ al-Raḥmān*, p. 258.

[24] Al-Shāfi'ī, the founder of one of the four Sunnite schools of jurisprudence, is remembered especially for the emphasis he placed on *Ijmā'* (Agreement). See al-Nawawī (Wüstenfeld), *Ueber das Leben*, p. 56 ff.; Ibn Khallikān, *Biog. Dict.*, II, 569 ff.; *Enc. of Islam*, IV, 252; Macdonald, *Development*, pp. 104 ff.

plies to be made to them have been mentioned in what we have already said.

The second matter is that the real essence of Belief does not increase or decrease. It has already been said that it is the assent of the heart which reaches the point of decision and acknowledgment.[25] In this no decrease or increase is conceivable, so whoever attains to the real essence of assent, whether he does obedient acts or commits disobedient ones, his assent continues in a state in which there is no change at all. [*129*] The verses which indicate an increase of Belief may be interpreted in the way that Abū Ḥanīfa mentioned, saying that after people had believed in general there came one obligation (*farḍ*) after another, and as they believed each special obligation [as it came] the consequence was that Belief increased just as Belief in each obligation necessitated; and that this [increase in Belief] was inconceivable except in the time of the Prophet. This is a matter for consideration, for obtaining knowledge of the details of the ordinances is possible in other than the Prophet's time. Belief is incumbent upon people in general in matters that are known in general, and in detail in matters that are known in detail, it being clear that detailed Belief is [something] additional—nay rather, more perfect. What has already been said about general Belief not being lower in rank that detailed Belief has to do with its being described as the foundation of Belief. It has been suggested that as fixity and perseverance in Belief increase hour by hour, the consequence is that Belief increases as times increase since it is an accident which only continues by the continual renewing [of Beliefs] similar to it. But this calls for consideration, because the occurrence of something similar to a thing after it has been made nonexistent does not mean an increase at all, just as in the case of the blackness of a body, for example.

It has been suggested that the meaning [of increase in Belief] is the increase of the fruits of Belief and the shining forth in the heart of its light and brilliance, for it increases through works and decreases through disobedient acts. It is quite evident that he who holds that works are a part of Belief accepts the increase and decrease [of Belief]; consequently this problem of increase and decrease is a part of the [larger] problem of obedient acts as a part of Belief. Some of the Verifiers said, "We do not admit that the real essence of assent does not permit of increase and decrease, but it varies indeed as to power and weakness since the assent of the individuals of a

---

[25] The text of A.J. (p. 181) adds *al-qubūl,* "acceptance."

people is not like that of the Prophet." For this reason Abraham said, "But let my heart be confident" [26] (Qur'ān 2:262).

There remains yet another subject for discussion, namely that some of the Qadarites [27] held that Belief is cognition (*al-ma'rifa*).[28] Our Learned Men agreed that this position is unsound because the People having Scriptures (*ahl al-kitāb*) knew that Muhammad was a prophet, just as their descendants do, yet undoubtedly they were Unbelievers because of their failure to assent [to Muhammad's being a prophet], and because there were among the Unbelievers those who knew the truth very well indeed and yet through stubbornness and pride denied it. Allah said of them, "They denied it though their souls knew them [that is, the signs] to be genuine" (Qur'ān 27:14). So of necessity there is a distinct difference between the cognition of the judgments and deciding that they are true on the one hand, and the assent to them and conviction about them on the other. So it is sound to call the second kind Belief in distinction from the first.

Some of the Early Theologians mention the suggestion that assent is an expression for binding the heart to that which is known of the narratives given by the Narrator; and it is something acquired (*kasbī*), established by the choice of the one who assents. Therefore it is to be rewarded and considered the chief of religious duties (*al-'ibādāt*) rather than cognition which sometimes occurs without any acquisition, as when one's glance falls on some body and there results to him knowledge that it is a wall or a stone. This is what has been mentioned by some of the Verifiers who say that assent means that by your choice you ascribe veracity to the Narrator. Thus, if it were to occur in the heart without choice, it would not be assent, even though it were cognition. There is a problem about this, for assent is one of the divisions of knowledge. It is one of the qualities of the soul (*al-kayfīyāt al-nafsānīya*), rather than one of the voluntary actions, for whenever we conceive the relationship between two things and doubt whether it is to

[26] The occasion was Abraham's dispute concerning his Lord's power to give life to the dead. Abraham prayed, "O Lord, show me how thou bringest the dead to life." The Lord answered, "Hast thou not believed?" Then he replied, "Yes, but let my heart be confident." See al-Baydāwī, *Anwār al-Tanzīl*, I, 134; al-Ṭabarī, *Annales*, I, 261.

[27] *Al-Qadarīya*, the name given to the free-will party, Macdonald, *Development*, pp. 127 ff.; Wensinck, *The Muslim Creed*, pp. 52 ff.; al-Shahrastānī, *al-Milal*, p. 29; al-Faḍālī, *Kifāyat al-'Awāmm*, p. 67; al-Baghdādī, *al-Farq bayn al-Firaq*, pp. 260 ff.; Goldziher, *Vorlesungen über den Islam*, pp. 95 ff.

[28] Al-Ghazzālī took the position that there are three different degrees of Belief. His position that cognition (*ma'rifa*) was the highest, however, is different from that of the Qadarites for his is essentially a Ṣūfī attitude. See al-Ghazzālī, *Iḥyā'*, VII, 236 ff.; Macdonald, *Rel. Att. and Life*, pp. 245 ff.; cf. also Ibn Khaldūn, *Muqaddima*, III, 33 f.

be affirmed or denied, and then proof is adduced for establishing it, that which takes place in us is the acknowledgment and acceptance of this relationship. This is the meaning of assent, judgment, affirmation (*ithbāt*), and realization (*iqā'*).

Yes, it is true that these qualities are arrived at [*130*] through choice, by coming into contact with the causes, the use of speculation, the removing of objections, and so on. In this way the imposition of responsibility for Belief occurs. This is, as it were, the meaning of its being acquired and of its being by choice. Cognition is not sufficient for obtaining assent, for it is sometimes devoid of assent. Most assuredly this absolute cognition which is acquired by choice must be assent. There is no objection to this, for in this way one attains the idea expressed by the Persian word *girawīdan*, for Belief and Assent are nothing else but that. It is impossible for the obstinate, haughty Unbelievers to obtain that. And if their obtaining it were a possible supposition they would become Unbelievers through denial with their tongues, their perseverance in obstinacy and arrogance, and through such things as are signs of denial and rejection.

And Belief and Islam are one [29]/for Islam is resignation (*al-khuḍū'*) and submission (*al-inqiyād*), meaning the acceptance of judgments and acknowledgment. That is the real essence of assent, as we have seen. This is supported by the statement of Allah, "So we brought out the Believers of those who were in it and we only found one house of Muslims" [30] (Qur'ān 51:36). And in general it is not sound in the Law to judge one a Believer who is not a Muslim nor to judge one a Muslim who is not a Believer. And we mean nothing more than this by their being one.

The evident purpose of the statement of the Early Theologians was [*131*] that they intended to make no distinction in meaning [between the two], so that one [term] is inseparable from the other, yet there is no absolute unity as that term is understood, as seen in what was mentioned in *al-Kifāya*, that is, that Belief is assent to what Allah has narrated of positive commands and prohibitions; and Islam is submission and resignation to the Deity, and that is not verified except by acceptance of the positive command and prohibition [of Allah]. So Belief is inseparable from Islam as to judgment and they are not distinct from one another. One may say to him who makes a distinction,

---

[29] This is al-Rāzī's position also. See *Muḥaṣṣal*, p. 174.

[30] The reference here is to Abraham and his honored guests and their visit to the wicked city of Lot. Cf. Gen. 18 and 19; al-Tha'labī, *Qiṣaṣ al-Anbiyā'*, pp. 88 ff.; al-Ṭabarī, *Annales*, I, 332 f.

"What is the judgment to be applied to one who believes but does not become a Muslim, or who becomes a Muslim but does not believe?" If he affirms for one of them a judgment not established as applicable to the other, well and good; otherwise the unsoundness of his statement is clear.

The following statement of Allah may be cited as evidence that Islam is not necessarily Belief, "The desert Arabs say, 'We have believed.' Say thou, 'Ye have not believed, but rather say, We have become Muslims'" (Qur'ān 49:14). To this we would reply that the meaning of Islam which is considered as such in the Law is not to be found without Belief. The Islam referred to in the verse above is an outward submission devoid of an inward submission, just as in the case of the one who utters the words of the Witnessing Formula without assent, as seen in the section [above] on Belief.

Objection may be made that there seems to be an indication that Islam is works [31] and not an assent of the heart in the saying of the Prophet, "Islam means that you bear witness that there is no deity but Allah and that Muhammad is the Messenger of Allah, and that you perform worship (*al-ṣalā*), bring the poor rate (*al-zakā*), fast the month of Ramaḍān, and make the pilgrimage to the House, if you are able to make the journey there." [32] To this we reply that the meaning is the fruits and signs of Islam, just as the Prophet said to some people who came as a delegation to him, "Do you understand what Belief in Allah alone means?" They replied, "Allah and His Messenger know better." He said, "It means witnessing that there is no deity but Allah and that Muhammad is the Messenger of Allah, and [it means] the performance of worship, the bringing of the poor rate, the fast of Ramaḍān, and that you give a fifth of the booty." [33] Or it is as the Prophet said, "Belief is seventy-some sects: [34] the highest is to say that there is no deity but Allah, and the lowest is the removing of that which is harmful from the path." [35]

And whenever assent and confession are found in the creature, it is right

[31] The traditions in general seem to make a distinction between Belief and Islam; the former having to do with doctrine, the latter with practice. See *Musnad*, I, 27 f., 51 f., 97, 133, 319; III, 134 ff.

[32] Al-Bukhārī, *al-Ṣaḥīḥ*, I, 10; Muslim, *al-Ṣaḥīḥ*, I, 26.

[33] Al-Bukhārī, *al-Ṣaḥīḥ*, I, 23, 34, and also *Musnad*, I, 228. The accounts in al-Bukhārī, IV, 417, 499 differ in some details. Cf. also Muslim, I, 23 ff.

[34] See *Musnad*, II, 414, 445; Al-Bukhārī (I, 11) says sixty-some sects. One tradition given by the *Musnad* (II, 379) says there are 64 doors to Belief, the remainder of the tradition being as given by al-Taftāzānī.

[35] Cf. Ibn Māja, *Sunan*, "Muqaddima," b. 90.

for him to say, "I am a Believer in reality" [86]/because Belief in him has been verified.

and it is not fitting that he should say, "I am a Believer, if Allah wills "/If he says that because of doubt there is no avoiding the fact that it is Unbelief. If one says it because of good breeding and in order to refer matters to the will of Allah, or because of doubt about [37] the final consequence and outcome [of his life], not as to his present [Belief], or because of an expected blessing from mentioning Allah, or to clear himself of self-righteousness and of glorying in his state—well, in any case it is preferable to omit it, since it may give the impression of doubt. Al-Nasafī said, "It is not fitting" rather than "it is not permissible," since were [the saying of] it due to something else than doubt there would be no reason to deny the permissibility of using the expression. How would that be possible when many of the Fathers, even of the Companions and their Followers, used this expression? [38] This is not like your saying, "I am a youth, if Allah wills"; because being a youth is not an acquired action, nor is it to be conceived that one will continue [to be a youth] as a final consequence [*132*] and outcome [of his life]; nor does self-righteousness and glorying result from it, but [saying "I am a Believer, if Allah wills" in this way] is as though you said, "I am abstinent from worldly pleasures and devoted to the service of Allah, if He wills."

Some of the Verifiers held that the result for the creature was that real essence of assent by which he escapes from Unbelief; even though assent in itself admits of being strong or weak. It is only by the will of Allah that one attains to that perfect saving assent which is referred to in the saying of Allah, "Those in reality are the Believers. They have ranks with their Lord, forgiveness, and a generous sustenance" (Qur'ān 8:4). From what has been reported from some of the Ash'arites we learn that it is right to say, "I am

---

[86] This is a point of dispute between the Ash'arites and the Maturidites. See Wensinck, *The Muslim Creed*, pp. 138 ff.; *al-Rawḍa al-Bahiya*, pp. 6 f. The story is told in *al-Rawḍa* of Abū Ḥanīfa who answered, "Yes," when asked if he were a Believer. They said, "Are you a Believer in the sight of Allah?" He replied, "Are you asking me about my knowledge and fixed purpose, or that of Allah?" They said, "We are asking you about your knowledge." Then said he, "Verily I, by my knowledge, know that I am a Believer."

[37] The text of A.J. (p. 186) adds, "in the present."

[38] Al-Ghazzālī (*Ihyā'*, IX, 621 ff.) gives some narratives that teach the humiliation that may lie back of the Ash'arite position. Fuḍayl said, "If you are asked, 'Do you love Allah?' be silent, for if you say 'No' you become an Unbeliever; and if you say 'Yes' your saying so is not the description of those who love." Some of the Learned said, "There is no higher blessedness in the Garden than that of the People of knowledge and love of Allah, and no more serious punishment in the Fire than that of the one who claims to have them."

a Believer, if Allah wills," on the basis that the real account of Belief and Unbelief, and of happiness (*al-sa'āda*) and misery (*al-shaqāwa*) is made at the end of life, so the happy Believer is the one who dies in Belief even though all his life was spent in Unbelief and disobedience; and the miserable Unbeliever is the one who dies in Unbelief—we seek refuge in Allah from such—although all his life was spent in assent and obedience. This is as Allah pointed out in the case of Iblīs, "And he was one of the Unbelievers" (Qur'ān 2:32, 38:74). There is also the statement of the Prophet, "The happy one is he who was happy in his mother's womb, and likewise the miserable is he who was miserable in his mother's womb." [39]

Al-Nasafī in order to show the unsoundness of this statement [of some of the Ash'arites] said,

The happy one sometimes becomes miserable/in apostatizing after having believed—we seek refuge in Allah from such.

and the miserable one sometimes becomes happy/by believing after having been an Unbeliever

and the changing is in happiness and misery, not in making happy and making miserable, for these are both attributes of Allah/since making happy is the bringing of happiness into being and making miserable is the bringing of misery into being.

and there is no alteration in Allah and His attributes/This is due to what has already been said about the Eternal not being the locus of originated things. The real fact of the matter is that there is no disagreement in the meaning, for if the meaning of Belief and happiness is merely the obtaining of the idea expressed in these, it is obtained in the present; and if the meaning is that thing from which salvation and fruitful works result, there is, according to the will of Allah, no certainty in obtaining it now. So whoever is certain of obtaining Belief and happiness now means the first definition, and whoever commits the matter to Allah means the second.

[39] Cf. Muslim, *al-Ṣaḥīḥ*, II, 406 f.

Chapter 14

THE MESSENGERS, ANGELS, AND BOOKS OF ALLAH

In the sending of Messengers there is wisdom, and Allah has sent Messengers of mankind to mankind announcing good tidings, and warning, and explaining to people what they need [to know] of the matters of this world and of the judgment. And He has aided them with evidentiary miracles which contradict the customary way of things.

The first of the prophets is Adam and the last is Muhammad. A statement of their number has been handed down in several traditions, but it is preferable not to limit their number in naming them, for Allah said, "Of some of them we have told thee their stories, and of others we have not" (Qur'ān 40:78). And there is no security in a statement of their number against there being entered in some who are not among them, or of there being excluded some who are of them. All of them were narrators conveying information from Allah, veracious and sincere. The most excellent of the prophets is Muhammad.

The angels are the creatures of Allah and they do according to His command. They are not described as being male or female.

Allah has books which He has sent down to His prophets, and in them He has shown His positive commands and His prohibitions, His promise and His threat.

In the sending of Messengers (*al-rusul*) [1]/*Rusul* is the plural of *rasūl*, which is on the measure of *faʿūl* from [the noun] *risāla* (a message), | *133* | and it means the sending of a creature between Allah and intelligent beings (*dhawīyi 'l-albāb*) among His creation in order to remove thereby those defects by which their reasons have fallen short of the benefits of this world

---

[1] See *Dict. of Tech. Terms*, pp. 584 f.; al-Faḍālī, *Kifāyat al-ʿAwāmm*, p. 68; al-Ījī, *al-Mawāqif*, pp. 169 ff.; Mohammed Abdou, *Rissālat al-Tawḥīd*, pp. 57 ff.; Ibn Khaldūn, *Muqaddima*, I, 165 ff.; *Enc. of Islam*, III, 1127 ff.; 'I.D. p. 31; A.J. pp. 53 f.

and the next. You have already understood the meaning of Messenger and prophet in a section at the beginning of the book.

there is wisdom (*ḥikma*)/that is, a benefit and a praiseworthy consequence.[2] In this there is an allusion to the fact that the sending of a Messenger is necessary, not meaning that it is incumbent on Allah,[3] but meaning that wisdom demands it, since in it there are wise and beneficial things. The sending of a Messenger is not impossible as the Sumaniya and the Barahima [4] assert, nor is it [merely] a possible thing, both alternatives of the possible being equal, as is the position of some of the Mutakallims.[5]

Then al-Nasafī referred to the actual fact that Messengers had been sent, to the advantage derived therefrom, to the method of establishing the sending [of Messengers], and to the designation of some whose being sent has been established, by saying,

and Allah has sent Messengers of mankind (*al-bashar*) **to mankind announcing good tidings** (*mubashshirīn*)/of the Garden and reward to the people of Belief and obedience.

and warning/the people of Unbelief and disobedience of the Fire and punishment, for these are among the things of which Reason has no way [of obtaining knowledge]. And if it did have a way, it would be by minute speculations which would not be easy except for individuals one by one.

and explaining to the people what they need [**to know**] **of the matters of this world and of the judgment**/for Allah created the Garden and the Fire, and He prepared in them reward and punishment. The details of the different states to be found in both of them and the way to attain the Garden and guard against the Fire are among the things in which Reason is not independent [of revelation from Allah]. He also created useful and harmful bodies and He did not give Reason and the senses complete independence for knowing

---

[2] It is also called a *luṭf* (a favor) from Allah. See al-Ghazzālī, *Iḥyā'* (commentary of Sayyid Murtaḍā), II, 199.

[3] The Shi'ites say that it is absolutely incumbent on Allah to send Messengers. See *al-Bābu 'l-Hādī 'Ashar*, p. 54.

[4] *Al-Bidāya* and other books assert that this is the position of the Sumaniya and the Barahima, but the *Sharḥ* of the *Maqāṣid* states that the Barahima did not deny the possibility but the necessity of sending prophets (A.J., p. 187). Cf. 'I.D., p. 133, and also al-Ijī, *al-Mawāqif*, pp. 187 f.; *Iḥyā'* (commentary of Sayyid Murtaḍā), II, 197.

[5] See al-Faḍālī, *Kifāyat al-'Awāmm*, p. 68; al-Ijī, *al-Mawāqif*, pp. 182 f.

them. And he also made some propositions that are possible, there being no way of [knowing for a] certainty which one of the two alternatives [is right]; and some propositions that are either necessary or impossible, but which are not clear to Reason until after endless speculation and complete investigation. So were a man to spend his time in [studying] them, he would deprive himself of most of their benefits. Therefore it was of the grace (*faḍl*) of Allah and His mercy that He sent Messengers to demonstrate that, as He said, "We have not sent thee except in mercy to the worlds" (Qur'ān 21:107).

And He has aided them/that is, the prophets

with evidentiary miracles (*al-mu'jizāt*) [6] **which contradict the customary way of things**/*Mu'jizāt* is the plural of *mu'jiza* and it is something that appears contrary to the customary way of things (*al-'āda*) at the hands of one who claims [*134*] the office of prophet, [and it happens] in such a way that those who deny are unable (*yu'jizu*) to do the same thing that he does when they compete with him. For if he were not aided by the miracle it would not be necessary to accept the statement of the prophet, nor would the veracious man be clearly distinguished from the false in claiming the office of Messenger. But at the appearance of the evidentiary miracle the certainty of his veracity results in the customary way whereby Allah creates knowledge of his veracity as a consequence of the appearance of the evidentiary miracle, even though the non-creation of the knowledge [of his veracity] is possible in itself. It is as though one were to claim in the presence of a group of people that he was the Messenger of a certain king to them, and then he would say to this king, "If I am veracious, act contrary to your custom and rise from your seat three times." So when the king did that, the group would have [as a result of this action] the necessary customary knowledge regarding his veracity in the statement [he has made].

If falsehood [on the part of the prophet] were possible in itself—for the essential possibility means the rational permissibility—it would not preclude the attaining of absolute knowledge, just as we know that the mountain of Uḥud did not turn into gold although that in itself were possible. So here the knowledge of his veracity results because the customary way requires this, since it is one of the means of decisive knowledge just as the senses are. The possibility that the evidentiary miracle is not from Allah, or

[6] See above, Chap. 2, n. 20, and below, Chap. 15, n. 6.

that it is not for the purpose of gaining assent or for a false prophet's gaining assent, or any other possibility, does not detract from this knowledge,
just as the possibility of there not being heat in fire does not detract from
the necessary knowledge through the senses that there is heat in fire. This
means that, were the non-existence of the evidentiary miracle a supposition, it
would not follow then that it is impossible.

The first of the prophets (*al-anbiyā'*) **is Adam and the last is Muhammad/**
The prophetic office of Adam [7] is seen from the Book, which points out
that he was commanded and prohibited along with the certainity that there
was no other prophet in his time. This is only by revelation (*al-waḥy*). This
is also [the position] according to Tradition (*al-sunna*) and Agreement so the
denial to him of the office of prophet, as has been reported by some, is Unbelief.

But as for the prophetic office of Muhammad, it is so because he claimed
it and manifested the evidentiary miracle.[8] His claim to the office is known
from *mutawātir* tradition; and as for the manifestation of the evidentiary
miracle, that is seen from two viewpoints. In the first place he manifested the
speech (*kalām*) of Allah and strove thereby with the eloquent, who, in spite
of their eloquence, were unable to match the shortest *sūra* of the Qur'ān, although they applied themselves to this task until they risked their hearts'
blood and turned from opposition by letters to fighting with swords. There
has not been reported of any one of those who strove with the Prophet that
he produced anything that came anywhere near it, although many claims
have been preserved. And that indicates absolutely that it [that is, the
Qur'ān] is from Allah. Thereby the veracity of the Prophet's claim is known
in such a purely customary way that it detracts nothing from the things
that are possible according to Reason such as are to be found in other
customary knowledge. In the second place there has been reported about
Muhammad, among the things which annul the customary way, that which
attains a rank sharing with it, I mean, the evidentiary miracle. [These
things are so many that they reach] the point of a *mutawātir* tradition, so
even though their details are individual traditions like those of the courage

---

[7] See Qur. 2:33, 7:18; *Enc. of Islam*, I, 127; al-Ṭabarī, *Annales*, I, 151; al-Nawawī
(Wüstenfeld), *Ueber das Leben*, p. 123, and 'I.D., p. 134.

[8] See Hughes, *Dictionary of Islam*, p. 350; Muslim, *al-Ṣaḥīḥ*, II, 279 f.; al-Rāzī, *Mafātiḥ*,
I, 232 ff.; *Ihyā'* (commentary of Sayyid Murtaḍā), II, 209; Ibn Khaldūn, *Muqaddima*, I,
168 ff. For the Shi'ite statement see *al-Bābu 'l-Ḥādī 'Ashar*, p. 56.

of 'Alī and the generosity of Ḥātim, for [*135*] each of these facts is supported by *tawātur*, although the details are individual traditions which have been mentioned in the biographies of the Prophet.

Those of real insight sometimes deduce from two standpoints proof for his having had the prophetic office. Firstly, from *mutawātir* tradition there are derived certain facts concerning his circumstances before being a prophet, at the time of his call, and after the fulfillment of it: his great moral characteristics, his wise judgments, his boldness when the gallant heroes held back, his confidence [9] in the power of Allah to preserve him under all circumstances from errors, and his steadfastness before terrors, so that his enemies in spite of all their bitter enmity and their eagerness to slander him could not find place for slander nor was there any way to impugn him. Therefore Reason is certain that the union of all these things is impossible in anyone except the prophets, and that Allah united all these perfections in him of whom He knew that he would be maligned, and yet for twenty-three years He would make him patient, and that then He would give his religion mastery over other religions, would aid him with victory over his enemies, and would keep alive his memory after his death until the day of resurrection.

Secondly, Muhammad claimed this great distinction amidst a people who were without a book [10] and devoid of wisdom and showed them the Book and wisdom. He taught them judgments and laws, fulfilled the most noble characteristics, perfected many people in the theoretical and practical virtues, and enlightened the world by Belief and good works. And Allah gave his religion mastery over all religion as He promised him. This is the whole meaning of the office of prophet and Messenger. Since his prophetic office has been established, his speech and the Speech of Allah which descended on him having indicated that he is the seal (*khātam*) [11] of the prophets, and the one sent to all mankind,[12] nay rather to *al-Jinn* [13] and mankind too, it has been established that he is the last of the prophets and that his prophetic office is not, as some Christians assert, especially confined to the Arabs.

---

[9] Muslim, *al-Ṣaḥīḥ*, II, 281 ff.   [10] Qur. 32:2, 36:5.

[11] Qur. 33:40; al-Bayḍāwī, *Anwār al-Tanzīl*, II, 130. Cf. *Iḥyā'* (commentary of Sayyid Murtaḍā), II; 202 ff.

[12] Qur. 34:27. Cf. also 38:87 f.; 36:69 f.

[13] Qur. 46:28. See also al-Bayḍāwī, *Anwār al-Tanzīl*, II, 258; al-Ṭabarī, *Annales*, I, 1202; Ibn Hishām *Sīrat Rasūl Allāh*, p. 281.

If it is objected that there has been handed down a tradition that Jesus will descend [14] after him,[15] we answer, "Yes, but he will be a follower of Muhammad, for the law of Jesus has been abrogated (*nusikhat*). There will be no revelation nor setting up of judgments on his behalf, but he will be the Khalīfa (vicegerent) of the Messenger of Allah. Thus it is more correct to say that he will perform worship with the people and lead them [in worship], and the Mahdī [16] will follow his example, for Jesus is more excellent and his leadership (*imāma*) is preferable."

A statement of their number has been handed down in several traditions/ According to what has been handed down the Prophet was asked about the number of the prophets, and he replied, "One hundred twenty-four thousand," [17] and in another narrative it is two hundred twenty-four thousand.

but it is preferable not to limit their number in naming them, for Allah said, "Of some of them we have told thee their stories, and of others we have not" (Qur'ān 40:78). And there is no security in a statement of their number against there being entered in some who are not among them/that is, if one mentions [*136*] more than there are

or of there being excluded some who are of them/that is, if one mentions a number less than their real number, that is to say [in explanation of the desirability of not mentioning a definite number] the narrative of an individual—on the supposition that it fulfills all the conditions mentioned in the foundations of *fiqh*—is useful only for opinion, and no account is to be taken of opinion in the case of beliefs. This is true especially if it [that is, the conclusion reached] includes something about which the records handed down differ. The statement that affirms [a fixed number of prophets] arrives only at a contradiction of the plain meaning of the Book, which is that some of the prophets were not mentioned to the Prophet. So it is possible that something may be stated contrary to the actual fact, in counting the prophet among the non-prophets, and the non-prophet among the prophets,

---

[14] See al-Nawawī (Wüstenfeld), *Ueber das Leben*, p. 497; Wensinck, *Handbook*, p. 113.

[15] The text in A.J. (p. 190) adds "so the Prophet then would not be the last of the prophets."

[16] See Hughes, *Dictionary of Islam*, p. 305; *Enc. of Islam*, III, 111; Ibn Khaldūn, *Muqaddima*, II, 142 ff.

[17] Wensinck, *The Muslim Creed*, p. 204; al-Ṭabarī, *Annales*, I, 152; al-Bayḍāwī, *Anwār al-Tanzīl*, II, 217.

since on the basis that the number is a specific one in that which it indicates, it is not possible then that there be increase and decrease in the number.

All of them were narrators conveying information from Allah/for this is the meaning of the office of prophet and of Messenger (*al-nubūwa wa 'l-risāla*).

veracious and sincere [18]/to all creation, lest the benefit of the mission and message be in vain. In this there is an allusion to the fact that the prophets were preserved (*ma'ṣūmūn*) [19] from falsehood, especially in what is connected with the commanding of laws and the conveying of judgments and the guidance of the people. [They are preserved from errors committed] willfully, on the basis of Agreement, and also through inadvertence according to the majority.

In the matter of being preserved from the remainder of sins there is some detail [to be given]. By Agreement the prophets were preserved from Unbelief both before and after the appearance of Revelation; likewise from the willful commission of great sins according to the Multitude in opposition to al-Ḥashwīya,[20] the difference between them being only whether the proof for believing that great sins were impossible for them is based on tradition or on Reason. But as for great sins committed through inadvertence, the majority make this permissible. As for the small sins, the Multitude in opposition to al-Jubbā'ī and his followers make them permissible when willfully committed; and by common consent (*bi'l-ittifāq*) they are permissible when committed through inadvertence, except such sins as indicate contemptibleness, like stealing a morsel and giving a grain less for short measure. But the Verifiers stipulated that the prophets after the appearance of Revelation must be made aware of such things and refrain from them; yet there is no proof for the impossibility of a great sin proceeding from them before the appearance of Revelation. The Mu'tazilites held that for prophets a great sin is impossible since it compels such a judgment in regard to them

18 Al-Sanūsī (*Umm al-Barāhīn*, pp. 173 ff.) says there are three qualities necessary in a prophet, veracity, faithfulness, and conveying the message, and three that are impossible, namely their opposites, lying, unfaithfulness, and concealing of the message. Al-Faḍālī, *Kifāyat al-'Awāmm*, pp. 73 ff., adds one to each group, intelligence and stupidity.

19 There is no appeal here to the Qur'ān and Traditions since this doctrine rests on the Agreement of the Muslim people (*Ijmā'*). See *al-Rawḍa al-Bahīya*, pp. 57 ff.; al-Ījī, *al-Mawāqif*, pp. 218 ff.; al-Rāzī, *Muḥaṣṣal*, pp. 157 ff., *Mafātīḥ*, I, 318 ff.

20 They were the literal Anthropomorphists. The Mu'tazilites called all of the Aṣḥāb al-Ḥadīth, Ḥashwīya because they tolerated anthropomorphic expressions. See *Enc. of Islam*, II, 287; al-Shahrastānī, *al-Milal*, p. 77; *al-Rawḍā al-Bahīya*, p. 57; *al-Bābu 'l-Hādī 'Ashar*, p. 58; al-Ījī, *al-Mawāqif*, p. 219.

as to prevent their being followed and so the benefit of the mission [of the prophet] would pass away. The true position forbids [in prophets] whatever compels men to forsake them like the debauchery of [their] mothers, vices, and small sins which indicate contemptibleness.

The Shī'ites [21] forbid the procession from a prophet of great and small sins before Revelation and after; however they permit dissimulation in feigning Unbelief for a pious reason (*taqīya*). If this which we have said is settled, then whatever has been reported about prophets, marking them with falsehood and disobedience, is to be rejected (*mardūd*) if it is recorded by individual traditions; and [*137*] is to be changed from its literal meaning if possible when it comes by way of *tawātur;* otherwise it is possible to explain it as a case of doing the less preferable of two actions, or as something that happened before the prophet's mission. The detailed account of this [subject] is to be found in the more extensive books.

The most excellent of the prophets is Muhammad/because of the statement of Allah, "Ye were the best people (*umma*)" (Qur'ān 3:106). There is no doubt that the measure of the goodness of a people is their perfection in religion (*al-dīn*), and that follows the perfection of their prophet whom they follow. To cite as proof the saying of the Prophet, "I am the lord (*sayyid*) of the offspring of Adam without glorying on my part" [22] is weak, for the saying does not indicate that he was better than Adam, but better than his children.

The angels (*al-malā'ika*) [23] **are the creatures of Allah and they do according to His command**/As the statement of Allah indicated, "They do not precede Him in speech and they do according to His command; and they disdain not His service, neither are they wearied" (Qur'ān 21:27, 19).

They are not described as being male or female/ since there is neither record of this in tradition nor any indication of it in Reason. The statement of the idolaters that the angels are the daughters of Allah is impossible, unsound, and extravagant, just as the statement of the Jews that one of the angels may commit the sin of Unbelief and be punished by Allah with metamorphosis is also an extravagant statement which belittles their state.

[21] See *al-Bābu 'l-Ḥādī 'Ashar*, pp. 58 ff.

[22] Cf. Muslim, *al-Saḥīḥ*, II, 278; A.J., p. 189; and al-Rāzī, *Mafātīḥ*, II, 315.

[23] Cf. Wensinck, *The Muslim Creed*, pp. 198 f.; al-Rāzī, *Mafātīḥ*, I, 261 ff.; al-Ījī, *al-Mawāqif*, pp. 237 ff.; Ibn Ḥazm, *Kitāb al-Fiṣal*, III, 259 ff.; *Enc. of Islam*, III, 189 ff.; *Dict. of Tech. Terms*, pp. 1337 f.

If someone objects saying, "Did Iblīs [24] not become an Unbeliever and he was an angel, the proof of this being that it was valid for him to be made an exception from them?" we reply, "No, he was one of the Jinn, and then he strayed from the command of his Lord. But, since he had the attributes of angels in regard to service and exalted rank, and since he was a lone Jinnī inexperienced in worship in the midst of the angels, it was proper to make him an exception, since he had been outnumbered." But as for Hārūt and Mārūt,[25] it is more proper to say of them that they were angels from whom there proceeded neither Unbelief nor a great sin. Their punishment was only by way of rebuke, just as prophets are rebuked for a slip or inadvertence. They exhorted the people and taught them magic, yet said, "We are only a means of testing, so do not become Unbelievers." It is not Unbelief to teach magic, [*138*] but it is |Unbelief] to have a conviction approving it and to work it.

Allah has books (*kutub*) [26] which He has sent down to His prophets, and in them He has shown His positive commands and His prohibitions, His promise (*wa'd*) and His threat (*wa'īd*)/All the books are the speech of Allah, which is one; the multiplicity and differentiation of them is only to be found in the context which is recited and heard. With this consideration in mind, the most excellent is the Qur'ān, then the Tawrā, then the Injīl, then the Zabūr. And as the Qur'ān is one speech, it is inconceivable to think that there are preferable parts; however, from the standpoint of writing and recitation some suras may be preferred to others as tradition states.[27] The real fact of the preferability of some parts over others is for the reason that the recitation of them is more excellent, because there is more benefit in them, or because the name of Allah is mentioned oftener. The books have been abrogated [28] by the Qur'ān as to the necessity of reading and copying them and as to the authority of some of their judgments.

[24] The Devil. See Qur. 2:32, 7:10, 17:63, 18:48, 20:115; *Enc of Islam*, II, 351; al-Bayḍāwī, *Anwār al-Tanzīl*, I, 51; al-Ijī, *al-Mawāqif*, pp. 237 ff.; al-Nawawī (Wüstenfeld), *Uber das Leben*, p. 137; al-Rāzī, *Mafātīh*, I, 297 ff.

[25] These two angels, failing to appreciate the frailties of human beings, were sent to the earth to be tested. See Qur. 2:96; Rodwell, *The Koran*, p. 348n; *Enc. of Islam*, II, 272; III, 190 ff.

[26] See Ibn Qutayba, *Kitāb al-Ma'ārif*, pp. 27 f.; al-Faḍālī, *Kifāyat al-'Awāmm* (commentary of al-Bayjūrī), p. 54; Hughes, *Dict. of Islam*, pp. 440 ff.

[27] See al-Bukhārī, *al-Ṣaḥīh*, III, 193; Muslim, *al-Ṣaḥīh*, I, 299 f.

[28] Cf. Qur. 61:9; Muslim, *al-Ṣaḥīh*, I, 71.

Chapter 15

THE ASCENSION OF THE PROPHET AND MIRACLES

The Ascension of the Messenger, while awake, in his person to heaven and thence to whatsoever exalted place Allah willed is a Reality.

The Graces of the Walīs are a Reality. The Grace appears on behalf of the Walī by way of contradicting the customary way of things, such as covering a great distance in a short time, and the appearance of food and drink and clothing at the time of need, and walking on the water and in the air, and such as the speaking of inanimate solid objects and of animals, and the warding off of an approaching calamity, and the protection from enemies of him who is anxious, and other things of the same kind. And such a thing is reckoned as an evidentiary miracle on behalf of the Messenger to one of whose people this act appears, because it is evident from it that he is a Walī, and he could never be a Walī unless he were right in his religion; and his religion is the confession of the message of the Messenger.

The Ascension (*al-miʿrāj*) [1] of the Messenger, while awake, in his person to heaven (*al-samāʾ*) and thence to whatsoever exalted place Allah willed is a Reality/It is established by so well-known a tradition that he who denies it is an innovator (*mubtadiʿ*). The denial of it and the claim that it is impossible are based on the fundamental position of the Philosophers; otherwise it is permissible of heavenly things that there be an infringement of custom and a compliance with it. All bodies are similar to each other so it is sound to say of one body what it is sound to say of all. Allah is powerful to perform all possible things.

Al-Nasafī's statement "while awake" (*fī 'l-yaqẓa*) alludes to the refutation of the one who asserts that the Ascension was in sleep, which is in ac-

[1] Cf. *Enc. of Islam*, III, 505 ff.; al-Bukhārī, *al-Ṣaḥīḥ*, I, 99; Muslim, *al-Ṣaḥīḥ*, I, 76 f., 83 f.; Ibn Hishām, *Sīrat Rasūl Allāh*, pp. 263 ff.; Wensinck, *Handbook*, p. 25.

cordance with a tradition from Mu'āwiya, who when asked about the Ascension said, "It was a proper vision" (*ru'ya ṣāliḥa*).[2] And there is a tradition from 'Ā'isha who said, "The body of Muhammad was not absent the night of the Ascension." And Allah has said,[3] "We have made the vision which we showed thee only as a testing for mankind" (Qur'ān 17:62). Answer is made to this that the meaning here is vision through the eye, and that his body was not deprived of his spirit (*rūḥ*), but was along with the spirit, so the Ascension was both by spirit and body. Al-Nasafī's use of the term "in his person" (*bi shakhṣihi*) is an allusion to the refutation of the one who says that it was of the spirit only. [*139*] It is clear however that the Ascension in sleep or in spirit is not something to be denied absolutely. The Unbelievers denied the matter of the Ascension entirely, yea many Muslims apostatized on account of it. His use of the term "to heaven" is an allusion to the refutation of the one who asserts that the Ascension made by Muhammad while awake was only to the House of the Holy Place (*bayt al-maqdis*) as recorded in the Book. And the term "then to whatsoever place Allah willed" is a reference to the different statements of the Fathers, some saying, "to the Garden," others, "to the Throne" (*al-'arsh*), others, "above the Throne," and still others, "to the edge of the world." The night journey (*al-isrā'*)[4] which was from the Sacred Mosque (*al-masjid al-ḥarām*) to the House of the Holy Place is an absolute fact established by the Book. The Ascension from earth to heaven is a well-known tradition; and from heaven to the Garden, or the Throne, or wheresoever it was, is [a tradition based] on individuals. But the sound position is that Muhammad saw his Lord with his heart (*fu'ād*) and not with his eyes.[5]

The Graces (*al-karāmāt*)[6] of the Walīs (*al-awliyā'*)[7] are a Reality/The Walī is the one who knows (*al-'ārif*) Allah and His attributes, insofar as it is pos-

---

[2] Cf. *Dict. of Tech. Terms*, pp. 600 f.

[3] Al-Bayḍāwī (*Anwār al-Tanzīl*, I, 544) says that the reference here is to the Ascension, although some say that it refers to an incident in the Battle of Badr.

[4] See Qur. 17:1 and the references to the *mi'rāj* above.

[5] A.J. (p. 194) maintains as the correct doctrine that Muhammad saw his Lord with his eye (*bi 'aynihi*). I.D. (p. 138 f.) favors the position that his heart was given the sense of sight and that it was with the heart that he saw Him. Both appeal to tradition from Ibn 'Abbās.

[6] These are "wonders by the divine grace." They seem related to the Χαρίσματα of I Cor. 12:9. See Macdonald, *Development*, p. 174; Goldziher, *Muhammadanische Studien*, II, 373 f. Acts that contradict (*kharaqa*—pierce) the customary way have been listed as follows: (1) *mu'jiza* which proceeds from a true prophet when claiming the prophetic office, (2) *irhāṣ* which appears at the hands of a prophet before he is described as one, (3) *karāma* which comes from a *walī*, (4) *ma'ūna* which proceeds from any one

sible, who perseveres in acts of obedience, who shuns acts of disobedience, and who avoids being engrossed in the pleasures and appetites of the world. The Grace which belongs to him is the appearance of something that annuls the customary way of things on his behalf, but which is not in any way connected with a claim to the prophetic office. Such an act which is not accompanied by Belief and good works is only a deception (*istidrāj*), and that which is accompanied by the claim to the prophetic office is an evidentiary miracle (*mu'jiza*). The proof for the real existence of the Grace is that so much has come down by *tawātur* from many of the Companions and those [who came] after them that denial of it is impossible, especially when the matter is something that is common even though the details are [based on the testimony of] individuals. The Book also speaks of the manifestation of Graces on behalf of Maryam and the friend of Sulaymān. Having once established their occurrence there is little need to prove the possibility of them.

Al-Nasafī next introduced a statement which refers to the explanation of a Grace, and to the details of some of the very strange particulars regarding Graces. He said,

The Grace appears on behalf of the Walī by way of contradicting (*naqḍ*) the customary way of things, such as covering a great distance in a short time/as when the friend of Sulaymān,[8] namely Āṣaf b. Barakhyā according to the most noted traditions, brought the throne of Bilqīs before the twinkling of an eye although it was a great distance off.

and the appearance of food and drink and clothing at the time of need/ as in the case of Maryam,[9] for Allah says, "Whenever Zakarīyā went in to

---

of the generality of Believers, (5) *istidrāj* which is performed by an evildoer, (6) *ihāna* which proceeds from a false prophet making a claim to the prophetic office. The stock example of *ihāna* is Musaylama's attempt to give a one-eyed man another eye, which ended in his good eye being taken. See al-Faḍālī, *Kifāyat al-'Awāmm* (commentary of al-Bayjūrī), p. 69; 'I.D. (and al-Khayālī), p. 139; A.J., p. 194. Cf. for the general discussion of miracles al-Rāzī, *Muḥaṣṣal*, p. 151 ff., *Mafātīḥ*, II, 460 ff.; Wensinck, *The Muslim Creed*, pp. 224 ff.: al-Shahrastānī, *Nihāyatu 'l-Iqdām*, pp. 497 f.; al-Ījī, *al-Mawāqif*, p. 243; al-Sanūsī, *Umm al-Barāhin*, p. 236; *Enc. of Islam*, II, 744; *Dict. of Tech. Terms*, pp. 444 ff.; M. Abdou, *Rissalat al-Tawhid*, pp. 58 f.

[7] The *Walī* is "one to whom the real essence of things is unveiled, but who is not engaged in the improvement of creatures as is the prophet" (al-Ghazzālī, *Iḥyā'*, VII. 262 f.). Cf. Macdonald, *Rel. Attitude and Life in Islam*, pp. 271 ff.; *Dict. of Tech. Terms*. pp. 1528 ff.

[8] See Qur. 27:40 and al-Bayḍāwī, *Anwār al-Tanzīl*, II, 69; al-Tha'labī, *Qiṣaṣ al-Anbiyā'*, pp. 271 f.; al-Ṭabarī, *Annales*, I, 576. As intimated by al-Taftāzānī, not all the accounts agree that Āṣaf b. Barakhyā was the messenger sent by Sulaymān.

[9] See al-Bayḍāwī, *Anwār al-Tanzīl*, I, 153; al-Tha'labī, *Qiṣaṣ al-Anbiyā'*, p. 328.

her at the sanctuary (*al-miḥrāb*) he found that she had sustenance. He said, 'O Maryam, how dost thou get this?' She replied, 'It is from Allah' " (Qur'ān 3:32).

and walking on the water/as is related of many of the Walīs

and in the air/as is related of Ja'far b. Abū Ṭālib [10] and Luqmān al-Sarakhsī [11] and others.

and such as the speaking of inanimate solid objects and of animals,[12] and the warding off of an approaching calamity, and the protection from enemies of him who is anxious/As for speaking of inanimate solid objects, there is the tradition of Sulaymān and Abū 'l-Dardā' [13]—Allah be well pleased with them both—who had in front of them a bowl [14] which praised [Allah] and both of them heard it praising; and as for the speaking of animals there is the matter of the dog [15] addressing the Companions of the Cave (*al-kahf*). There is also the tradition of the Prophet [*140*] that he said, "There was a man among us driving a cow [16] which he used for bearing burdens. Lo, it turned to him and said, 'I was not created for this but for plowing.' " The people said, "Allah be praised! Does a cow speak?" The Prophet replied, "I have believed it."

and other things of the same kind/such as 'Umar's seeing [17] his army at Nihāwand, while on the pulpit at al-Madīna, so that he spoke to the commander of his army saying, "O Sāriya, the mountain, the mountain," in order to warn him of the stratagem of the enemy there behind the mountain; and such as Sāriya's hearing his speech in spite of the distance; and like

[10] See al-Nawawī (Wüstenfeld), *Ueber das Leben*, pp. 193 f.

[11] See al-Hujwirī, *Kashf al-Maḥjūb*, translated by Nicholson (London, 1911), p. 188.

[12] The text of 'I.D. puts the rest of the sentence in al-Taftāzānī's commentary. A.J. (p. 195) gives the reading followed.

[13] Abū 'l-Dardā' (d. A.H. 32) was a Companion from al-Khazraj, *Enc. of Islam*, I, p. 82; Ibn Qutayba, *Kitāb al-Ma'ārif*, p. 137; Ibn Ḥajar, *Biographical Dictionary*, III, 89 f.

[14] A.J. (p. 195) says that the story of the "bowl" is given by al-Bayhaqī in "The Indications of Prophecy" (*Dalā'il al-Nubūwa*) (Brockelmann, *Geschichte*, I, 363).

[15] The dog followed the men and when the men of the Cave tried to drive it away, Allah gave it speech. It said, "I am the most beloved of the loved of Allah, so sleep and I shall guard you." See Qur. 18:17; al-Bayḍāwī, *Anwār al-Tanzīl*, I, 557; al-Ṭabarī, *Annales*, I, 775 ff.; al-Tha'labī, *Qiṣaṣ al-Anbiyā'*, pp. 361 ff.

[16] Al-Bukhārī, *al-Ṣaḥīḥ*, II, 68 and 376; cf. *Musnad*, II, 245, 246, 382, 502.

[17] Ibn Qutayba (*Kitāb al-Ma'ārif*, p. 152) says that the commander at Nihāwand was al-Nu'mān b. Muqarrin. The story as given by al-Taftāzānī is to be found in al-Suyūṭī's *Tarīkh al-Khulafā'*, pp. 124 f. and al-Ghazzālī's *Iḥyā'*, VII, 260.

Khālid's drinking poison [18] without being injured; and like the Nile's flowing [19] on receipt of the letter from 'Umar. There are examples like these which are more than can be numbered.

Since the Mu'tazilites, who deny the Graces of the Walīs, deduced proof that the manifestation of acts which annul the customary way of things, were they permitted to Walīs, would be confused with evidentiary miracles and the prophet in no way would be distinguished from the non-prophet, al-Nasafī alluded to the answer which is made to them by saying,

And such a thing is reckoned as/that is to say, the manifestation of acts that annul the customary way **on behalf of Walīs** [in general] or an individual Walī who is one of a certain people

an evidentiary miracle on behalf of the Messenger to one of whose people this act appears because it is evident from it/that is, from this Grace

that he is a Walī, and he could never be a Walī unless he were right [20] **in his religion; and his religion is the confession**/by the tongue and assent by the heart

of the message of the Messenger/accompanied by obedience to him with respect to his commands and prohibitions, so that even if the Walī claimed to be independent and not a follower, he would not be a Walī and the act would not be manifested at his hands.

The outcome is that something which annuls the customary way is an evidentiary miracle when in any way related to a prophet, whether it appears on his behalf or on behalf of individuals of his people, but when related to a Walī it is a Grace because he is free of any claim to the prophetic office of the one on whose behalf it was manifested. The prophet must know that he is a prophet, he must purpose to manifest those things that annul the customary way, and he must give absolute judgment as to the necessity of evidentiary miracles; [all of which is] in contrast to the Walī.

[18] See Ibn Ḥajar, *Biographical Dictionary*, I, 852.

[19] See al-Suyūṭī, *Tarīkh al-Khulafā'*, pp. 125 f.; Muir's *Caliphate*, pp. 165 f.

[20] The text of A.J. (p. 195) inserts a comment as from al-Taftāzānī, "that is, assenting to the Reality."

Chapter 16

THE KHALIFATE AND IMAMATE

The most excellent of mankind after our Prophet is Abū Bakr, the Very Veracious, then 'Umar the Divider, then 'Uthmān, he of the two lights, then 'Alī the Approved. Their Khalifate was in this order. The Khalifate was for thirty years and then after it [the form of rule was that of] a kingdom and a principality.

The Muslims must have an Imam, who will carry out the administration of their decisions, the maintaining of their restrictive ordinances, the guarding of their frontiers, the equipping of their armies, the receiving of their alms, the subjugation of those who get the upper hand and robbers and highwaymen, the performance of worship on Fridays and Festivals, the settlement of disputes which take place among creatures, the receiving of evidence based on legal rights, the giving in marriage young men and maidens who have no guardians, and the division of the booty.

Then the Imam must be visible, neither hidden nor expected, and he must be of the tribe of Quraysh and not of any other. He is not restricted to the Banī Hāshim nor to the children of 'Alī. It is not a stipulation that he should be preserved from error, nor that he should be the most excellent of the people of his time. It is a stipulation that he should be of the people who have free and complete authority, an administrator, able to execute decisions and maintain the limits of the territory of the world of Islam and to give the oppressed equity against the oppressor. The Imam is not to be removed for evil-doing or tyranny.

The most excellent of mankind after our Prophet/It would have been better to say "after the prophets" but he meant "after" in point of time, since there is no prophet after ours. Nevertheless he should have made a special exception of Jesus, since were he to mean all mankind in existence after our Prophet this [statement] would be refuted by [the descent] of Jesus; [*141*] and since if all mankind to be born after our prophet were meant, this stating of a preference would not convey a meaning which includes the Companions; and [1] if all mankind on the face of the earth at that time were meant, then it would not convey a meaning that includes the Followers [of the Companions] and those who came after them. And if the meaning were all people to be found on the face of the earth in general, it would be refuted by the case of Jesus.

is Abū Bakr, the Very Veracious (*al-ṣiddīq*)/who assented to the Prophet's claim to the office without delay and hesitation [2] and to the Ascension without hesitating, also.

then 'Umar the Divider (*al-fārūq*)/who made a distinction between the real and the unsound both in legal cases and quarrels

then 'Uthmān, he of the two lights (*dhū 'l-nūrayn*)/He was so called because the Prophet married his daughter Ruqayya to him and, when she died, he married Umm Kulthūm to him, and when she died, he said, "Had I a third, I would marry you to her."

then 'Alī the Approved (*al-murtaḍā*)/by the creatures of Allah and by the sincerest of the Messenger's Companions. This [is the order in which] we have found [them] according to the Fathers. It is evident that if they did not have some proof for this [order] they would not have so ruled.

However we have found that the proofs given by the two sides of the question are in opposition to each other. But we do not consider it one on which hangs any matter relating to practice, nor does hesitation to commit one's self about the matter cause any confusion regarding the duties incumbent [on Muslims towards either of the two parties]. It appears that the Fathers were hesitant about preferring 'Uthmān to 'Alī—Allah approve of them both—since they made one of the signs of the Approved Way and the Community the preference of the two *Shaykhs* [3] (Abū Bakr and 'Umar) and the love of the *Khatans* [4] ('Uthmān and 'Alī). The impartial position

---

[1] The text of A.J. (p. 196) reads "since" for "and."

[2] The texts of A.J. (p. 196) and al-Kastalī, Constantinople text of A.H. 1310 (p. 178), omit *taraddud*, "hesitation."

[3] For the Shi'ite position, see *al-Bābu 'l-Ḥādī 'Ashar*, pp. 69 f. and *Journal of the American Oriental Society*, XXIX, 137 ff.

[4] *Al-khatan* means any relation on the side of the wife. Here the meaning is evidently "son-in-law." Lane, *Lexicon*, p. 704; *Lisān*, XVI, 295; A.J., p. 196.

to take is that if being more excellent means a greater reward, then hesitation to commit oneself in the matter has a place; but if it means that 'Uthmān had more of those things which are reckoned as virtues by people who use Reason, then hesitation does not [have a place].

Their Khalifate [5] (*khilāfatuhum*)/that is, their vicegerency (*niyābatuhum*) of the Messenger in maintaining religion so that it is incumbent on all peoples to follow

was [6] in this order/also, that is to say, the Khalifate after the Prophet was to Abū Bakr, then to 'Umar, then to 'Uthmān, and then to 'Alī. This is based on the fact that the Companions, having gathered on the day of the Messenger's death under the shelter of the Banī Sā'ida, settled upon the succession of Abū Bakr [7] to the Khalifate after some discussion and disagreement. They all agreed to this and 'Alī followed him [8] too in the presence of witnesses, after hesitation on his part.[9] If the Khalifate had not been Abū Bakr's right, the Companions would not have agreed to him, [*142*] and 'Alī would have contended with him as he contended with Mu'āwiya [10] and would have argued against them had there been some statute in his favor, as the Shī'ites assert. How is it conceivable that it was right for the Companions of the Messenger to agree on something unsound and fail to act according to the statute which had come down to them?

Then when Abū Bakr felt that his end was near he called 'Uthmān and dictated to him the letter of his appointment of 'Umar.[11] When 'Uthmān had written the paper, he sealed it and took it out to the people and commanded them to swear allegiance to the one whose name was written

---

[5] Cf. Ibn Khaldūn, *Muqaddima*, I, 344 f.; *Enc. of Islam*, II, 881 ff.; al-Ash'arī, *Maqālāt*, pp. 460 ff.; Ibn Ḥazm, *Kitāb al-Fiṣal*, IV, 87 ff.; al-Ījī, *al-Mawāqif*, pp. 296 ff.; *Dict. of Tech. Terms*, p. 92.

[6] The text of A.J. (p. 197) adds "established" and with al-Kastali (p. 179) makes the "also" that follows part of the text of al-Nasafī.

[7] See Ibn Sa'd (Sachau), *Biographien Muhammeds*, III, a, 128 f.; al-Ṭabarī, *Annales*, I, 1815 ff.; Caetani, *Annali dell' Islam*, II, 528; al-Bukhārī, *al-Ṣaḥīḥ*, II, 421; *Musnad*, I, 55 ff.; Muir, *Caliphate*, pp. 1 ff.

[8] The texts of A.J. (p. 197) and al-Kastali (p. 179) read *bāya'ahu*, "he pledged fealty to him," for *tāba'ahu*.

[9] See al-Ṭabarī, *Annales*, I, 1825. Some say 'Alī was not present: A.J., p. 197; *al-Bābu 'l-Ḥādī 'Ashar*, pp. 70 f. Cf. Muir, *Caliphate*, p. 5.

[10] See al-Ṭabarī, *Annales*, I, 3353 ff.; al-Suyūṭī, *Tarīkh al-Khulafā'*, pp. 173 f., 205 ff.; *Enc. of Islam*, III, 617 ff.

[11] See Ibn Sa'd (Sachau), *Biographien Muhammeds*, III, a, 133 f.; al-Suyūṭī. *Tarīkh al-Khulafā'*, p. 79; al-Ṭabarī, *Annales*, I, 2137 ff.; Muir, *Caliphate*, p. 77; Caetani, *Annali dell' Islam*, III, 119 ff.

therein. So they swore allegiance; even 'Alī when the paper passed him said, "We have sworn allegiance to the one mentioned in it, even if it is 'Umar." In general, agreement upon 'Umar's Khalifate occurred. Then when 'Umar died a martyr's death, he left the matter of the Khalifate to a council of six,[12] 'Uthmān, 'Alī, 'Abd al-Raḥmān b. 'Awf, Ṭalḥa, al-Zubayr, and Sa'd b. Abū Waqqāṣ. Then the [other] five committed the matter to 'Abd al-Raḥmān b. 'Awf. They accepted his decision and he chose 'Uthmān and swore allegiance to him in the presence of a group of the Companions. They, then, did likewise and submitted themselves to his commands and prohibitions, and performed worship with him on Fridays and on Festivals. This was by Agreement. Then 'Uthmān died a martyr's death and left the matter [of a successor] undecided. The older men of the Refugees (*al-muhājirūn*) and the Helpers (*al-anṣār*) agreed upon 'Alī[13] and besought him to accept the Khalifate. They swore allegiance to him since he was the most excellent of the people of his time and the most fitting candidate for the Khalifate. The dissensions and conflicts which took place were not because of a quarrel over the question of his Khalifate but because of an error in *ijtihād*. The dissensions which took place between the Shi'ites and the People of the Approved Way on this matter, and how each party claimed statutes to substantiate its position on the Imamate, and the replies that were given on both sides are all mentioned in the more extensive books.

The Khalifate was for thirty years and then after it [the form of rule was that of] a kingdom (*mulk*) and a principality (*imāra*)/[This is based] on a statement of the Prophet, "After me there will be for thirty years a Khalifate, then it will become a tyrannical kingdom."[14] 'Alī having died as a martyr at the beginning of the thirtieth year following the death of the Prophet, Mu'āwiya and those after him are not considered Khalifas but kings and princes. This is a difficult problem, for the People of Loosing and Binding (*ahl al-ḥall wa l-'aqd*)[15] of the Muslim people were agreed on the Khalifate of the 'Abbāsids and some of the Marwānids, such as 'Umar b. 'Abd al-'Azīz,[16] for example. Perhaps the meaning here is rather that the

---

[12] See al-Ṭabarī, *Annales*, I, 2724 ff.; al-Suyūṭī, *Tarīkh al-Khulafā'*, pp. 134 f., 152 f.; T. W. Arnold, *The Caliphate* (Oxford, 1924), pp. 21 ff.; Caetani, *Annali dell' Islam*, V, 48.

[13] See al-Ṭabarī, *Annales*, I, 3066 ff.; *Enc of Islam*, I, 283. For the definition of *ijtihād* see the paragraph on Mujtahid in Chap. 19, below.

[14] See *Musnad*, V, 220 f.; Arnold, *Caliphate*, pp. 107 f., 163; A.J., p. 198.

[15] See al-Māwardī, *al-Aḥkām al-Sulṭānīya*, pp. 7 ff.; *al-Ta'rīfāt*, p. 8.

[16] See al-Ṭabarī, *Annales*, II, 1340 ff.; Ibn Qutayba, *Kitāb al-Ma'ārif*, p. 184; al-Suyūṭī, *Tarīkh al-Khulafā'*, p. 229; al-Nawawī (Wüstenfeld), *Ueber das Leben*, pp. 463 ff.; Muir, *Caliphate*, pp. 369 ff.

perfect Khalifate, in which there is no dross due to difference [of opinion] or inclination away from following [the right Khalīfa], will be for a period of thirty years, and then after it there might be or there might not be a Khalifate.

The position of Agreement is that it is necessary [17] to appoint an Imam. The difference of opinion is on the question whether the appointment must be by Allah or by His creatures, and whether the basis [for appointment] is authority or Reason. The correct position is that the creatures must appoint a Khalīfa on the basis of authority because of the statement of the Prophet,[18] "Whoever dies not having known the Imam of his time, dies the death of the days of Ignorance (al-jāhilīya)." And they must appoint someone, since the people at the time of the Prophet's death made this question the most important matter of consideration, so important in fact that they considered it more important than the matter of his burial, and so also has it been after the death of each Imam. And they must appoint someone for so many legal obligations are dependent on the Imam, as al-Nasafī has indicated in his statement which follows.

The Muslims must have an Imam, who will carry out the administration of their decisions, the maintaining of their restrictive ordinances, the guarding of their frontiers, [*143*] the equipping of their armies, the receiving of their alms, the subjugation of those who get the upper hand and robbers and highwaymen, the performance of worship on Fridays and Festivals, the settlement of disputes which take place among creatures, the receiving of evidence based on legal rights, the giving in marriage of the young men and maidens who have no guardians, and the division of the booty [19]/and things like these [20] with which individuals of the people are not entrusted. And if objection is made, "Why is it not permissible to have sufficient men of power in different districts, and thus do away with the necessity of a general authority over all?" we reply that this only leads to disputes and quarrels which end in disorder both in religious and secular matters, as is to be seen

---

[17] The Khārijites say the Khalifate is permissible, but not necessary. The Imamites and the Isma'ilites say the appointment is of Allah; the orthodox say it is of His creatures on an authoritative basis, the Zaydites and the most of the Mu'tazilites say on a rational basis, al-Jāḥiẓ, al-Ka'bī, and Abū'l-Ḥusayn al-Baṣrī say both (see A.J., p. 198; 'I.D., p. 142). See also Ibn Khaldūn, *Muqaddima*, I, 346 ff.; Macdonald, *Development*, pp. 18 ff.

[18] *Musnad*, IV, 96.

[19] Cf. Ibn Khaldūn, *Muqaddima*, I, 342; al-Māwardī, *al-Aḥkām al-Sulṭānīya* (see Index); al-Rāzī, *Muḥaṣṣal*, pp. 176 ff.; al-Ījī, *al-Mawāqif*, pp. 196 ff.; al-Shahrastānī, *Nihāyatu 'l-Iqdām*, p. 478.

[20] A.J. (p. 198) reads this phrase as part of the text of al-Nasafī.

at the present time. If objection is made that it is sufficient to have a man of power with general authority over all, whether he is called an Imam or not, so that the organization [of rule] would be very much like the days of the Turks, we reply, "Yes, there would be a sort of order in secular affairs, but the religious affairs which are more important and which are the great mainstay of the state would be in disorder."

If objection is made that since the period of the Khalifate was thirty years, then the time subsequent to the rightly guided Khalīfas (*al-khulafā' al-rāshidūn*) is devoid of the Imam and the whole of the Muslim people are thus disobedient and when they die, they die as in the days of Ignorance, we reply that it has already been pointed out that the perfect Khalifate is what is meant. And were it admitted [that the period of the Khalifate was for thirty years only] then perhaps after it the era of the Khalifate ends without the era of the Imamate ending, on the basis that "Imām" is a more general term than "Khalīfa." However, we have not found this technicality of differentiating thus the two terms used by any people except those of the Shī'ites who assert that "Khalīfa" is a more general term. On this basis they speak of the Khalifate of the three Imams, not of their Imamate. But after the 'Abbāsid Khalīfas the matter of the Khalifate is a dubious affair (*mush-kil*).

Then the Imam must be visible/that he may be resorted [21] to, and so that he may perform what is beneficial, to accomplish that for which the office of Imam was established

neither hidden/from the eyes of men out of fear of enemies and the mastery which oppressors have gained

nor expected (*muntaẓar*)/His coming forth will be at the suitable time, at the cutting off of the sources [22] (*mawārid*) of evil and corruption and at the loosening of the rule of tyranny and obstinacy. [That is to say the right position] is unlike that of the Shī'ites who assert—especially the Imamites among them—that after Muhammad the rightful Imam is 'Alī, then his son al-Ḥasan, then his brother al-Ḥusayn, then his son 'Ali Zayn al-'Ābidīn, then his son Muḥammad al-Bāqir, then his son Ja'far al-Ṣādiq, then his son Mūsā al-Kāẓim, then his son 'Alī al-Riḍā, then his son Muḥammad al-Taqī,[23]

---

[21] A.J. (p. 199) reads this phrase as part of the text of al-Nasafi.
[22] The texts of A.J. (p. 199 f.) and al-Kastalī (p. 182) read *mawādd*, "materials."
[23] Cf. *al-Bābu 'l-Ḥādī 'Ashar*, p. 78, which reads al-Jawād for al-Taqī, and al-Hādī for

then his son 'Alī al-Naqī, then his son al-Ḥasan al-'Askarī, then his son Muḥammad al-Qā'im, the expected one, the Mahdī,[24] who has hidden himself out of fear of his enemies. [They believe also that] he will appear and fill the world with equity and justice just as it has been filled with injustice and oppression. Nothing shall prevent his length of years and the prolonging of his days. He will be like Jesus and al-Khaḍir [25] and others in this respect. You [O reader] are well aware that the hiding and the non-existence of the Imam are alike in failing to attain the purpose to be sought in the existence of the Imam, and that his fear of enemies should not require his hiding, since nothing but the name now exists; rather the end of the whole matter is that fear does require him to hide his claim to the Imamate, just as in the case [144] of his ancestors who appeared among men but did not claim the office. Moreover when times are corrupt and there are differences of opinion and tyrants reign, the people's need for an Imam is just that much stronger and their submission to him is just that much easier.

and he must be of the tribe of Quraysh, and not of any other. He is not restricted to the Banī Hāshim nor to the children of 'Alī [26]/This means that it is stipulated that the Imam be of Quraysh, because of the saying of the Prophet, "The Imams are of Quraysh." [27] This is correct although it is an individual narrative. However, when Abū Bakr related it, adducing it as evidence to the Helpers (al-anṣār), no one contradicted him, and it thus became agreed upon. No party has dissented except the Kharijites and some of the Mu'tazilites. There is no stipulation, however, that the Imam must be a Hāshimite or an 'Alid, from what has already been established by proof regarding the Khalifate of Abū Bakr, 'Umar and 'Uthmān who were of Quraysh although they were not of Banī Hāshim. The name Quraysh is applied to the children of al-Naḍr b. Kināna, while Hāshim was

---

al-Naqī and Ṣāḥib al-Zamān for al-Mahdī. See also *Enc. of Islam*, III, 111 f.; Ibn Khaldūn, *Muqaddima*, I, 363 f.; A.J., p. 199.

[24] The doctrine of the coming of al-Mahdī, the Guided One, is not confined to Shi'ite Islam although that of the expected Imam is. See *Enc. of Islam*, III, 111 f.; *Enc. of Religion and Ethics*, VIII, 336 ff.; *Jour. Am. Or. Soc.*, XXIX, 52 ff.; *al-Bābu 'l-Hādī 'Ashar*, pp. 80 f.

[25] See *Enc. of Islam*, II, 861 f.; Muslim, *al-Ṣaḥīḥ*, II, 311; *Lisān*, V, 332; Ibn Ḥajar, *Biographical Dictionary*, I, 882 ff.; al-Tha'labī, *Qiṣaṣ*, pp. 189 ff.; *Enc. of Religion and Ethics*, VII, 693 f.

[26] Here I have adopted the reading of A.J. (p. 198 "nor the children of 'Alī") who makes this phrase a part of al-Nasafī's text. I.D. reads it as a part of the commentary.

[27] See Arnold, *Caliphate*, p. 47; al-Bukhārī, *al-Ṣaḥīḥ*, IV, 407; Muslim, *al-Ṣaḥīḥ*, II, 107 f.; *Musnad*, III, 129, 183; IV, 421. The Khārijites quoted traditions to contradict it. See al-Bukhārī, *al-Ṣaḥīḥ*, I, 181 f.

the father of 'Abd al-Muṭṭalib, the grandfather of the Messenger of Allah, for he was Muḥammad b. 'Abd Allah b. 'Abd al-Muṭṭalib b. Hāshim b. 'Abd Manāf b. Quṣayy b. Kilāb b. Murra b. Ka'b b. Lu'ayy b. Ghālib b. Fihr b. Mālik b. al-Naḍr b. Kināna b. Khuzayma b. Mudrika b. al-Yās b. Muḍar b. Nizār b. Ma'add b. 'Adnān.[28]

The 'Alids and the 'Abbāsids are of the Banī Hāshim, for al-'Abbās and Abū Ṭālib were sons of 'Abd al-Muṭṭalib. Abū Bakr [29] was from Quraysh, for he was the son of Abū Quḥāfa, 'Uthmān b. 'Āmir b. 'Amr b. Ka'b b. Lu'ayy, and so also was 'Umar,[30] for he was the son of al-Khaṭṭāb b. Nufayl b. 'Abd al-'Uzzā b. Ribāḥ b. 'Abd Allah b. Qurṭ b. Rizāḥ b. 'Addī b. Ka'b. And so also was 'Uthmān,[31] for he was the son of 'Affān b. Abū l-'Āṣ b. Umayya b. 'Abd Shams b. 'Abd Manāf.

It is not a stipulation/of the Imam

that he should be preserved from error (*ma'ṣūm*) [32]/We have already seen that there is proof of Abū Bakr's Imamate, in spite of the lack of absolute certainty as to his being preserved from error. Furthermore, the stipulation is the thing here that needs proof, whereas the lack of proof for the stipulation is sufficient to show that the stipulation is lacking. The one who differs from this position adduces as an argument the saying of Allah, "My covenant does not apply to wrong-doers (*al-ẓālimīn*)" (Qur'ān 2:118). Therefore the one who differs says that he who is not preserved from error is a wrong-doer, so the covenant of the Imamate does not apply to him. The answer is to preclude this, for a wrong-doer is one who commits an act of disobedience which brings to pass the downfall of justice, without there being any repentance for the act, or reformation. The one who is not preserved from error is not necessarily a wrong-doer.

The real fact about this matter of preservation from error (*al-'iṣma*) is that Allah does not create a sin (*al-dhanb*) in the creature while his power

---

[28] Cf. Ibn Hishām, *Sīrat Rasūl Allāh*, p. 3; Ibn Qutayba, *Kitāb al-Ma'ārif*, pp. 32 ff.; Ibn Sa'd (Sachau), *Biog. Muhammeds*, I, 1, 28.

[29] Cf. Ibn Hishām, *Sīrat Rasūl Allāh*, p. 161; al-Nawawī (Wüstenfeld), *Ueber das Leben*, p. 656; Ibn Ḥajar, *Biog. Dict.*, II, 328; Ibn Sa'd (Sachau), *Biog. Muhammeds*, III, 1, 119; Ibn Qutayba, *Kitāb al-Ma'ārif*, p. 83. There are slight variations in Abū Bakr's genealogy as given in some of these.

[30] Al-Nawawī (Wüstenfeld), *Ueber das Leben*, p. 447 and Ibn Sa'd (Sachau), *Biog. Muhammeds*, III, 1, 190 say clearly that Rabāḥ in 'Umar's genealogy is Riyāḥ.

[31] See also al-Nawawī (Wüstenfeld), *Ueber das Leben*, p. 409; Ibn Sa'd (Sachau), *Biog. Muhammeds*, III, 1, 36.

[32] The Shi'ites hold that the Imam is *ma'ṣūm*. See *al-Bābu 'l-Hādī 'Ashar*, p. 66.

and choice remain. This is the meaning of the saying, "It [that is, *al-'iṣma*] is a favor (*luṭf*) of Allah which leads him on to do good and restrains him from doing evil, although the power of choice remains in order to verify the reality [*145*] of trial." For this reason al-Shaykh Abū Manṣūr al-Māturīdī said, "Preservation from error does not remove testing (*al-miḥna*)." From this there appears the invalidity of the statement of the one who says that this preservation from error is a special characteristic of the soul of a person or his body, on account of which characteristic no sin is able to proceed from him. How could this be? If the sin were impossible it would not be sound for him to be made responsible for forsaking sin, nor would he be rewarded for so doing.

nor that he should be the most excellent [33] **of the people of his time** [34] /for the one who is equal [to the most excellent] in virtue and even less fit as to knowledge and practice may be more experienced in the things of the Imamate that are conducive to good and evil, and more able to perform the necessary duties, especially whenever the appointment of the less excellent is better for warding off evil and removing the outbreak of sedition. For this reason 'Umar made the Imamate a matter for consultation (*shūra*) among six persons, along with the certain fact that some of them were more excellent than others. If someone asks, "How can it be sound to make the Imamate a matter for consultation among six persons, since it is not permissible to appoint two Imams [35] at one time?" we answer that the thing which is not permissible is to appoint two independent Imams, both of whom must be obeyed separately, since compliance with mutually opposing decisions follows the appointing of two independent Imams. But in consultation all of them took the place of one Imam.

It is a stipulation that he should be of the people who have free and complete authority [36] /that is, a free, intelligent, male Muslim who is mature, since Allah has not made a way for the Unbelievers over the Believers (see Qur'ān 4:140). The slave is busy in the service of his master, despised in the

---

[33] The texts of al-Kastalī (p. 185) and A.J. (p. 200) read "More excellent than."

[34] The Shī'ite position requires the Imam to be the most excellent man of his time (*al-Bābu 'l-Ḥādī 'Ashar*, p. 69).

[35] There is an interesting tradition suggesting that one of two contemporaneous Imams should be killed. See Muslim, *al-Ṣaḥīḥ*, II, 118.

[36] Cf. Ibn Khaldūn, *Muqaddima*, I, 349; al-Ījī, *al-Mawāqif*, pp. 301 ff.; al-Māwardī, *al-Aḥkām al-Sulṭāniya*, pp. 5 ff.; al-Ghazzālī, *Iḥyā'* (commentary of Sayyid Murtaḍā), II, 230 ff.; al-Shahrastānī, *Nihāyatu 'l-Iqdām*, p. 496.

eyes of the people; women are deficient in Reason and religion; and a boy
and a demented man are wanting [in ability] for the regulation of affairs
and the management of the common welfare.

an administrator/that is, in possessing management over the affairs of Muslims by the force of his opinion and by his deliberation and the aid of his
boldness and might

able/by his knowledge, justice, competence and courage

to execute decisions and maintain the limits (*ḥudūd*) **of the territory of the
world of Islam** (*dār al-Islām*) **and to give the oppressed equity against the
oppressor**/since failure in these matters falls short of the purpose of establishing an Imam.

The Imam is not to be removed for evil-doing [37]/that is, for departing from
obedience to Allah

or tyranny (*al-jawr*)/that is, the oppression of Allah's creatures. This is so, for
evil-doing has appeared and tyranny has spread among Imams and com-
manders after the time of the rightly-guided Khalīfas [Abū Bakr, 'Umar,
'Uthmān, and 'Alī]. The Fathers were accustomed to submit to such [Imams
and commanders] and to perform worship on Fridays and Festivals with
their permission, without thinking of rebelling against them. This is [also
true] because preservation from error is not a stipulation for the Imam on
assuming office, so how much more would it not be for continuing [him in
office]!

According to al-Shāfi'ī the Imam may be removed on the grounds of
evil-doing and tyranny, and in like manner any judge (*qāḍī*) or commander [may be removed]. The basis for this view is that the evil-doer according to al-Shāfi'ī is not a person of authority (*min ahl al-wilāya*), for
since he does not look after himself, how can he look after others? According
to Abū Ḥanīfa an evil-doer is a person of authority even to the extent
[*146*] that it is valid for an evil-doer who is a father to give in marriage his
daughter who is a minor. That which is written down in the books of the
Shāfi'ites permits the removal of a judge for evil-doing, but not an Imam, the

[37] This was the Murji'ite position. See Macdonald, *Development*, pp. 122 ff.; Goldziher,
Vorlesungen, pp. 87 ff.; *Enc. of Islam*, III, 734.

difference being that in the removal of the Imam and the appointment of another there is occasion for stirring up sedition, since he possesses power which the judge does not.

In the book *al-Nawādir* [38] it is stated that the three Learned Ones say that the judging of an evil-doer is not permissible. Some of the Early Theologians say that a man being an evil-doer may be invested [with the office of judge], but if, after being invested with the office as an upright man, he does evil he may be removed because the one who invested him with the office depended on his being upright, and he would not be pleased that he should act as a judge devoid of uprightness. Qāḍī Khān in his *Fatāwī* [39] says that all are agreed that whenever a judge is bribed, his decision on the matter in which he was bribed should not be enforced. And whenever a judge procures the position of judge by bribery he should not become a judge, and if he should make a decision it should not be enforced.

[38] This may be the book by Muḥammad b. ʿAlī al-Tirmidhī. See Brockelmann, *Geschichte*, I, 164.

[39] Qāḍī Khān, a Ḥanafī mufti and scholar. His *Fatāwī*, in four volumes, is a widely known work. See *Enc. of Islam*, II, 608; Brockelmann, *Geschichte*, I, 376.

Chapter 17

VARIOUS ARTICLES OF BELIEF CONCERNING WORSHIP, THE COMPANIONS OF THE PROPHET, THE WIPING ON THE INNER SHOES, AND NABIDH

Worship is allowable behind anyone [acting as Imam], whether righteous or immoral; and worship is to be performed for anyone whether righteous or immoral.

Only the good concerning the Companions should be mentioned of them. We bear witness that in the Garden are the ten Blessed to whom the Prophet announced the glad tidings.

We approve the wiping on the two inner shoes on a journey and at one's abode.

We do not prohibit as unlawful the *nabīdh* of dates.

Worship (*al-ṣalā*) is allowable behind anyone [acting as Imam], whether righteous (*barr*) or immoral (*fājir*) [1]/[This is based] on the statement of the Prophet, "Worship behind anyone whether righteous or immoral," [2] and also on the fact that the Learned of the Muslim people were accustomed to worship behind evil-doers, people of personal desires, and the innovator without [there being any] disapprobation. With regard to what has been reported from some of the Fathers concerning the prohibition of worship behind an evil-doer or an innovator, its purport is that such an act is to be disapproved, since there is no actual statement about the disapproval of

---

[1] Most of the Mu'tazilites did not permit worship behind an immoral person, according to al-Ash'arī. *Maqālāt*, pp. 450 f. Cf. Ibn Ḥazm, *Kitāb al-Fiṣal*, IV, 176 f.

[2] Al-Ghazzālī (*Iḥyā'*, III, 171 ff., tr. in Calverley, *Worship in Islam*, p. 136) quotes a saying from Sufyān who said, "Worship behind every one, just or unjust, except one addicted to wine, one notorious for transgression, one disobedient to parents, one with an innovation, or one who is a runaway slave." Cf. al-Ghazzālī, *al-Wajīz* (Cairo, A.H. 1317), p. 55; al-Māwardī, *al-Aḥkām al-Sulṭāniya*, p. 175; al-Bukhāri, *al-Ṣaḥīḥ*, I, 181 f.; Goldsack; *Muḥammadan Traditions*, p. 49.

worship behind an evil-doer or an innovator. This [is the case] if evil-doing and innovation do not reach the point of Unbelief, but if they do, then there is no question about the impropriety of worship behind them [in that case].

Although the Mu'tazilites make the evil-doer something other than a Believer, yet they permit worship behind him, since they stipulate for the Imam an absence of Unbelief and not the presence of Belief, meaning [by Belief] assent, confession, and good works, all taken together.

and worship is to be performed for anyone whether righteous or immoral/ whenever he dies in Belief. This is on the basis of Agreement and the statement of the Prophet, "Do not fail to perform worship for anyone of the People of the *qibla* who dies." [3] It may be objected that such questions as these are of the details of *fiqh* and have no place in the fundamentals of *kalām;* and that if al-Nasafī means by this statement that a conviction regarding the reality of this doctrine is [one of the] necessary [articles of Belief] and of the fundamentals, then all questions of *fiqh* are. To this we reply that when he had completed the explanation of the purposes of the science of *kalām* in investigating the essence [of the Deity], His attributes and His actions, the world to come (*al-ma'ād*),[4] the prophetic office, and the Imamate according to the law of the people of Islam, and the path of the People of the Approved Way and the Community, then he attempted to draw attention to some of the matters by which the People of the Approved Way are distinguished from others who differ from them, such as the Mu'tazilites, or the Shī'ites, or the Philosophers or the Heretics (*al-Malāḥida*) or any others of the people of innovation and personal desires, whether these matters are details of *fiqh* or some particular matters connected with the articles of Belief.

Only the good concerning the Companions should be mentioned of them/ This is on account of their merits which are mentioned in sound traditions, and because it is necessary to refrain from reviling them since the Prophet has said, "Do not vilify my Companions, for if one of you should spend as much as Mount Uḥud in gold he would not attain the standard of one of them, no, not even half of it." [5] He also said, "Honor my Companions, for they are the best of you, and so forth," [6] and, "Allah, Allah, and regarding

[3] Al-Bukhārī, *al-Ṣaḥiḥ*, I, 110 f.; Muslim, *al-Ṣaḥiḥ*, I, 47. Cf. al-Ījī, *al-Mawāqif*, pp. 290 ff.

[4] See Lane, *Lexicon*, p. 2191; al-Rāzī, *Muḥaṣṣal*, p. 163; *al-Bābu 'l-Hādī 'Ashar*, pp. 82 ff.

[5] *Musnad*, III, 54 f.   [6] *Musnad*, I, 26; al-Bukhārī, *al-Ṣaḥiḥ*, III, 416.

my Companions do not make them a target after I am gone, for whoever loves them, with my love loves them, and whoever hates them, with my hatred hates them; and whoever harms them has harmed me, and whoever harms me has harmed Allah, and whoever has harmed Allah is about to be taken by Allah." [7]

There are sound traditions regarding the merits of Abū Bakr, 'Umar, 'Uthmān, 'Alī, al-Ḥasan, al-Ḥusayn and others of the important Companions. As for the disputes and conflicts which occurred among them, there are reasons and interpretations for these. Then as to vilifying and reviling them, this is Unbelief if it contradicts the absolute proofs [147] such as in the case of defaming of 'Ā'isha; [8] otherwise it is an innovation and evil-doing. In general there is no basis in what has been reported from the Fathers, who were Mujtahids and from the Learned who were of good repute, for permitting a curse on Mu'āwiya and his Allies; for the aim of their affair was rebellion and secession from obedience to the real Imam, and this does not require that they be cursed. However, they [that is, the Fathers and the Learned] differed so about Yazīd b. Mu'āwiya [9] [whether cursing him was permissible or not] that it was stated in *al-Khulāṣa* [10] and other books that it was not fitting to curse him nor al-Ḥajjāj,[11] since the Prophet prohibited the cursing of those who performed worship and who are of the people of the *qibla*. As for that which has been reported about the Prophet's cursing some of the people of the *qibla,* that was because he knew things about the affairs of men which no one else knew. Some pronounced a curse on Yazīd because he became an Unbeliever when he ordered the murder of al-Ḥusayn. They agreed to permit the cursing of those who killed al-Ḥusayn, or commanded it, or permitted it, or consented to it. The real fact is that the consent of Yazīd to the killing of al-Ḥusayn, his rejoicing in it, and his contempt for the family of the Prophet are among those things the meaning of which is based on *tawātur* although the details of the incident are from individual traditions.

---

[7] *Musnad,* IV, 87; V, 55, 57, and al-Tirmidhī, *Ṣaḥīḥ,* "al-Manāqib," b. 58.

[8] See Margoliouth, *Mohammed.* pp. 340 ff.; Muir, *Life of Mohammed,* pp. 298 ff.; al-Bukhārī, *al-Ṣaḥīḥ,* II, 153 ff.; *Musnad,* VI, 59 ff.; Muslim, *al-Ṣaḥīḥ,* II, 455 ff.; al-Bayḍāwī. *Anwār al-Tanzīl,* II, 16; Ibn Hishām, *Sīrat Rasūl Allāh,* 731 ff.; al-Ṭabarī, *Annales,* I, 1517 ff.; *Enc. of Islam,* I, 216.

[9] See al-Ṭabarī, *Annales,* II, 272 ff.; Ibn Qutayba, *Kitāb al-Ma'ārif,* p. 178; al-Suyūṭī, *Tarīkh al-Khulafā',* pp. 205 ff.; Henri Lammens, *Le Califat de Yazid Ier* (Beyrouth, 1921), pp. 132 ff.; Goldziher, *Muh. Studien,* II, 97.

[10] This is probably *Khulāṣat al-Aḥkām,* etc., by al-Nawawī. See Brockelmann, *Geschichte,* I, 396.

[11] See al-Ṭabarī, *Annales,* II, 829 ff., 863 ff.; al-Nawawī (Wüstenfeld), *Ueber das Leben,* pp. 198 f.

So then we do not hesitate at all concerning him, rather we do not hesitate [to decide] about his Belief [as to whether he had any or not]—the curse of Allah on him, his Helpers, and his Allies.

We bear witness that in the Garden are the ten Blessed to whom the Prophet announced the glad tidings/of the Garden,[12] inasmuch as the Prophet said, "Abū Bakr is in the Garden, 'Umar is in the Garden, 'Uthmān is in the Garden, 'Alī is in the Garden, Ṭalḥa is in the Garden, al-Zubayr is in the Garden, 'Abd al-Raḥmān b. 'Awf is in the Garden, Sa'd b. Abū Waqqāṣ is in the Garden, Sa'īd b. Zayd is in the Garden, Abū 'Ubayda b. al-Jarrāḥ is in the Garden.[18] We also bear witness that Fāṭima and al-Ḥasan and al-Ḥusayn are in the Garden because of what is related in sound tradition; that Fāṭima is the mistress [14] of the women who dwell in the Garden, and that al-Ḥasan and al-Ḥusayn are the two masters [15] of the youths who dwell in the Garden. The remainder of the Companions are only remembered for their good; more is to be hoped for them than for any other Believers. We do not bear witness that any [special] individual in himself is in the Garden or in the Fire, but we bear witness that the Believers are of the people of the Garden and the Unbelievers are of the people of the Fire.

We approve the wiping on the two inner shoes (al-khuffayn) [16] on a journey and at one's abode [17]/Although this is an addition to the Book, yet it is established by a well-known narrative. 'Alī b. Abū Ṭālib, when asked about the wiping on the inner boots, replied, "The Messenger of Allah made the period three days and nights for the traveler and a day and a night for the dweller." [18] Abū Bakr relates that the Messenger of Allah sanctioned the wiping on the inner shoes three days and nights for the traveler and a day

---

[12] Cureton, p. 5, and al-Kastalī, p. 188, make "of the Garden" part of the text of al-Nasafī.

[18] The names are not always in the order given here, nor is the number always ten. See *Musnad*, I, 187 ff.

[14] See *Musnad*, III, 64; V, 391. Traditions given in al-Bukhārī, *al-Ṣaḥīḥ*, IV, 182, and Muslim, *al-Ṣaḥīḥ*, II, 340, say "mistress of the women of the Believers" or "of this religion." See also Ibn Ḥajar, *Biog. Dict.*, IV, 727; *Enc. of Islam*, II, 85 ff.

[15] *Musnad*, III, 3, 62, 64; V, 391, 392; al-Tirmidhī, *Ṣaḥīḥ*, "Manāqib," b. 30. See also Ibn Ḥajar, *Biog. Dict.*, I, 676; al-Nawawī (Wüstenfeld), *Ueber das Leben*, p. 207.

[16] *Al-khuffayn*. See Dozy, *Dictionnaire des vêtements arabes*, pp. 155 ff.

[17] This rite, which permits the wiping of the inner shoes instead of washing the feet in ablutions, was a distinguishing mark between the Sunnites, the Shi'ites, and the Khārijites. Wensinck, *The Muslim Creed*, pp. 158, 219 f.; al-Ghazzālī, *Iḥyā'*, VI, 416 ff.; *idem, al-Wajīz* (Cairo, A.H. 1317), I, 23.

[18] Cf. *Musnad*, I, 133; Muslim, *al-Ṣaḥīḥ*, I, 119 f.

and a night for the dweller, if one has purified himself and then put them on. Al-Ḥasan al-Baṣrī said that he met seventy of the Companions who approved the wiping of the inner shoes. Therefore Abū Ḥanīfa said, "I did not admit the wiping until the proof was as clear to me as the light of day." Al-Karkhī said, "I fear him to be an Unbeliever who does not approve the wiping on the inner boots, for the precedents on this subject have come down in the form of *tawātur*." So in general whoever does not approve the wiping on the inner shoes is one of the people of innovation. It became so distinctive that when Anas b. Mālik was asked who were the People of the Approved Way and the Community, he said, "It means to love the two *shaykhs* [Abū Bakr and 'Umar], not to revile the two *khatans* ['Uthmān and 'Alī], and to wipe on the inner shoes."

We do not prohibit as unlawful the *nabīdh* **of dates** (*al-tamr*) [19]/This means that the dates or the raisins are brewed in water and then put in an earthen vessel, until a stinging taste develops in the brew as in *fuqqāʿ* [a kind of beer]. It seems as though this [*nabīdh*] had been prohibited [20] at the beginning of Islam when jars (*al-jirār*) were the vessels for wines (*al-khumūr*); then it was abrogated. So then the non-prohibition of *nabīdh* is of the rules of the People of the Approved Way and the Community, which is contrary to the position of the Rawāfiḍ. This [judgment] is different from that which has [to do with *nabīdh* that has] become strong and intoxicating. Many of the People of the Approved Way and the Community took the position that little or much of it is prohibited.

[19] A.J., p. 203 reads *al-jurra*, "the jar," instead of *al-tamr*, "the dates." Cureton, p. 5, omits both and reads "al-nabīdh" only.

[20] Muslim, *al-Ṣaḥīḥ*, II, 182; *Musnad*, I, 27, 38, and III, 237.

Chapter 18

VARIOUS ARTICLES OF BELIEF CONCERN-
ING THE RANK OF THE WALI, THE PEOPLE
OF THE INNER MEANING, THE FEELING OF
SECURITY AND DESPAIR, THE DIVINER,
THE NON-EXISTENT, AND PRAYERS
FOR THE DEAD

The Wali does not reach the rank of the prophets.

And the creature does not come to the place where command and prohibition do not apply to him. The statutes are [to be interpreted] according to
their literal meanings, and to turn aside from them to meanings which the
People of the Inner Meaning assert is heresy. The rejection of the statutes
is Unbelief. The making of disobedience lawful is Unbelief, and making
light of disobedience and ridicule of the Law are Unbelief.

And despair of Allah is Unbelief and feeling secure from Allah is Unbelief.

To assent to what a diviner narrates of the Unseen is Unbelief.

The non-existent is not a thing.

And in prayer of the living for the dead and the giving of alms for them
there is advantage for them. Allah answers prayers and supplies needs.

The Wali [1] does not reach the rank of the prophets/for prophets are preserved from error, secure from fear of their latter end, honored by revelation,
and by seeing the Angel [of Revelation, Gabriel], and ordered to convey
judgments and to lead mankind, in addition to possessing the perfections
of Walis. That which has been reported of some of the Karramites, [*148*]
in that they permit a Wali to be more excellent than a prophet, is Unbelief
and error. Certainly this question of whether the rank of prophet is better
than that of Wali [in the same individual] is sometimes reopened after [it

---

[1] See above, Chap. 15, n. 7.

is admitted that] there is decisive proof that the prophet is characterized by both dignities and that he is more excellent than the Walī who is not a prophet.

And the creature does not come to the place/as long as he is rational and mature

where command and prohibition do not apply to him/This is because the manner of address in the imposing of responsibilities is general, and because the Mujtahids are in Agreement on it. Some of the Antinomians (*al-Mubāḥīyūn*) [2] held that whenever the creature reached the limit of love and his heart was pure, and he chose Belief instead of Unbelief without hypocrisy, then command and prohibition did not apply to him and Allah would not make him enter the Fire for committing great sins. And some said that outward forms of service such as worship, fasting, the poor rate, and the pilgrimage [3] do not apply to him, but rather his service is meditation (*al-tafakkur*). This is Unbelief and Error, for the most perfect of people in love of Allah are the prophets, especially the Beloved of Allah, and yet the imposing of responsibilities in their case was more complete and more perfect. As for the saying of the Prophet, "Whenever Allah loves a creature no sin shall harm him," it means that He has preserved him from sins, nor has He visited him with the harm of them.

The statutes/of the Qur'ān and the Sunna

are [to be interpreted] according to their literal meanings/unless a decisive proof sets them aside, as in case of the verses the literal meaning of which refers to a direction or to corporeality [4] [on the part of the Deity] and the like. One does not say that these [literal meanings] [5] are not of the statute but rather that the statute is equivocal (*mutashābih*).[6] For we say that the

---

[2] See al-Baghdādī, *al-Farq bayn al-Firaq*, pp. 251 f.

[3] An example of this attitude is that of Abū Saʿīd b. Abū 'l-Khayr regarding the non-necessity of the Pilgrimage. R. A. Nicholson, *Studies in Islamic Mysticism* (Cambridge, 1921), pp. 61 f.

[4] The verses of the Qur'ān suggesting anthropomorphic ideas were the battleground of the early theologians. See al-Ijī, *al-Mawāqif*, pp. 71 ff.; Ibn Khaldūn, *Muqaddima*, III, 44 ff.

[5] The extreme literalists were called *al-Ẓāhirīya*. See Macdonald, *Development*, pp. 108, 208 ff.; Horten, *Die phil. Systeme der spek. Theologen im Islam* (Index); Goldziher, *Die Zahiriten*, pp. 41 ff.; Ibn Khaldūn, *Muquddima*, III, 3 f.

[6] See Qur. 3:5; al-Rāzī, *Mafātiḥ*, II, 415 ff.; al-Bayḍāwī, *Anwār al-Tanzil*, I, 145 f.

meaning of the statute here is not that which is contrary to the literal meaning, or to that which is to be explained as the meaning or that the meaning is perspicuous, but rather it is that which embraces all the conventional divisions of the context.

and to turn aside from them/that is, from the literal meanings

to meanings which the People of the Inner Meaning (*ahl al-bāṭin*) **assert** / They are the Heretics, who are called *al-Bāṭinīya* [7] because of their assertion that the statutes are not to be interpreted according to their literal meanings, but that they have inner meanings which only the Teacher knows. Their purpose in this is the disavowal of the Law entirely.

is heresy [8]/that is, a swerving away and a turning aside from Islam and an attaining to Unbelief and being so described, because it is a denial of the Prophet in that very thing by which his coming was of necessity known. But as for the position which some of the Verifiers have taken—that along with their literal meanings there are in the statutes hidden allusions to fine points (*daqā'iq*) which are unveiled to the lords of the Way (*arbāb al-sulūk*) [9] and which it is nevertheless possible to harmonize with the purpose of the literal meanings—well, this position is of the perfection of Belief and absolute knowledge.

The rejection of the statutes/by denying the judgments which are indicated in the decisive statutes, whether they are from the Book or the Sunna, such as the resurrection of bodies, for example

is Unbelief/for it plainly makes Allah and His Messenger liars. So whoever defames ʿĀʾisha on the charge of adultery [10] becomes an Unbeliever.

The making of disobedience lawful (*istiḥlāl*)/whether the disobedience is a small or a great sin

---

[7] See al-Shahrastānī, *al-Milal*, pp. 147 ff.; al-Ījī, *al-Mawāqif*, p. 348; al-Baghdādī, *al-Farq bayn al-Firaq*, pp. 265 ff.; *Dict. of Tech. Terms*, pp. 669 f.; Ibn Khaldūn, *Muqaddima*, I, 363.

[8] A.J., p. 204, adds "and Unbelief."

[9] *Al-sulūk* is the Mystic's progress in the way to Allah. See *Enc. of Islam*, IV, 549; Macdonald, *Rel. Attitudes and Life*, p. 258; al-Ghazzālī, *Ihyā'* (commentary of Sayyid Murtaḍā), VII, 247 ff.

[10] See above, Chap. 17, n. 8.

is Unbelief/whenever it is established by decisive proof to be an act of disobedience, and that has already been explained.

and making light of disobedience and ridicule of the Law are Unbelief/because they are among signs of denial.

From these fundamental principles there are derived many particulars which have been mentioned in legal decisions (*al-fatāwī*). For example, whenever one believes a forbidden thing to be lawful, if it is forbidden to the person himself—this having been established by decisive proof or by a proof based on opinion—then he becomes an Unbeliever; otherwise he does not [become an Unbeliever] because it is forbidden to someone else. Some have made no distinction between what is forbidden for himself or for someone else and have said, "He is an Unbeliever whoever makes lawful a forbidden thing, which has been stigmatized as forbidden in the religion of the Prophet, such as marrying those of one's kin whom one should not, or the drinking of wine, or eating what dies of itself, or blood, or swine's flesh except when necessity demands. And doing these things without making them lawful is evil-doing (*fisq*). Whoever makes lawful the drinking of *nabīdh* until one is drunken is an Unbeliever."

However, if one were to say of something forbidden, "This is lawful," in order to sell his merchandise or because he is ignorant, he would not become an Unbeliever. If he should wish that wine were not forbidden or that the fast of Ramaḍān were not an obligation, because of the hardship it brings to him, he would not become an Unbeliever. On the other hand, whenever one wishes that adultery or that killing a soul without just reason were not forbidden, he is an Unbeliever because the forbidding [*149*] of these things is established in all religions and is in accord with wisdom. Whoever then desires to forsake wisdom desires that Allah decide contrary to wisdom, and that is ignorance of his Lord on his part. Al-Imām al-Sarakhsī [11] in the section on menstruation said, "Were one to make copulation with his wife who is menstruating a lawful act,[12] he would become an Unbeliever." According to *al-Nawādir* [18] [there is a statement] from Muhammad [that] he would not, and this is the sound position. As to the question of making lawful the committing of sodomy with one's wife, according to the soundest position such a one does not become an Unbeliever.

[11] Al-Imām al-Sarakhsī, the most important Ḥanafī lawyer of the 5th century A.H. See *Enc. of Islam*, IV, 159; Brockelmann, *Geschichte*, I, 172.

[12] Cf. *Musnad*, II, 476.   [18] See above, Chap. 16, n. 37.

Whoever attributes to Allah something that is not fitting or mocks at one of Allah's names or commands, or denies Allah's promises of reward and punishment, becomes an Unbeliever.

So also does he become an Unbeliever were he to wish that there had never been a prophet, because of contempt or enmity; or were he to laugh in approval of one who speaks of Unbelief, or were he to sit on an exalted seat surrounded by a group who propounded problems to him and made him laugh and pelted him with pillows; in fact they all would become Unbelievers.

So also would he become an Unbeliever were he to order a man to deny Belief in Allah, or were he to intend so to order him, or were he to render a legal decision advising a woman to get a divorce from her husband by means of Unbelief. So also would he become an Unbeliever were he, on drinking wine or committing adultery, to say, "In the name of Allah." [14]

So also would one become an Unbeliever were he to worship intentionally towards some other direction than the *qibla*, even though it might really be the *qibla*, or were he to worship intentionally without purification. So also would one become an Unbeliever were he to utter the word of Unbelief in contempt but not really as a conviction on his part. In like manner there are many [further] details [on this subject].

And despair (*al-ya's*) of Allah is Unbelief/because no one despairs of the spirit of Allah except the people who are Unbelievers (see Qur'ān 12:87).

and feeling secure (*al-amn*) from [15] Allah is Unbelief/since "no one feels secure from the craftiness of Allah except the people who lose" (Qur'ān 7:97). It may be objected that the decision that the disobedient will be in the Fire is a despairing of Allah, and the decision that the obedient will be in the Garden is a feeling of security from Allah. It follows then from the objection that the Mu'tazilite is an Unbeliever, whether obedient or disobedient, for he is either secure or in despair, although it is one of the rules of the people of the Approved Way that no one of the people of the *qibla* is an Unbeliever. To this we reply that this position of the Mu'tazilite is not despair nor a feeling of security. On the supposition that he is disobedient he does not despair that Allah will fit him for repentance and good works; and

---

[14] Cf. al-Bukhārī, *al-Ṣaḥīḥ*, I, 49 and III, 492.

[15] A.J. (p. 205) inserts *makr*, "craftiness" or "stratagem," doubtless because it occurs in the Qur'ān verse that follows.

on the supposition that he is obedient he is not secure from Allah's forsaking him with the result that he will acquire acts of disobedience for himself. From this the answer is clear to what has been said regarding the Mu'tazilite in that whenever he commits a great sin, it must follow that he is an Unbeliever because he despairs of Allah's mercy and is convinced that he is not a Believer. That [answer] means that we do not admit that [his] being convinced that he deserves the Fire [when he commits a great sin] requires despair, nor that his being convinced of his lack of Belief—which is interpreted by them to include assent, confession and works—does not, on the basis that there is a negation of works, require Unbelief.

So much for that. There is a difficulty in reconciling sayings like those [of al-Ash'arī and some of his followers], "No one of the people of the *qibla* is an Unbeliever," and their saying, "Whoever declares the creation of the Qur'ān or that the Vision is impossible or vilifies and curses the two *shaykhs* [Abū Bakr and 'Umar] and the like is an Unbeliever."

To assent to what a diviner (*al-kāhin*)¹⁶ narrates of the Unseen is Unbelief/because of the statement of the Prophet, "Whoever consults a diviner and assents to what he says becomes an Unbeliever in that which came down on Muhammad."¹⁷ The diviner is one who tells of things that shall come into being in the future and pretends to know secret things and to explain the science of the Unseen. Among the Arabs there were diviners who pretended to know matters; some of them asserted that they had a familiar demon of the Jinn and an adherent who informed them of the news, and some [150] pretended to comprehend matters by a kind of understanding which had been granted them. The astrologer (*al-munajjim*) whenever he pretends to know approaching events is like the diviner. In general, knowledge of the Unseen is something in which Allah is unique. There is no way to the Unseen for His creatures except by a communication from Allah, or by an Illumination through an evidentiary miracle, or through Grace, or through guidance (*irshād*) in making a deduction from signs in matters in which this is possible. Therefore it has been recorded in the legal decisions (*al-fatāwī*) that whoever predicts that there will be rain on seeing a ring around the moon, pretending that it is by knowledge of the Unseen and not a sign,¹⁸ is an Unbeliever. And Allah knows better.

¹⁶ See *Enc. of Islam*, II, 624 ff.; Macdonald, *Rel. Att. and Life*, pp. 25 ff.
¹⁷ *Musnad*, II, 408. Cf. al-Tirmidhī, *Ṣaḥīḥ*, "al-Ṭahāra," b. 102; Ibn Māja, *Sunan*, "al-Ṭahāra," b. 122.
¹⁸ A.J., p. 206, reads *karāma*, "a Grace" instead of *'alāma*.

The non-existent is not a thing [19]/if by thing is meant the really existent and that which is verified as having reality according to the position of the Verifiers. This means that being a thing (*al-shay'īya*) is equivalent to existence, real existence, and being verified as having real existence. Non-existence is a synonym of negation. This is a necessary judgment [20] which no one disputes but the Mu'tazilites, who say that the possible non-existent is really existent in the outside world. And if they mean that the non-existent is not called a thing, then it is merely a question of language based on the explanation of "thing," whether it is the existent or the non-existent, or of what may be validly known and narrated of it. It goes back to tradition (*al-naql*) and to tracing the sources of the use of these expressions.

And in prayer (*du'ā'*) of the living for the dead and the giving of alms (*taṣadduq*)/that is, on the part of the living

for them/that is, for the dead

there is an advantage for them/that is, for the dead. This is unlike the Mu'tazilites, for they maintained that Destiny (*al-qaḍā'*) does not change, that every soul has a pledge of what it has acquired, and that man is recompensed for his own action but not for that of another. We have in support of our position that which has come down in the sound traditions regarding prayer for the dead, especially the funeral prayer. The Fathers inherited this [custom]. If there had been no advantage for the dead in this it would have meant nothing. The Prophet said, "No group of Muslims amounting to a hundred in number performs worship over a dead person, all of them interceding for him, without their intercession for him being welcomed." [21] Of Sa'd b. 'Ubāda it is related that he said, "O Messenger of Allah, Umm Sa'd has died; what alms is best?" The Prophet replied, "Water." So Sa'd dug a well and said, "This is for Umm Sa'd." The Prophet said, "Prayer averts trial and alms quenches the anger of the Lord." [22] The Prophet also said that if the learned and the learner pass by a village, Allah will remove the

---

[19] The Cureton text, p. 5, inserts after "non-existent," "is something known of Allah just as the existent is known of Him." Also after "thing" it inserts "nor an object of vision." See Macdonald, *Development*, p. 314.

[20] Cf. above, Chap. 1, n. 17; al-Rāzī, *Mafātīh*, II, 391; VI, 164; Ibn Ḥazm, *Kitāb al-Fiṣal*, V, 42 ff.; al-Shahrastānī, *Kitāb Nihāyatu 'l-Iqdām*, pp. 150 ff.

[21] Muslim, *al-Ṣaḥīḥ*, I, 350; *Musnad*, VI, 32, 40; cf. variants of the tradition in al-Tirmidhī, *Ṣaḥīḥ*, "Janā'iz," b. 40; al-Nasā'ī, *Sunan*, "Janā'iz," b. 78; *Musnad*, IV, 79; VI, 97, 230.

[22] Al-Bukhārī, *al-Ṣaḥīḥ*, II, 192.

torment from the cemetery of that village for forty days.[23] The traditions and the precedents to be followed on this subject are more than can be numbered.

Allah answers prayers and supplies needs/This is based on the statement of Allah, "Call upon me, I will answer you" (Qur'ān 40:62). There are also the statements of the Prophet, "The creature will be answered so long as he does not pray for evil or for severing the ties of relationship, and so long as he does not hurry," [24] and, "Verily, your Lord is Living and Generous, He is ashamed to turn back empty the hands of His creature when lifted towards Him." [25] Know that the pillar of prayer is truthfulness of intention, the sincerity of aim, and the presence of the heart, because of the statement of the Prophet, "Pray to Allah, being certain that He will answer, and know ye that Allah will not answer the prayer of a careless and thoughtless heart." [26]

The Early Theologians differed on the question as to whether it was permissible to say that the prayer of an Unbeliever is answered. The Multitude precludes it on the ground of the statement of Allah, "The prayer of the Unbelievers is only in error" (Qur'ān 13:15, 40:53), and because the Unbeliever does not pray to Allah, for he does not know Him, and if he confesses Him he vitiates his own confession in not ascribing proper attributes to Him. What has been related in tradition regarding the prayer of the one who is oppressed—that he, even though an Unbeliever, is answered—that applies to his lack of Belief in the favor of Allah. Some permitted this on the basis of the statement of Allah regarding Iblīs, "O my Lord, grant me time until the day when men are raised from the dead" (Qur'ān 15:36). Allah replied, "Thou art of those to whom time is granted" [27] (Qur'ān 15:37). This is one answer. Abū 'l-Qāsim al-Ḥakīm al-Samarqandī [28] and Abū 'l-Naṣr al-Dabūsī took this position. Al-Ṣadr al-Shahīd [29] said, "According to it your legal decisions are to be made."

---

[23] A.J. (p. 207) remarks that this tradition clearly has no foundation.

[24] Muslim, *al-Ṣaḥīḥ*, II, 437; al-Bukhārī, *al-Ṣaḥīḥ*, IV, 194.

[25] Cf. *Musnad*, V, 438; Abū Dāwūd, *Sunan*, "Witr," b. 23; al-Tirmidhī, *Ṣaḥīḥ*, "Da'wāt," b. 104; and Ibn Māja, *Sunan*, Du'ā, b. 13.

[26] Al-Tirmidhī, *Ṣaḥīḥ*, "Da'wāt," b. 65.

[27] See also Qur. 7:13–14, 38:80–81 and al-Bayḍāwī, *Anwār al-Tanzīl*, I, 320.

[28] See Jacut (Wüstenfeld), *Geographische Wörterbuch*, III, 137 f.

[29] Ḥusām al-Dīn 'Umar b. 'Abd al-'Azīz al-Ṣadr al-Shahīd (d. A.H. 536; A.D. 1141) was a writer on *fiqh*. See Brockelmann, *Geschichte*, I, 374.

Chapter 19

VARIOUS ARTICLES OF BELIEF CONCERNING THE LAST HOUR, MUJTAHIDS, AND THE COMPARATIVE EXCELLENCE OF MEN AND ANGELS

What the Prophet has reported of the indications of the Hour such as the appearance of al-Dajjāl, and the Beast of the earth, and Ya'jūj and Ma'jūj, and the descent of Jesus from heaven, and the rising of the sun in the West is a Reality.

The Mujtahid sometimes errs and sometimes hits the mark.

The Messengers of mankind are more excellent than the Messengers of the angels, and the Messengers of the angels are more excellent than the generality of mankind; and the generality of mankind is more excellent than the generality of the angels.

What the Prophet has reported of the indications of the Hour (*al-sā'a*) [1]/that is, its signs

such as the appearance of al-Dajjāl,[2] and the Beast of the earth, and Ya'jūj and Ma'jūj,[3] and the descent of Jesus from heaven, and the rising of the sun in the West is a Reality/for they are all possible things which [*151*] the Truthful One reported. Hudhayfa b. Asīd al-Ghifārī [4] said,[5] "The Messenger of Allah came upon us conversing together and he said, 'What are you conversing

---

[1] Cf. *Enc. of Islam*, II, 1050; Sale, *Koran with Preliminary Discourse*, Sec. III, pp. 92 ff.

[2] See *Enc. of Islam*, I, 886. References to the numerous traditions concerning al-Dajjāl (the Anti-Christ) are given by Wensinck, *Handbook*, pp. 50 f.; *Concordance*, IX, 111.

[3] (Cf. Gog and Magog, Gen. 10:2; Ezek. 38–39; Rev. 20:8.) See al-Ṭabarī, *Annales*, I, 68; Jacut, *Geographische Wörterbuch*, III, 53 ff.; Wensinck, *Handbook*, p. 263; *Enc. of Islam*, IV, 1142.

[4] See Ibn Ḥajar, *Biog. Dict.*, I, 650.

[5] See Muslim, *al-Ṣaḥīḥ*, II, 501 f.; Ibn Māja, *Sunan*; "Fitan," b. 25, 28, 29, 32; Wensinck, *Handbook*, p. 100.

about?' We said, 'We were mentioning the Hour.' He said, 'It will not come until you see ten wonders (*āyāt*) preceding it.' He then mentioned the Smoke, al-Dajjāl, the Beast, the rising of the sun in the West, the descent of Jesus ('Īsā b. Maryam), Ya'jūj and Ma'jūj, and three eclipses of the moon (*khusūf*), one in the East, one in the West, and a third in the peninsula of Arabia. At the end of that [time] there is a Fire which will come forth from al-Yaman driving the people to the place of their assembly for the last Day." The sound traditions concerning these indications are many. Traditions (*al-aḥādīth*) [from the Prophet] and narratives (*al-āthār*) [from the Companions] have related in detail these matters and the manner of their occurrence. They are to be found in the commentaries, the biographies of the Prophet, and the books of history.

The Mujtahid [6]/both in matters relating to Reason and the Law, whether fundamental or derived

sometimes errs and sometimes hits the mark/Some of the Ash'arites and the Mu'tazilites held that every Mujtahid hits the mark in derived matters of the Law which are not absolutely fixed. The difference [of opinion] is based on their differing as to whether Allah has a fixed judgment for every incident or whether His judgment in matters of *ijtihād* (that is, striving for a legal judgment) is that at which the opinion of the Mujtahid has arrived. The verifying of [the possible aspects of] this position is that in the matter of *ijtihād*, either Allah has no fixed judgment before the *ijtihād* of the Mujtahid occurs or He has [a fixed judgment]. Then there is either no proof from Allah for this judgment, or there is proof from Him. Then either this proof is absolute or it is based on opinion. Some have taken every possible viewpoint.

The one which we have chosen is that the judgment [of Allah] is fixed and that there is proof for it based on opinion. If the Mujtahid finds the judgment which is fixed, he hits the mark; if he loses it, he misses. The Mujtahid is not legally responsible for hitting the mark in the judgment, for it is obscure and hidden. Therefore he who misses is excusable, nay rather he is to be rewarded. There is thus no difference [of views] regarding the position that he who misses is not a sinner (*āthim*). The question is only whether he misses the mark both at the beginning and at the end of his

---

[6] See above, Chap. 2, n. 29.

effort, that is both in consideration of the proof and in the judgment. Some of the Early Theologians took this position, among them al-Shaykh Abū Manṣūr (al-Māturīdī). Or does he miss the mark at the end only? That is, consideration is given to the fact that although he missed the mark in judgment, yet he hits the mark in [his use of] proof, inasmuch as he establishes it, combining all the stipulations and principles, and then brings in all those considerations for which he is legally responsible. In matters of *ijtihād* he is not legally responsible for establishing an absolute argument, in which the thing to be proved is absolute reality.

In proof of the proposition that the Mujtahid may sometimes miss the mark there are the following points. First, there is the statement of Allah, "We gave Solomon (Sulaymān) understanding of it" (Qur'ān 21:79). The pronoun "it" refers to judicial authority or to making a legal decision. If each of the two *ijtihād*'s [on the part of David and Solomon] had been correct there would have been no reason for particularizing [*152*] Solomon, for each would then have hit the mark in his judgment and understood it. In the second place, there are traditions [from the Prophet] and narratives [from the Companions] which indicate that in *ijtihād* there was a wavering between hitting and missing the mark, so that the idea [that one might miss the mark] became *mutawātir*. The prophet said, "If you hit the mark, you will have ten good deeds [to your account]; and if you miss, one." [7] In another tradition the one who hits the mark gets two rewards, the one who misses, one.[8] By Ibn Mas'ūd [the saying is reported], "If I hit the mark, it is from Allah, otherwise it is from me and Satan." It is well known that the Companions accused one another of error in *ijtihād*. In the third place, there is Analogy (*al-qiyās*) which makes a declaration but does not establish [of itself], so that which is established by Analogy must be established as to its meaning by statute. Agreement has been reached that there is only one right position regarding that which is established by statute, [so, since there is a statute proving that the Mujtahid does sometimes miss the mark, Analogy declares this to be a principle in *ijtihād*]. In the fourth place, no distinctions are made between persons in the general definitions that have come down in the Law of our Prophet, so if every Mujtahid were to hit the mark, then it would follow that the one action must be described by mutually negating opinions, as prohibited and permitted, as sound and un-

---

[7] Cf. *Musnad*, II, 187, IV, 205.

[8] Cf. al-Bukhārī, *al-Ṣaḥīḥ*, IV, 438 and other traditions noted by Wensinck (*Concordance*, I, 20).

sound, as necessary and unnecessary. The completion of the verifying of these proofs and the answer to the convictions held by those who differ from us may be found in our book, *Al-Talwīḥ fī Sharḥ al-Tanqīḥ.*[9]

The Messengers of mankind are more excellent than the Messengers of the angels,[10] and the Messengers of the angels are more excellent than the generality of mankind; [11] and the generality of mankind is more excellent than the generality of the angels/That the Messengers of the angels are to be preferred to the generality of mankind is based on Agreement, nay rather, it is so of necessity. But there are certain reasons why the Messengers of mankind are to be preferred to those of angels, and why the generality of men is to be preferred to the generality of angels. In the first place, Allah ordered the angels to prostrate themselves to Adam by way of magnifying and honoring him, as is indicated in the statements of Allah, "Seest thou this man whom thou hast honored above me?" (Qur'ān 17:64), and, "I am better than he; Thou hast created me of fire, and Thou has created him of clay" (Qur'ān 7:11, 38:77). The wisdom of this requires [us to believe] that he commanded the lower to prostrate himself to the higher and not vice versa. Secondly, every lexicographer understands from the statement of Allah, "And He taught Adam all the names" [12] (Qur'ān 2:29), that the purpose was to prefer Adam to the angels and to demonstrate that he had more knowledge and deserved to be magnified and honored. In the third place, there is the statement of Allah, "Verily Allah selected Adam, Noah, [*153*] the family of Abraham, and the family of 'Imrān above the worlds" (Qur'ān 3:30). The angels are a part of all the worlds. From this it has been specified by Agreement that the generality of mankind is not to be preferred to the Messengers of the angels, otherwise the rule [that mankind is to be preferred] remains in operation. It is clear however that this is a matter of opinion based merely on proofs from opinion. In the fourth place, man achieves virtues and perfections in knowledge and practice in spite of such hindrances and impediments as lust and anger and the recurrence of necessary wants which divert his attention from acquiring the perfections of life. There is no doubt that religious service and acquiring perfections, when done in spite of preoccupations and vicissitudes, are more trying and go further in sincerity; so man is more excellent.

[9] See Brockelmann, *Geschichte*, II, 214, 216. [10] Cf. *Enc. of Islam*, III, 191 ff.
[11] Cureton, p. 5, adds "of the Believers."
[12] Cf. al-Ṭabarī, *Annales*, I, 94 ff.; al-Bayḍāwī, *Anwār al-Tanzīl*, I, 49.

The Mu'tazilites, the Philosophers, and some of the Ash'arites [13] took the position that angels are more excellent, and maintain it by the following arguments. First, the angels are pure spirits (*arwāḥ mujarrada*), actually perfect and free from the principles of evils and defects like lust, anger, and the obscurities of matter and form, capable of doing wonderful things and knowing the things that come into being, their past and future, without error. The answer to this position is that it is based on philosophical foundations and not on Islamic ones. The second argument is that the prophets, although they are the most excellent of mankind, learned from angels and were benefited by them. The proof of this is in the statements of Allah, "The strong in power taught" (Qur'ān 53:5), and, "The faithful spirit brought it down" (Qur'ān 26:193). There is no doubt [they claim] that the teacher is more excellent than the learner. The answer is that the learning process is from Allah, and the angels [are only intermediaries who] pass on the information. The third argument is that there are many cases where the angels are mentioned before the prophets in the Book and the Sunna. Their being mentioned first is only, [according to the argument], because they are advanced in honor and dignity. The answer to this is that they were placed first because their existence was prior to that of man or because it is more of a mystery, so Belief in them is [to be emphasized] more and [Belief] in [their]having preceded [man in time] is more fitting. The fourth argument is the statement of Allah, "Al-Masīḥ never disdains being a creature of Allah, nor do the angels who are nigh to Him" (Qur'ān 4:170). The lexicographers understand by this that the angels are more excellent than Jesus, since the analogy in such cases of exaltation is to proceed from the lower to the higher. The following is the usage, "The vizier does not disdain this thing, nor does the Sultan," but not the opposite order, "The Sultan does not, nor does the vizier." Then no one says [that this verse has to do with the question] whether Jesus is more excellent than others of the prophets. The answer is that Christians (*al-Naṣāra*) so magnified the Messiah that he is exalted above being one of the creatures of Allah; rather, they even held that he must be a son of Allah—who is praised—only because he had no father. Allah said, "He heals the blind and the leper, and raises the dead" [14] in contrast to other creatures of Allah among the children of Adam. So Allah refuted them by saying that al-Masīḥ did not disdain being a creature

---

[13] See also al-Rāzī, *Mafātīḥ*, I, 299 ff.; al-Ijī, *al-Mawāqif*, p. 237; al-Faḍālī, *Kifāyat al-'Awāmm*, p. 69; *Dict. of Tech. Terms*, p. 1337; Ibn Ḥazm, *Kitāb al-Fiṣal*, V, 20 ff.

[14] This is a paraphrase of two Qur'ān verses; 3:43 is in the first person, 5:110 in the second.

of Allah, nor did the one who is more exalted than he in this respect, that is, the angels who have neither father nor mother and who are able with the permission of Allah to perform greater and more wonderful acts than healing the blind and the leper and reviving the dead. Their exaltation and eminence is only in being born without father and mother and in manifesting powerful signs, not in absolute honor and perfection. So there is no indication that the angels are more excellent.[15] Allah knows better and to Him is the recompense and the return.

[15] Al-Ghazzālī (*Iḥyā'*, III, 165) argues in commenting on Qur. 37:164 that Allah has granted angels fixed ranks, while men are elevated from rank to rank. Elsewhere (*Iḥyā'*, VIII, 263 f.) he tells of a mystic who asked the two recording angels about a matter. They did not know, but the mystic asked his heart, which answered in such a marvelous manner that it proved that men may be more excellent than angels.

Bibliography

Abū Dāwūd. Sunan. 2 vols. Cairo, A.H. 1292.

Abū Ḥanīfa. Al-Fiqh al-Akbar (I). With a commentary (spurious) by al-Māturīdī. Haydarābād, A.H. 1321.

—— Al-Fiqh al-Akbar (II). With a commentary by Abū 'l-Muntahā. Haydarābād, A.H. 1321.

—— Commentary on al-Fiqh al-Akbar (II). By 'Ali al-Qārī. Cairo, A.H. 1323.

—— Kitāb al-Waṣīya. With a commentary by Molla Ḥusayn b. Iskander al-Ḥanafī. Haydarābād, A.H. 1321. (Al-Fiqh al-Akbar (II) and Kitāb al-Waṣīya, though considered spurious, reflect the school of Abū Ḥanīfa.)

Ash'arī, Al- (Abū 'l-Ḥasan). Kitāb Maqālāt al-Islamiyyīn. Ed. H. Ritter. 2 vols. Stambul, 1929–30.

—— Kitāb al-Ibāna 'an Uṣūl al-Diyāna. Haydarābād, A.H. 1323. Translation by W. C. Klein, *Al-Ibānah 'an Uṣūl ad-Diyānah (The Elucidation of Islam's Foundation).* New Haven, 1940.

Bābu 'l-Ḥādī 'Ashar, Al-. By Ḥasan b. Yūsuf b. 'Alī Ibnu 'l-Muṭahhar al-Hilli, with commentary by Miqdād-i-Fāḍil al-Ḥillī. Trans. from the Arabic by W. M. Miller. Oriental Translation Fund, N.S., Vol. XXIX. London, 1928.

Baghdādī, Al- (Ibn Ṭāhir b. Muḥammad). Al-Farq bayn al-Firaq. Cairo (undated).

Bayḍāwī, Al- (Abū Sa'īd 'Abdallāh b. 'Umar). Anwār al-Tanzīl wa Asrār al-Ta'wīl (commentary on Qur'ān). Ed. H. O. Fleischer. 2 vols. Leipzig, 1846–48.

Boer, T. J. de. The History of Philosophy in Islām. Trans. Edward R. Jones. London, 1903.

Brockelmann, Karl. Geschichte der arabischen Litteratur. 2 vols. Weimar, 1898, 1902.

Bukhārī, Al- (Abū 'Abdallāh Muḥammad b. Ismā'īl). Al-Ṣaḥīḥ. Ed. M. L. Krehl and Th. W. Juynboll. 4 vols. Leiden, 1862–68, 1908.

Caetani, L. Annali dell' Islam. Vol. I. Milan, 1905.

Concordantiae Corani Arabicae. By Gustavus Flügel. Leipzig, 1875.

172   BIBLIOGRAPHY

Dictionary of Technical Terms in the Sciences of the Mussalmans. Ed. under superintendence of A. Sprenger and W. Nassau Lees. Calcutta, 1862.

Dozy, R. Supplément aux dictionnaires arabes. 2 vols. Leiden, 1881.

—— Dictionnaire des noms des vêtements chez les Arabes. Amsterdam, 1845.

Encyclopaedia of Islam, The . . . Prepared by a Number of Leading Orientalists. Leiden, 1913–38.

Encyclopaedia of Religion and Ethics. Ed. James Hastings. Edinburgh and New York, 1908–22.

Faḍālī, Al- (Muḥammad). Kifāyat al-ʿAwāmm fi ʿIlm al-Kalām. With a commentary by Ibrāhīm al-Bayjūrī. Cairo, A.H. 1328.

Fatḥ al-Raḥmān li Ṭālib Ayāt al-Qurʾān. Beirut, A.H. 1323.

Ghazzālī, Al- (Abū Ḥāmid Muḥammad b. Muḥammad). Iḥyāʾ ʿUlūm al-Dīn. With a commentary by Sayyid Murtaḍā. 10 vols. Cairo, A.H. 1311.

—— Maqāṣid al-Falāsifa. Ed. Muḥyi ʾl-Dīn Ṣabrī al-Kurdī. Cairo, A.H. 1355.

—— Miʿyār al-ʿIlm. Ed. Muḥyi ʾl-Dīn Ṣabrī al-Kurdī. Cairo, A.H. 1346.

—— Worship in Islam. Translation of the Book of Worship from the *Iḥyāʾ* by E. E. Calverley. Madras, 1925.

Goldsack, Wm. Selections from Muhammadan Traditions Taken from *Mishkātu ʾl-Maṣābīḥ*. Madras, 1923.

Goldziher, I. Muhammedanische Studien. 2 vols. Halle, 1889–90.

—— Vorlesungen über den Islam. Heidelberg, 1910.

—— Die Zāhiriten. Leipzig, 1884.

Guillaume, A. The Traditions of Islam. Oxford, 1924.

Horten, M. Die philosophischen Ansichten von Razi und Tusi. Bonn, 1910.

—— Die philosophischen Systeme der spekulativen Theologen im Islam. Bonn, 1912.

—— Die spekulative und positive Theologie des Islam. Leipzig, 1912.

Hughes, T. P. The Dictionary of Islam. London, 1885.

Ibn Ḥajar. A Biographical Dictionary of Persons Who Knew Moḥammad. 4 vols. Calcutta, 1856.

Ibn Ḥazm. Kitāb al-Fiṣal fi ʾl-Milal wa ʾl-Ahwāʾ wa ʾl-Niḥal. 5 vols. Cairo, A.H. 1320.

Ibn Hishām (ʿAbd al-Malik). Sīrat Rasūl Allāh. Ed. Ferdinand Wüstenfeld. 2 vols. Göttingen, 1858.

Ibn Khaldūn (Abū Zayd ʿAbd al-Raḥmān). Al-Muqaddima. 3 vols. Paris, 1858.

Ibn Khallikān. Biographical Dictionary. Trans. from the Arabic by Bn. Mac Guckin de Slane. 4 vols. Paris, 1842, 1871.

Ibn Mājā. Sunan. 2 vols. Cairo, A.H. 1313.

Ibn Qutayba. Kitāb al-Ma'ārif. By Abū Muḥammad 'Abd Allah (*Handbuch der Geschichte*, ed. Ferdinand Wüstenfeld). Göttingen, 1850.

Ibn Sa'd. Biographien Muhammeds, seiner Gefährten und der späteren Trager des Islams, bis zum Jahre 230 der Flucht. Ed. Eduard Sachau. 9 vols. Leiden, 1904–1909.

Ibn Sīnā. Al-Najāt. Cairo, A.H. 1331.

—— Rasā'il fi 'l-Ḥikma wa 'l-Ṭabī'īyāt. Cairo, A.H. 1326.

Ījī, Al- (al-Qāḍī 'Aḍud al-Dīn). Al-Mawāqif. With the commentary by 'Alī b. Muḥammad al-Jurjānī. Parts V and VI ed. Th. Soerensen. Leipzig, 1848.

Jacut (Yaqūt ibn 'Abd Allāh). Geographisches Wörterbuch. Ed. Ferdinand Wüstenfeld. 6 vols. Leipzig, 1866–70.

—— Moschtarik: Lexicon geographischer Homonyme. Ed. Ferdinand Wüstenfeld. Göttingen, 1846.

Kitāb aḥwāl al-Qiyāma (Muhammedanische Eschatologie). Ed. M. Wolff. Leipzig, 1872. This book is also published in Cairo, under the title of *Daqā'iq al-Akhbār fi dhikr al-Janna wa 'l-Nār*, by 'Abd al-Raḥmān b. Aḥmad al-Qāḍī. Cairo, A.H. 1333.

Lane, E. W. An Arabic-English Lexicon. London, 1863–93.

Lisān al-'Arab. 20 vols. Cairo, A.H. 1300–1308.

Macdonald, D. B. "Continuous Re-creation and Atomic Time," *Isis*, IX, 2. Also in *The Moslem World*, XVIII, 6 ff.

—— Development of Muslim Theology, Jurisprudence and Constitutional Theory. New York, 1903.

—— The Religious Attitude and Life in Islam. Chicago, 1909.

—— "Wahm and its Cognates," *Journal of the Royal Asiatic Society*, 1922.

Maimonides. Le Guide des égarés, par Moise Ben Maimoun. Trans. S. Munk Paris, 1856.

—— The Guide for the Perplexed. Trans. M. Friedländer. London, 1928.

Margoliouth, D. S. Mohammed and the Rise of Islam. New York, 1905.

Māwardī, Al- (Abū 'l-Ḥasan 'Alī). Al-Aḥkām al-Sulṭānīya. Bonn, 1855.

Mohammed Abdou, Cheikh. Rissālat al-Tawhīd. Paris, 1925.

Muir, Sir Wm. The Caliphate, Its Rise, Decline and Fall. New and revised edition by T. H. Weir. Edinburgh, 1915.

—— The Life of Mohammad. New and revised edition by T. H. Weir. Edinburgh, 1912.

Müller, M. J. Philosophie und Theologie des Averroes. Arabic text. Munich, 1859.

Muslim (al-Imām Abū 'l-Ḥusayn). al-Ṣaḥīḥ. 2 vols. Cairo, A.H. 1327.

Musnad. Abū Abd 'Allah Aḥmad Muḥammad b. Ḥanbal. 6 vols. Cairo, A.H. 1313.

Nawawī, Al- (Abū Zakarija Jaḥja). Ueber das Leben und die Schriften. Ed. Ferdinand Wüstenfeld. Göttingen, 1849.

Nicholson, R. A. A Literary History of the Arabs. London, 1907.

Palmer, E. H., trans. The Koran. World's Classics. Oxford, 1928.

Pines, S. Beiträge zur islamischen Atomenlehre. Berlin, 1936.

Rawḍa al-Bahīya fī mā bayn al-Ashā'ira wa 'l-Māturīdīya, Al-. Al-Ḥasan b. 'Abd al-Muḥsin Abū 'Udhba. Hydarābād, A.H. 1322.

Rāzī, Al- (Fakhr al-Dīn Muḥammad b. 'Umar). Mafātīḥ al-Ghayb. 8 vols. Cairo, A.H. 1308.

—— Muḥaṣṣal Afkār al-Mutaqaddimīn wa 'l-Muta'akhkhirīn min al-Falāsifa wa 'l-Mutakallimīn. With notes by Nāṣir al-Dīn al-Ṭūsī. On the margin is the *Ma'ālim uṣul al-Dīn,* also by al-Rāzī. Cairo, A.H. 1323.

Risāla al-Shamsīya, Al-. Al-Qazwīnī. Translated under the title "The Logic of the Arabians" as the first appendix to the *Dictionary of Technical Terms,* by A. Sprenger. Calcutta, 1854.

Rodwell, J. M. The Koran Translated from the Arabic. Everyman's Library. New York, 1913.

Sa'adya al-Fayyūmī. Kitāb al-Amānāt wa 'l-I'tiqādāt. Leiden, 1881.

Sale, G. The Koran with Preliminary Discourse. 2 vols. Philadelphia, 1833.

Sanūsī, Al- (Muḥammad). Sharḥ Umm al-Barāhīn. With supercommentary by Muḥammad al-Dasūqī. Cairo, A.H. 1330.

Shahrastānī, Al- (Muḥammad). Al-Milal wa 'l-Niḥal (Book of Religious and Philosophical Sects). Ed. W. Cureton. London, 1842.

—— Kitāb Nihāyatu 'l-Iqdām fī 'Ilm al-Kalām. Ed. A. Guillaume. Oxford, 1934.

Suyūṭī, Al- (Jalāl al-Dīn). Tarīkh al-Khulafā'. Calcutta, 1857.

Ṭabarī, Al-. Annales quos scripsit Abu Djafar Mohammed Ibn Djarir. Ed. M. J. De Goeje et al. 3 parts. Leiden, 1879–1901.

Tāj al-'Arūs. Sharḥ al-Qāmūs al-Musammā. By Sayyid Muḥammad Murtaḍā. Cairo, A.H. 1306.

Ta'rīfāt, Al-. 'Alī b. Muḥammad al-Jurjānī. Ed. Gustavus Flügel. Leipzig, 1845.

Tha'lābī, Al- (Abū Isḥāq Aḥmad b. Muḥammad). Qiṣaṣ al-Anbiyā'. Cairo, A.H. 1298.

Tirmidhī, Al-. Ṣaḥīḥ. 2 vols. Cairo, A.H. 1292.

Wensinck, A. J. Concordance et indices de la tradition musulmane. Leiden, 1935.

—— A Handbook of Early Muhammadan Tradition. Leiden, 1927.

—— The Muslim Creed; Its Genesis and Historical Development. Cambridge, 1932.

Wolfson, H. A. "The Amphibolous Terms in Aristotle, Arabic Philosophy and Maimonides," *Harvard Theological Review*, XXXI (1938), 151 ff.

—— "The Aristotelian Predicables and Maimonides' Division of Attributes," *Essays and Studies in Memory of Linda R. Miller*. New York, 1938.

—— "The Internal Senses in Latin, Arabic and Hebrew Philosophic Texts," *Harvard Theological Review*, XXXIII (1935), 93 ff.

—— The Philosophy of Spinoza. Cambridge, Mass., 1934.

Zamakhsharī, Al- (Abū Qāsim). Al-Kashshāf 'an Ḥaqā'iq al-Tanzīl. Ed. Lees. 2 vols. Calcutta, 1856.

—— Al-Mufaṣṣal, ed. J. P. Broch. Christianiae, 1879.

Index

Printed in April 2023
by Rotomail Italia S.p.A., Vignate (MI) - Italy